A Survey of Solo Works for the Violoncello

A guide to 200 selected pieces from the literature from 1689-2023

by
Brian Hodges

ISBN: 978-1-62992-048-1

Published by Fairhaven Press

Copyright 2023 by Brian Hodges

All rights reserved. No part of this publication may be copied, scanned, photographed, stored in an electronic retrieval system, posted online, or transmitted by any means, electronic, mechanical, recording, or otherwise, escept brief extracts for the purposes of review, and no part of this publication may be sold or hired, without the express written permission of the publisher. Fairhaven Press is a registered trademark.

Fairhaven Press is an independent publishing company. We thank you for supporting us by purchasing or considering our titles.

www.fairhavenpress.com

Preface

The idea for this book came out of a class I have taught at my university for the last several years on cello literature. I was unable to find a resource for the students that perfectly aligned with the way the class was structured. I wanted a broader scope, so that students could see and understand the full breadth of cello music. In addition, I also wanted a resource that contained background information on a given work, to assist in cultivating recital programs for my students (or even myself). Being somewhat old school, I wanted something I could walk over to my bookshelf and pull off in one volume that could accomplish both.

Choosing to focus on more of a wide-ranging overview of the entire cello repertoire, I limited myself to 200 works; 100 seemed too limited, and 300 sounded too overwhelming. I landed on 200 as a number that could accurately represent the span of works written for cello. Inevitably, that means leaving out certain pieces and composers, but I also was interested in balancing the list of the usual suspects (Dvorak concerto, Elgar concerto, Bach Suites, etc.), with newer and lesser known works that perhaps deserve a place at the table.

There were a few criteria that I considered when including a work:

1. It had to be by an established composer. The composer needed to have a certain track record and substantive career, with some kind of deserved reputation. What's fascinating is that almost all composers who are widely considered to be major and important have written solo pieces for the cello. There are only a few composers of notable reputation that didn't write anything for the cello (Mozart one of the most glaring examples). This is a good problem to have.

2. It had to be available. The last thing I wanted was to write about a piece, get someone interested and excited to play it, only to find it wasn't obtainable. This was something that really affected many modern pieces. Some major contemporary composers have written some fantastic works for cello, but unfortunately, and frustratingly, they are not available for purchase. Some are available to rent, but I have found that many times the cost to rent the score and parts is usually limited to a very narrow time frame, not to mention very cost prohibitive. I did make a couple of exceptions to this rule, but only in extreme circumstances.

3. I kept it to three categories: Unaccompanied, with Piano, and Concerto. This leaves out many other kinds of solo works, which might involve other accompanying instruments or cello ensemble works. There is great music to be found in these other categories, I just felt compelled to limit it to these categories.

4. I generally avoided transcriptions, preferring to keep it to a piece that originally was written for the cello, although you will notice that I made several exceptions to this. There are many wonderful transcriptions that are in normal play, many by Piatigorsky for instance, but I felt that generally speaking, I could populate the list without including transcriptions.

In short, I envisioned this book, both for my class, and you the reader, whether or you are a cellist or cello enthusiast, to be used as a jumping off point. There is a vast wealth of cello music out there, some alluded to in the book, some not, but my sincere hope is for you to be inspired to seek out further pieces and composers. As cellists, we are very blessed with the amount of music we have (and quality of music, I might add).

May we all continue to cultivate, discover, and commission new works.

Happy exploring!

- Brian
SDG

Acknowledgements

Despite my name being the only author listed on the cover, there have been many people who have assisted me in the completion of this book.

I would like to thank my father, first and foremost for not only being an inspiration as a published author many times over himself, but for acting as a soundboard, proofreader, and helping greatly in tracking down and finding background information on the pieces. His work was invaluable, and took a huge load off of my shoulders.

Thank you to Jo Nardolillo, violinist colleague and fellow author, for helping me form the idea of this book many years ago, and whose own book on violin repertoire, *The Canon of Violin Literature: A Performer's Resource* served as a wonderful inspiration for this book.

Thank you to the many students over the years who were a part of my Cello Literature course. You helped in the conception of this book, whether you knew it or not, and helped make it what it is. They include: Ava Camilo, Alec Duggan, David Feldman, Matthew Fiorentino, Jonah Haddad, Alex Knudson, Lacee Link, Samaquias Lorta, Taylor Rhodes, Cera Riveland, Jake Saunders, Ian Schroeder, Kyle True, Aslen Whitmore, and Melissa Wilson.

Thank you to Miranda Wilson, professor of cello at the University of Idaho, author of a number of wonderful cello books, for your advice, sound wisdom, encouragement and for connecting me with my publisher.

Thank you to Rachel Becker, my music history and oboe colleague at Boise State, who is also a published author, for her advice and feedback. It was great getting your perspective on this project.

Thank you to Diana Allan for bouncing off ideas and giving feedback, especially in the initial stages of the project. Your insight and creativity is always treasured.

Thank you to Phil Mason, my grandfather, whose fascination with 'off-the-beaten-path' composers introduced me to some of the lesser known composers on this list.

Thank you to fellow cellists, Sarah Hanson, Philip Kettler, Juliana Soltis, and to violinist Jessica Harned, for looking over the repertoire list and making suggestions. A handful of wonderful pieces are included here thanks to their input.

Thank you to cellist Seth Parker Woods for his help with background information on the George Walker Cello Sonata.

Thank you to my former primary teachers, Pamela Frame, Alan Harris, Brooks Whitehouse, Marcy Rosen, and Mary Ruth Leonard, any other teacher I've worked with, whether in lessons or master classes, and my fellow cello colleagues who inspired me and brought many composers and works to my attention. I have learned so much from all of you.

Thank you to my publisher, Mike Hollis at Fairhaven Press for helping me bring this out into the world. It's been a great collaboration.

Thank you to my dog, Henle, a constant companion in the writing of this book. As you read this, dear reader, imagine a soundtrack of a ninety-pound labrador snoring away, so you can experience it as I did.

Thank you to my wife and duo partner, Betsi Hodges, who played a huge role in learning a lot of this repertoire. Many of the works for cello and piano listed here were discovered, studied, learned and performed with her (not to mention her published dissertation was a great reference for a number of the works included here). Thanks for always supporting me and helping me achieve my dreams.

And last, but certainly not least, thank you to my daughter, Clara, a budding author herself. I can't wait to be reading your published works very, very soon.

About the Author

Brian Hodges is a cellist who performs on modern and baroque cello. He is Professor of Cello at Boise State University and is the principal cellist of the Boise Baroque Orchestra. Educated at the Eastman School of Music and University of North Carolina at Greensboro, he has a BM, MM and DMA all in cello performance. He is the co-author of the book *Cello Secrets: Over 100 Performance Strategies for the Advanced Cellist* and has contributed a number of articles for The Strad and Strings magazines.

Author photo by Sean Evans

Table of Contents

Preface		iii
Acknowledgements		iv
About the Author		v
Thomas Adès (b. 1971)	*Lieux retrouvés for Cello & Piano*	1
Eleanor Alberga (b. 1949)	*Ride Through for Solo Cello*	2
Eric Alexander (b. 1973)	*Symmetry of Trees for Solo Cello*	3
Lera Auerbach (b. 1973)	*24 Preludes for Cello and Piano, Op. 47*	4
Lera Auerbach (b. 1973)	*Sonata for Cello & Piano No. 1, Op. 69*	6
Carl Philipp Emanuel Bach (1714-1788)	*3 Cello Concerti (Wq. 170, 171, 172)*	7
J.S. Bach (1685-1750)	*Three Sonatas for Viola da Gamba & Harpsichord, BWV 1027-1029*	9
J.S. Bach (1685-1750)	*Six Suites for Unaccompanied Cello, BWV 1007-1012*	11
David Baker (1931-2016)	*Sonata for Cello & Piano*	13
James Balentine (b. 1947)	*a wiser man: 6 short songs for cello & piano*	14
Samuel Barber (1910-1981)	*Cello Concerto, Op. 22*	16
Samuel Barber (1910-1981)	*Sonata in C Minor for Cello & Piano, Op. 6*	18
Jean-Baptiste Barrière (1707-1747)	*Sonatas for Cello & Basso Continuo*	19
Mason Bates (b. 1977)	*Cello Concerto*	20
Armando Bayolo (b. 1973)	*Orfei Mors for Cello & Orchestra*	21
Amy Beach (1867-1944)	*Five Compositions for Cello & Piano*	22
Sally Beamish (b. 1956)	*Sonata for Cello & Piano*	23
Ludwig van Beethoven (1770-1827)	*Sonata for Cello and Piano in A Major, Op. 69*	24
Ludwig van Beethoven (1770-1827)	*Sonatas for Piano & Cello, Op. 5, No. 1 and No. 2*	25
Ludwig van Beethoven (1770-1827)	*Sonatas for Cello & Piano, Op. 102, No. 1 and No. 2*	27
Ludwig van Beethoven (1770-1827)	*Three Sets of Variations for Piano & Cello, WoO*	29
Ludwig van Beethoven (1770-1827)	*Triple Concerto in C Major for Piano, Violin & Cello, Op. 56*	30
Leonard Bernstein (1918-1990)	*Three Meditations from 'The Mass' for Cello & Orchestra*	31
David Biedenbender (b. 1984)	*Light Over Mountains for Cello & Piano*	32
Ernest Bloch (1880-1959)	*From a Jewish Life (Prayer, Supplication & Jewish Song) for Cello & Orchestra*	33

Table of Contents

Ernest Bloch (1880-1959)	*Schelomo: Rhapsodie hébraïque for Cello & Orchestra*	34
Luigi Boccherini (1743-1805)	*Sonatas for Cello & Basso Continuo*	35
Luigi Boccherini (1743-1805)	*Concerti for Cello and Orchestra*	36
Léon Boëllmann (1862-1897)	*Variations symphoniques, Op. 23 for Cello & Orchestra*	38
Mélanie Hélène Bonis (1858-1937)	*Sonata for Cello & Piano in F Major, Op. 67*	39
Lili Boulanger (1893-1918)	*Nocturne for Cello & Piano*	40
Nadia Boulanger (1887-1979)	*Trois Pièces for Cello & Piano*	41
Johannes Brahms (1833-1897)	*Concerto in A Minor for Violin and Cello, Op. 102*	42
Johannes Brahms (1833-1897)	*Sonata for Cello and Piano No. 1 in E Minor, Op. 38*	44
Johannes Brahms (1833-1897)	*Sonata for Cello and Piano No. 2 in F Major, Op. 99*	46
Frank Bridge (1879-1941)	*Sonata for Cello & Piano*	48
Frank Bridge (1879-1941)	*Oration (Concerto elegiaco) for Cello and Orchestra*	49
Benjamin Britten (1913-1976)	*Three Suites for Solo Cello*	50
Benjamin Britten (1913-1976)	*Sonata in for Cello & Piano, Op. 65*	52
Max Bruch (1838-1920)	*Kol Nidrei, Op. 47 for Cello & Orchestra*	53
Kenji Bunch (b. 1973)	*Broken Music for Cello & Piano*	54
Nicola Saraceni Canzaon (b. 1991)	*Partita per Violoncello Sollo*	55
Elliott Carter (1908-2012)	*Sonata for Cello & Piano*	56
Pablo Casals (1876-1973)	*Song of the Birds (El cant dels ocells) for Cello & Piano*	57
Andrea Casarrubios (b. 1988)	*Seven for Solo Cello*	58
Gaspar Cassadó (1897-1966)	*Suite for Solo Cello*	59
Unsuk Chin (b. 1961)	*Cello Concerto*	60
Frederic Chopin (1810-1849)	*Introduction and Polonaise Brillante, Op.3 for Cello & Piano*	61
Frederic Chopin (1810-1849)	*Sonata for Cello & Piano in G Minor, Op. 65*	62
Rebecca Clarke (1886-1979)	*Sonata for Cello & Piano*	63
Anna Clyne (b. 1980)	*Dance for Cello & Orchestra*	64
Samuel Coleridge-Taylor (1875-1912)	*Variations in B Minor for Cello & Piano*	65
John Corigliano (b. 1938)	*Fancy on an Air by Bach for Solo Cello*	66
George Crumb (b. 1929-2022)	*Sonata for Solo Cello*	67
Giuseppe Dall'Abaco (1710-1805)	*11 Capricii for Solo Cello*	68
Michael Daugherty (b. 1954)	*Tales of Hemingway for Cello & Orchestra*	69
Kevin Day (b. 1996)	*Sonata for Cello and Piano (2016)*	70
Claude Debussy (1862-1918)	*Sonata for Cello & Piano*	71
Bryce Dessner (b. 1976)	*Tuusula for Solo Cello*	72
Tan Dun (b. 1957)	*Crouching Tiger Concerto for Cello & Orchestra*	73
Melissa Dunphy (b. 1980)	*Baroque Variations on The Frail for Cello & Piano*	74
Henri Dutilleux (1916-2013)	*Tout un monde lointain… for Cello & Orchestra*	75
Antonín Dvořák (1841-1904)	*Cello Concerto in B Minor, Op. 104*	76
Antonín Dvořák (1841-1904)	*Silent Woods for Cello & Orchestra*	78
Edward Elgar (1857-1934)	*Cello Concerto in E Minor, Op. 85*	79
Reena Esmail (b. 1983)	*Perhaps for Solo Cello*	80

Table of Contents

Elisenda Fábregas (b. 1955)	*Colores Andaluces for Cello & Piano*	81
Louise Farrenc (1804-1875)	*Sonata in B-flat Major, Op. 46 for Cello & Piano*	82
Gabriel Faure (1845-1924)	*Élégie, Op. 24 for Cello & Piano*	83
Gabriel Faure (1845-1924)	*Sonata No. 2 in G Minor, Op. 117 for Cello & Piano*	84
Vivian Fine (1913-2000)	*Sonata for Cello and Piano*	85
Gerald Finzi (1901-1956)	*Cello Concerto in A Minor, Op. 40*	86
Lukas Foss (1922-2009)	*Capriccio for Cello & Piano*	87
César Franck (1822-1890)	*Sonata in A Major for Cello & Piano*	88
Gabriela Lena Frank (b. 1972 & David Fetherolf (b. 1956)	*Serenata for Solo Cello*	89
Domenico Gabrielli (c. 1659-1690)	*7 Ricercari per violoncello solo*	90
Albert Ginastera (1916-1983)	*Pampeana No. 2 Rhapsody for Cello & Piano, Op. 21*	91
Philip Glass (b. 1937)	*Orbit for Solo Cello*	92
Philip Glass (b. 1937)	*Partita No. 1 for Solo Cello (Songs & Poems)*	93
Osvaldo Golijov (b. 1960)	*Azul for Cello and Orchestra*	94
Georg Goltermann (1824-1898)	*Cello Concerto No. 4 in G Major, Op. 65*	95
Edvard Grieg (1843-1907)	*Sonata in A Minor for Cello & Piano, Op. 36*	96
Sofia Gubaidulina (b. 1931)	*10 Preludes for Solo Cello*	97
Adolphus Hailstork (b. 1941)	*Theme & Variations on Draw the Sacred Circle Closer for Solo Cello*	98
Franz Joseph Haydn (1732-1809)	*Cello Concerto No. 1 in C Major, Hob. VIIb:1*	99
Franz Joseph Haydn (1732-1809)	*Cello Concerto No. 2 in D Major, Hob. VIIb:2*	100
Victor Herbert (1859-1924)	*Cello Concerto No. 2 in E Minor, Op. 30*	101
Jennifer Higdon (b. 1962)	*Nocturne for Cello & Piano*	102
Paul Hindemith (1895-1963)	*Sonata for Solo Cello*	103
Lee Hoiby (1926-2011)	*Sonata for Cello & Piano, Op. 59*	104
Imogen Holst (1907-1984)	*Fall of the Leaf for Solo Cello*	105
John Ireland (1879-1962)	*Sonata for Cello & Piano*	106
Marie Jaëll (1846-1925)	*Cello Concerto in F Major*	107
Leoš Janáček (1854-1928)	*Pohádka for Cello & Piano*	108
Nathalie Joachim (b. 1983)	*Dam Mwen Yo for Solo Cello*	109
David H. Johnson (b. 1977)	*5 Melodies for Cello & Piano*	110
Dmitri Kabalevsky (1904-1987)	*Cello Concerto No. 1 in G minor, Op. 49*	111

Table of Contents

Aaron Kernis (b. 1960)	*Colored Field (Cello Concerto)*	112
Zoltán Kodály (1882-1967)	*Sonata in B minor for Solo Cello, Op. 8*	113
Erich Korngold (1897-1957)	*Cello Concerto in C Major, Op. 37*	114
Antonin Kraft (1749-1820)	*Cello Concerto in C Major, Op. 4*	115
Édouard Lalo (1823-1892)	*Cello Concerto in D Minor*	116
Libby Larsen (b. 1950)	*Juba for Cello & Piano*	117
Luise LeBeau (1850-1927)	*Sonata in D Major, Op 17 for Cello & Piano*	118
Leonardo Leo (1694-1744)	*6 Concerti for Cello, Strings & Basso Continuo*	119
Tania Léon (b. 1943)	*Four Pieces for Solo Cello*	121
György Ligeti (1923-2006)	*Sonata for Solo Cello*	122
Allison Loggins-Hull (b. 1982)	*Stolen for Solo Cello*	123
Witold Lutosławski (1913-1994)	*Concerto for Cello and Orchestra*	124
James MacMillan (b. 1959)	*Sonata No. 1 for Cello & Piano*	125
Elisabeth Maconchy (1907-1994)	*Divertimento for Cello & Piano*	126
Bohuslav Martinů (1890-1959)	*Sonata for Cello and Piano No. 3, H.340*	127
David Maslanka (1943-2017)	*Remember Me for Cello and Nineteen Players*	128
Emilie Mayer (1812-1883)	*12 Sonatas for Cello & Piano*	129
Missy Mazzoli (b. 1980)	*Beyond the Order of Things (After Josquin) for Solo Cello*	130
Marc Mellits (b. 1966)	*Book of Ruth for Solo Cello*	131
Fanny Mendelssohn (1805-1847)	*Zwei Stücke for Cello & Piano*	132
Felix Mendelssohn (1809-1847)	*Sonata No. 2 in D Major for Piano & Cello, Op. 58*	133
Darius Milhaud (1892-1974)	*Cello Concerto No. 1, Op. 136*	134
Georg Matthias Monn (1717-1750)	*Cello Concerto in G Minor*	135
Jesse Montgomery (b. 1981)	*Divided for Cello & String Orchestra*	136
Dorothy Rudd Moore (b. 1940)	*Baroque Suite for Solo Cello*	137
Nico Muhly (b. 1981)	*Cello Concerto*	138
Thea Musgrave (b. 1928)	*D.E.S.- In Celebration for Solo Cello*	139
Michael Nyman (b. 1944)	*On the Fiddle for Cello & Piano*	140
Maria Theresia von Paradis (1759-1824)		
	Sicilienne for Cello & Piano	141
Arvo Pärt (b. 1935)	*Fratres*	142
Arvo Pärt (b. 1935)	*Pro et Contra (Concerto for Cello & Orchestra)*	143
Arvo Pärt (b. 1935)	*Spiegel im Spiegel*	145
Dora Pejačević (1885-1923)	*Sonata in E Minor, Op. 35 for Cello & Piano*	146
Krzysztof Penderecki (1933-2020)		
	Cello Concerto No. 2	147

Table of Contents

Coleridge-Taylor Perkinson (1932-2004)	Lamentations; Black/Folk Song Suite for Solo Cello	147
Astor Piazzolla (1921-1992)	Le Grande Tango for Cello & Piano	148
David Popper (1843-1913)	Hungarian Rhapsody, Op. 68 for Cello & Piano	149
Nicola Porpora (1686-1768)	6 Cello Sonatas	150
Francis Poulenc (1899-1963)	Sonata for Cello & Piano, FP. 143	151
Paola Prestini (b. 1975)	To Tell a Story for Solo Cello & Electronics	152
Florence Price (1887-1953)	Adoration for Cello & Piano	153
Sergei Prokofiev (1891-1953)	Sinfonia Concertante for Cello and Orchestra, Op. 125	154
Sergei Prokofiev (1891-1953)	Sonata in C Major, Op. 119 for Cello & Piano	155
Gabriel Prokofiev (b. 1975)	Cello Multitracks	156
Blaž Pucihar (b. 1977)	Summer Sonata for Cello & Piano, Op. 8	157
Kevin Puts (b. 1972)	Air for Cello & Piano	158
Sergei Rachmaninoff (1873-1943)	Sonata in G Minor, Op. 19 for Cello & Piano	159
Kaitlyn Raitz (b.1989)	Not So Simple for Solo Cello	160
Shulamit Ran (b. 1949)	Fantasy Variations for Solo Cello	161
Max Reger (1873-1916)	Three Suites for Solo Cello, Op. 131c	162
Ottorini Respighi (1879-1936)	Adagio con Variazione for Cello & Orchestra	163
George Rochberg (1918-2005)	Ricordanza Soliloquy for Cello & Piano	164
Joaquin Rodrigo (1901-1999)	Concierto in modo galante for Cello & Orchestra	165
Bernhard Romberg (1767-1841)	Sonata No. 1 in E Minor, Op. 38 for Cello & Piano	166
Daniel Bernard Roumain (b. 1971)	Why Did They Kill Sandra Bland for Solo Cello	167
Christopher Rouse (1949-2019)	Morpheus for Solo Cello	168
Kaija Saariaho (1952-2023)	Sept Papillons for Solo Cello	169
Camille Saint-Säens (1835-1921)	Cello Concerto No. 1 in A Minor, Op. 33	170
Camille Saint-Säens (1835-1921)	Le Cygne (The Swan) from Le Carnaval des animaux for Cello & Piano	171
Aulis Sallinen (b. 1935)	Cello Concerto	172
Alfred Schnittke (1934-1998)	Sonata No. 1 for Cello & Piano	173
Franz Schubert (1797-1828)	Sonata in A Minor, D. 821 Arpeggione	174
Robert Schumann (1810-1856)	Concerto in A Minor, Op. 129	175
Robert Schumann (1810-1856)	Fünf Stücke im Volkston, Op. 102 for Cello & Piano	176

Table of Contents

Caroline Shaw (b. 1982)	*In manus tuas for Solo Cello*	177
Bright Sheng (b. 1955)	*Seven Tunes Heard in China for Solo Cello*	178
Dmitri Shostakovich (1906-1975)	*Concerto No. 1 for Cello & Orchestra, Op. 107*	179
Dmitri Shostakovich (1906-1975)	*Sonata in D Minor, Op. 40 for Cello & Piano*	180
Jean Sibelius (1865-1957)	*Malinconia, Op. 20 for Cello & Piano*	182
Alvin Singleton (b. 1940)	*Argoru II for Solo Cello*	183
Derrick Skye (b. 1982)	*Hum for Solo Cello*	184
Ethel Smyth (1858-1944)	*Sonata in A Minor, Op. 5 for Cello & Piano*	185
Sarah Kirkland Snider (b. 1973)	*The Reserved, The Reticent for Solo Cello*	186
Carl Stamitz (1745-1801)	*Cello Concerti for the King of Prussia*	187
Carolyn Steinberg (b. 1956)	*A Wintry Mix: Of Ice and Snow for Cello & Piano*	188
John Steinmetz (b. 1951)	*Possessed for Solo Cello*	189
William Grant Still (1895-1978)	*Mother & Child for Cello & Piano*	190
Richard Strauss (1864-1949)	*Sonata in F Major, Op. 6 for Cello & Piano*	191
Richard Strauss (1864-1949)	*Don Quixote, Op. 35 for Cello & Orchestra*	192
Igor Stravinsky (1882-1971)	*Suite Italienne for Cello & Piano (after Pulcinella, trans. Piatigorsky)*	193
Mark Summer (b. 1958)	*Julie-O for Solo Cello*	194
John Tavener (1944-2013)	*The Protecting Veil for Cello & Orchestra*	195
Piotr Illych Tchaikovsky (1840-1893)	*Variations on a Rococo Theme for Cello & Orchestra*	196
Augusta Read Thomas (b. 1964)	*Cantos for Slava for Cello & Piano*	197
Joan Tower (b. 1938)	*Très lent (Hommage à Messiaen) for Cello & Piano*	198
Jean Balthasar Tricklir (1750-1813)	*13 Cello Concerti*	199
Peteris Vasks (b. 1946)	*Cello Concerto*	200
Ralph Vaughan Williams (1872-1958)	*Six Studies in English Folk Song for Cello & Piano*	201
Heitor Villa-Lobos (1887-1959)	*Concerto No. 2 for Cello & Orchestra, W165*	202
Antonio Vivaldi (1678-1741)	*9 Sonatas for Cello & Basso Continuo, RV 39-47*	203
Antonio Vivalid (1678-1741)	*27 Concerti for Cello & Orchestra, RV 398-409*	205
Gwyneth Walker (b. 1947)	*By Land and by Sea for Cello & Piano*	206
George Walker (1922-2018)	*Sonata for Cello & Piano*	207
George Walker (1922-2018)	*Movements for Cello & Orchestra*	208
William Walton (1902-1983)	*Cello Concerto*	209
Mary D. Watkins (b. 1939)	*Bus Stop for Cello & Piano*	210
Anton Webern (1883-1945)	*Drei Kleine Stücke, Op. 11 for Cello & Piano*	211
Paul Wiancko (b.1983)	*Microsuite for Solo Cello*	212

Table of Contents

John Williams (b. 1932)	*Elegy for Cello & Piano*	212
John Williams (b. 1932)	*Theme from Schindler's List for Cello & Piano*	213
John Williams (b. 1932)	*Three Pieces from Memoirs of a Geisha for Cello & Piano*	214
Luna Pearl Woolf (b. 1973)	*Helter Skelter arr. for Solo Cello*	215
Alexander Zemlinsky (1871-1942)	*Sonata in A Minor for Cello & Piano*	216
Ellen Taaffe Zwillich (b. 1939)	*Cello Concerto*	217

Appendix A: Works by Genre — 218

Appendix B: Chronology of Works — 223

Appendix C: Other Cello Repetroire Resources — 228

Thomas Adès (b. 1971) — Lieux retrouvés for Cello & Piano

Date of Composition: 2009
Date of Premiere: June 21, 2009
Premiered by: Steven Isserlis, cello and Thomas Adès, piano
Approximate Length: 15 min.

> I. Les Eaux
> II. La Montagne
> III. Les Champs
> IV. La Ville - Cancan Macabre

Background Information:

Lieux retrouvés, which translates to 'places found', was commissioned by the Aldeburgh Festival, Wigmore Hall, and Carnegie Hall. One of the leading composers in Britain of the recent past, Adès is also a concert pianist and conductor. Although the cello is used in various other chamber works of his, at press time, this is his only work featuring the cello as soloist.

From program notes by Paul Griffiths:

'I don't know why it is,' Thomas Adès has said, 'but the cello of all instruments makes one dream of "elsewhere".' Hence the four elsewheres of these Lieux retrouvés, or 'Places Revisited', which he wrote for Steven Isserlis in 2009 as a cello sonata, arranging the original piano accompaniment for chamber orchestra earlier this year.

The metaphor of water – flowing, sparkling – is one Adès has used before, too. In 'Les eaux', the first movement of this piece, it seems appropriate to the constant running quavers let loose by the [piano] at the start, and to how the cello's slow melody floats on those quavers, borne by them but distinct. This being music, the situation can change, whether gradually, by accumulating complication, or in a flash. At the same time, the orchestral version carries the music through wonderful colours, as throughout the work.

In the second movement, 'La montagne', the cello's upward steps are at once offset and energised by the triplet accompaniment. There is a smoother trio section before the exertion is continued, to reach, in the luminous coda, the peak.

Next comes 'Les champs' the slow movement, where the same figure keeps revolving, the mountain climb replaced by an amble through fields that goes on until it reaches up and up, into the sunlit haze.

Finally, back in the city ('La ville') after these rural excursions, we find another Adès speciality, a disturbing-exciting dance – in this case a 'cancan macabre', duly paying homage to Offenbach's.

A version of this work was made for cello and small orchestra in 2016.

Edition:
Faber Music

Bibliography:
www.thomasades.com
Faber Music Lieux retrouvés Accessed November 18, 2020,
https://www.fabermusic.com/music/lieux-retrouv%C3%A9s-5279

Program notes used with permission from Paul Griffiths

Recordings: Steven Isserlis and Thomas Adès himself made a recording on the Hyperion label.
www.thomasades.com

Eleanor Alberga (b. 1949) — Ride Through for Solo Cello

Date of Composition: 2015
Date of Premiere: 2015
Premiered by: Robert Irvine
Approximate Length: 4 min.

Background Information:

Jamaican-born composer Eleanor Alberga has had a wide and varied career. Trained as a professional pianist at the Royal Academy of Music in London, she ended up devoting her career solely to composition in 2011. Her works run across all categories (opera, symphonic, choral, chamber), even film and television. She often performs in a duo with her husband, violinist Thomas Bowes, additionally running a music festival together, the Arcadia Music Festival.

Ride Through for Solo Cello was commissioned by cellist Robert Irvine for a charity CD recording project of all solo cello works addressing the plight of impoverished children around the globe. Irvine said, "I hope the theme of this album will at the very least make people pause and think about issues that contribute to children suffering around the world."

As inspiration, Alberga based the thematic material on a traditional Jamaican nursery rhyme, with the lyrics, "Ride through, ride through the rocky road".

Edition:
Available from the composer herself: scores@eleanoralberga.com

Bibliography:
Eleanor Alberga Official Website, Accessed November 18, 2020, https://www.eleanoralberga.com
Robert Irvine interview, Accessed November 18, 2020, http://katemolleson.com/interview-robert-irvine-on-songs-lullabies/

Recordings:
There is one commercial recording available from Robert Irvine on his album "Songs and Lullabies" on the Delphian label, 2016.

Eric Alexander (b. 1973) — Symmetry of Trees for Solo Cello

Date of Composition: 2023
Date of Premiere: April 7, 2023
Premiered by: Brian Hodges: The Luminary Space at the Boise State Center for the Visual Arts
Approximate Length: 14 min.

I. Roots (7 min)
II. Host of Life (4 min)
III. Branches (3 min)

Background Information:

Eric Scott Alexander is Associate Professor of Composition and Theory at Boise State University. In many of his compositions, he is inspired by nature and the elements around us.

Symmetry of Trees was written for a gala event showcasing the new Luminary space in the Center for the Visual Arts at Boise State University. The Luminary is a room with three walls consisting of floor-to-ceiling LED interactive panels. Users can connect to gallery collections from museums around the world. For this performance, computer graphic designer, Ryan Donahue, created algorithms based on the frequency of the cello's open strings, which were then fed into the internal computer system of the room. Each note performed would create colors, shapes, and patterns projected on the wall panels, reacting in real time to the music being performed.

Alexander writes: The Symmetry of Trees was composed in 2023 for Brian Hodges. The composition for solo cello was composed for the grand opening of Boise State University's Keith and Catherine Stein Luminary, an all-digital museum space with touch-activated glass walls. The piece explores the natural balance and symmetry found in trees and other plants, not only related to the view of a tree from the top or the side, but the relationship between the root and branches, and even the individual leaves

Edition:
Available from the composer's website

Bibliography:
www.ericscottalexander.com

Recordings:
No commercial recordings have been made, although a video of the performance in the Luminary can be viewed on the Luminary website: https://www.boisestate.edu/luminary/

Lera Auerbach (b. 1973) — 24 Preludes for Cello and Piano, Op. 47

Date of Composition: 1999
Date of Premiere: July 11, 2008
Premiered by: Alisa Weilerstein, cello and Lera Auerbach, piano
Approximate Length: 50 min.

I Andante (3:02 min)
II. Allegro (0:47 min)
III. Andante misterioso (1:59 min)
IV. Allegro ossessivo (0:43 min)
V. Moderato (1:48 min)
VI. Andante tragico (2:17)
VII. Vivo ma non troppo e agitato (1:13 min)
VIII. Grave (1:52 min)
IX. Vivace (0:58 min)
X. Adagio sognando (1:37 min)
XI. Allegro (0:51 min)
XII. Adagio (4:59 min)
XIII. Andante grazioso (2:08 min)
XIV. Allegretto scherzando (1:18 min)
XV. Allegro con brio (1:00 min)
XVI. Tempo di valzer (3:18 min)
XVII. Allegro ritmico (2:44 min)
XVIII. Andantino (1:27 min)
XIX. Allegro appassionato (1:07 min)
XX. Giocoso (1:14 min)
XXI. Dialogo (2:49 min)
XXII. Andante nostalgico (3:29 min)
XXIII. Adagio sognando (2:40 min)
XXIV. Vivo (4:29 min)

Background Information:

Not only is Lera Auerbach an award-winning composer, she is also a pianist, conductor, poet and visual artist. She has published three books of poetry in her native Russian language, but has also written and published books in English. Studying at the Juilliard School, her compositions have been performed by some of the world's leading performing artists. Her visual art has been exhibited in several leading galleries.

Program notes from the composer:

The 24 Preludes, written in 1999, continue a long line of musical tradition, from the Well-Tempered Clavier of Bach through the preludes of Chopin and Debussy to similar cycles by Shostakovich. Ms. Auerbach writes: "Re-establishing the value and expressive possibilities of all major and minor tonalities is as valid at the beginning of the 21st century as it was during Bach's time, especially if we consider the aesthetics of Western music and its travels in this regard — or disregard — to tonality during the last century. The 24 Preludes follow the circle of fifths, thus covering the entire tonal spectrum…In writing this work I wished to create a continuum that would allow these short pieces to be united as one single composition. The challenge was not only to write a meaningful and complete prelude that may be only

Lera Auerbach (b. 1973) — 24 Preludes for Cello and Piano, Op. 47

a minute long, but also for this short piece to be an organic part of a larger composition with its own form. Looking at something familiar yet from an unexpected perspective is one of the peculiar characteristics of these pieces — they are often not what they appear to be at first glance. The context and order of preludes is important for their understanding.

Edition:
Exempla Nova 308 (Sikorski)

Bibliography:
Lera Auerbach Official website, Accessed March 22, 2021, https://leraauerbach.com/
24 Preludes pages at Boosey & Hawkes website, Accessed August 28, 2023, https://www.boosey.com/shop/prod/Auerbach-Lera-24-Praludien-mit-Postludium-24-Preludes-for-Violoncello-and-Piano/2322358

Recordings:
One commercial recording has been released with Ani Aznavoorian, cello with Lera Auerbach, piano on Cedille Records, 2013

Lera Auerbach (b. 1973) — Sonata for Cello & Piano No. 1, Op. 69

Date of Composition: 2002
Date of Premiere: February 19, 2003
Premiered by: David Finckel, cello and Wu Han, piano
Approximate Length: 22 min.

> I. Allegro moderato (7 min)
> II. Lament. Adagio (6 min)
> III. Allegro assai (3 min)
> IV. Con estrema intensitá (6 min)

Background Information:
Auerbach, the prodigiously brilliant and prolific composer from Russia, has written a handful of solo works for cello. Her Sonata No. 1, written in 2002 for the famed duo of David Finckel and Wu Han, is a towering work of complexity and emotional potency.

From the composer:
I was happy when David Finckel and Wu Han asked me to write a large-scale work for them. They form a very dramatic union, capable of captivating audiences with magnetic intensity and powerful interpretations. I was well aware of these qualities while writing the sonata…I began working on the piece while reading Hermann Hesse's novel Demian. Although there is no direct connection and the work is not programmatic, perhaps some of the imagery from Hesse's novel may have infiltrated the writing, especially in the first movement—Allegro moderato—where I thought of a dance of Abraxas, a mysterious god who combines in himself both good and evil.

Edition:
Sikorski Edition

Bibliography:
Lera Auerbach Official Website, Accessed August 26, 2023, https://leraauerbach.com/
Program Notes from Music at Menlo Festival, Accessed November 18, 2020, https://musicatmenlo.org/files/CB_IV_Notes.pdf

Recordings:
Ani Aznavoorian, cello with Lera Auerbach, piano (Cedille Records, 2013)

Carl Philipp Emanuel Bach (1714-1788)   3 Cello Concerti (Wq. 170, 171, 172)

Date of Compositions: 1750-1753
Approximate Lengths:

> A Minor, Wq. 170 (26 min)
> B-flat Major, Wq. 171 (25 min)
> A Major, Wq. 172 (19 min)
>
> Concerto in A Minor, Wq. 170
> I. Allegro Assai (10 min)
> II. Andante (8 min)
> III. Allegro assai (8 min)
>
> Concerto in B-flat Major, Wq. 171
> I. Allegretto (8 min)
> II. Adagio (9 min)
> III. Allegro assai (8 min)
>
> Concerto in A Major, Wq. 172
> I. Allegro (6 min)
> II. Largo con sordini, mesto (8 min)
> III. Allegro assai (5 min)

Background Information:

    Arguably the most famous of Johann Sebastian Bach's children, Carl Philipp Emanuel Bach was a composer of international celebrity in a way that his father never was (at least, in his lifetime). Employed by Frederik the Great, King of Prussia, chiefly as the main keyboardist in his court music ensemble for close to thirty years, he had an instrumental retinue around him consisting of some of the best musicians in Europe. He was involved in composing for and performing in weekly chamber concerts, allowing him to sharpen his naturally inherited compositional skills. His music deftly bridges the gap between the Baroque and Classical styles, having a considerable impact, namely with the use of the Empfindsamer Stil (in a sensitive and tender style).

    The three cello concerti were written between the years 1750 and 1753, roughly a decade after he began his employment at Frederik's court. Unfortunately, it is not known who they were written for and for what occasion. Of course, the most likely candidate would have been Ignaz Mara, the resident cellist at the court at that time.

    All three pieces make good use of the range of the cello and reflect the Classical characteristics just beginning to crystalize. It's in the slow movements where Emanuel's sentimental style is most evident, showcasing his lovely sense of melody and emotion. In contrast to the pieces from the Baroque era, we find more specific dynamic markings throughout, heightening contrast and drama.

    All the concerti exist in concerto versions for flute and for harpsichord. Although it's not entirely certain, most scholars regard the cello version as the original version.

Selected Editions:
Breitkopf und Härtel (Urtext)
www.cpebach.org gives access to urtext performance parts for major works, including the three cello concerti

Bibliography:
Gaines, James R, Evening in the Palace of Reason (HarperCollins Publishers, New York, NY, 2006).
Helm, Eugene, "Carl Philipp Emanuel Bach" The New Grove Bach Family, edited by Stanley Sadie (W.W. Norton & Company, New York, 1983).
Schulenberg, David, The Music of Carl Philipp Emanuel Bach (University of Rochester Press, Rochester, NY, 2014).

Recordings:
Many commercial recordings have been released, both in a modern interpretation and on period instruments.

J.S. Bach (1685-1750)
Three Sonatas for Viola da Gamba & Harpsichord, BWV 1027-1029

Date of Composition: 1735-1740?
Date of Premiere: Unknown
Premiered by: Unknown
Approximate Length: 13 min.

Sonata I in G Major, BWV 1027
I. Adagio (4 min)
II. Allegro ma non tanto (3 min)
III. Andante (3 min)
IV. Allegro moderato (3 min)

Sonata II in D Major, BWV 1028
I. Adagio (2 min)
II. Allegro (4 min)
III. Andante (4 min)
IV. Allegro (3 min)

Sonata III in G Minor, BWV 1029
I. Vivace (5 min)
II. Adagio (6 min)
III. Allegro (3 min)

Background Information:

By the time it is thought that J.S. Bach wrote his three sonatas for viola da gamba, the instrument itself was becoming more and more out of fashion. Once the reigning bowed string instrument, particularly popular with the nobility, it was quickly getting replaced by the new and modern string instruments, namely the violin. Bach featured the gamba from time to time throughout his music; it shows up in a number of his church cantatas, and they make special appearances in the two passions that survive, The St. Matthew's Passion and the St. John's Passion. Bach seemed to hold the gamba in special esteem, using it in very specific places to highlight its beautiful and unique sound (Komm, süßes Kreutz from the St. Matthew's Passion is especially sublime).

The three sonatas for viola da gamba are reworkings of pieces he had written earlier. Sonata No. 1 appears to be an arrangement of an earlier trio sonata for two treble instruments and basso continuo, No. 2 is an arrangement of an organ trio sonata, and the third sonata, a reworking of perhaps an orchestral work. It is not known if they were performed in his lifetime, not to mention by whom.

What is interesting is the fact that he wrote suites for cello, and sonatas for the viola da gamba. The cello was rapidly rising in the ranks of solo instruments, but the suite was starting to be antiquated. Whereas the viola da gamba was fading into the background, but the sonata was the piece genre du jour. For most people, it would've made more sense to write sonatas for the cello, and suites for the gamba. Nevertheless, we can't know what was behind Bach's reasons, and gambists are naturally thankful for these wonderful sonatas.

Of course, the viola da gamba is blessedly still around and in great use today. However, that hasn't stopped cellists (and other string instruments such as the viola and double bass) from performing these sonatas. They show up regularly on cello recitals and work quite successfully on the instrument.

Not surprisingly, there is a wealth of invention found in these works. Fugal writing, jaunty allegros, gorgeous slow movements (The Andante from the G Major Sonata is heavenly), they cover a wide spectrum of styles and character. Whichever instrument they are performed on, they are incredibly effective and exquisite works.

J.S. Bach (1685-1750)
Three Sonatas for Viola da Gamba & Harpsichord, BWV 1027-1029

Selected Editions:
Bärenreiter (Urtext)
G. Henle Verlag (Urtext)

Bibliography:
Bylsma, Anner, "Bach Gamba Sonatas," liner notes for Bach, J.S., *J.S. Bach: Sonatas for Viola da Gamba*, Sony Classics, 1990.
Eppstein, Hans, 1987, Preface. In Bach, J.S. *Drei Sonaten für Violoncello und Cembalo nach BWV 1027-1029*. Kassel: Bärenreiter.

Recordings:
There are many recordings of these works available, on all manners of stringed instruments.

J.S. Bach (1685-1750) — Six Suites for Unaccompanied Cello, BWV 1007-1012

Date of Composition: 1720's (?)
Date of Premiere: Unknown
Premiered by: Unknown
Approximate Length: 21 min. average (range from 16-27)

> I. Prelude
> II. Allemande
> III. Courante
> IV. Sarabande
> V. Minuets/Bourrées/Gavottes
> VI. Gigue

Background Information:

For all intents and purposes, it's probably not necessary for me to write anything about these works that could add to all of the discourse that is out there. As some of the most famous, well-known and beloved works for solo cello, these six suites by Johann Sebastian Bach hold a sacred place for performers and audiences alike.

What's fascinating is that we know practically nothing about this collection of pieces, when they were written, who they were written for, why they were written, and some even question what instrument Bach intended them for specifically. So many mysteries abound, which is not helped by the fact that we don't have a manuscript in Bach's own hand; modern editions are based off of four generally accepted sources, the most notable of them being the copy in Anna Magdalena's hand, who was his second wife and professional musician. Cellists tend to get bogged down in the details, what bowings are correct, to slur or not to slur, correct tempi, where to trill and where not to trill, etc., for which we have little to go on. Of course, this can get in the way of the inventive, moving, compelling, and brilliant music that lies before us.

Thought to be written in the time after he wrote his Sonatas and Partitas for Solo Violin, when he was working at the court of Cöthen, they are the first of their kind–an instrumental suite for solo cello. Unaccompanied music for cello had been written before (the ricercari by Gabrielli, capricii by Dall'Abaco, Domenico Galli's solo cello sonatas to name a few), but nothing on this scope: Six Suites made up of six movements each. Unlike the solo violin works, each suite is uniform, a prelude followed by a set of courtly dances: Allemande, Courante, Sarabande, a set of paired dances, concluding with a Gigue.

Much has been hypothesized about the meaning behind these suites, other than the pure dance forms. Are they religious? Is there a story? Do the keys of the suites or numbers of measures have any profound significance? We don't know, and probably never will know. And while that may be initially frustrating, it also is liberating, freeing the player to put their own sensibilities into the music, making it even more personal.

A fascinating take on the meaning behind the Suites has been proposed by cellist Steven Isserlis. He senses that there is an underlying story behind each of the six suites and that they relate thematically as well, reflecting Bach's Lutheran outlook on life. Starting with the G Major Suite, this could be the Nativity; the second suite in D Minor could be the agony in the garden from betrayal to foreshadowing of His sacrifice to come; the C Major suite could be the descent of the Holy Spirit, which appeared in the form of a dove; Suite 4 in E-flat Major could be the presentation in the temple, with its architectural arpeggios symbolizing a grand edifice; the dark C Minor 5th Suite could be the despair and eventual loneliness of the crucifixion; and the 6th Suite in glorious D major could be the resurrection.

Isserlis would be the first to admit that this is a far stretch and if Bach had anything like this in mind, it would be more of a suggestion or impression than a literal programmatic telling. He says, "these images are only there for those who might find them inspiring…but there is certainly no need for any extra-musical input. The suites are perfect in themselves."

J.S. Bach (1685-1750) — Six Suites for Unaccompanied Cello, BWV 1007-1012

Whether you prefer a more picturesque perspective or not, the suites are full of ideas, characters and emotions. If Bach wrote them in the order that they are collected, one can see the trajectory as he moves through the suites, gaining confidence and freedom to experiment and push boundaries. By the time we get to the fifth suite, Bach calls for scordatura, with the A-string tuned down to a G (this was quite common in this era; the mystery sonatas for violin by Heinrich Biber are full of scordatura or deliberate 'mis-tunings'), which makes an already dark work, even more somber and despondent. The sixth suite is indicated to be played on an instrument with five strings, but for which specifically (A violoncello piccolo? A violoncello da spalla? A viola pomposa?) is not known.

From the overly famous Prelude to the first suite, to the ebullient joy of the gigue of the sixth suite, the music covers the entire landscape of the human experience. Through the framework of the Baroque instrumental suite and its courtly dances, Bach presents it all, the joys, the sorrows, the despairs, the triumphs. It's hard to even imagine him adding anything else, as Isserlis so plainly puts, "they are perfect in themselves."

Selected Editions:
Practically every publisher has produced editions of these suites, with varying levels of editorial input.
Barenreiter (Urtext)
G. Henle Verlag (Urtext)

Bibliography:
Bylsma, Anner, Bach, the Fencing Master (Lulu Books, Amsterdam, 2019).
Gardiner, John Eliot, Music in the Castle of Heaven (Vintage Publishing, New York, 2015).
Isserlis, Steven, The Bach Cello Suites: A Companion (Faber & Faber, London, 2021).
Isserlis, Steve, "Bach's Six Cello Suites," liner notes for Bach, J.S. J.S. Bach The Cello Suites, Steven Isserlis, cello, Hyperion Records, 2007.

Recordings:
There are recordings of these suites to fit every style and taste. Virtually every major cellist has committed these to recording, both on modern and period setup.

David Baker (1931-2016) — Sonata for Cello & Piano

Date of Composition: 1973
Date of Premiere: 1973
Premiered by: Janos Starker
Approximate Length: 19 min.

> I. Fast (5 min)
> II. Blues (8 min)
> III. Fast (6 min)

Background Information:

David Baker was professor of jazz studies at Indiana University (also his alma mater) where he crossed paths with the formidable cellist, Janos Starker. No stranger to cello, Baker played a bit of cello, and has a handful of cello pieces in his catalog, including a solo sonata, some chamber pieces, and a concerto for cello with jazz band.

This Sonata was composed for Starker, with the cellist editing the published edition. It is separated into three movements: Fast, Blues and Fast, with the middle movement featuring some lovely pizzicato passages for the cello alone. Baker's musical language was steeped in jazz and this sonata is a reflection of that, with some inherently jazzy rhythms and harmonies. It is currently one of the required pieces for the Sphinx Competition senior division.

Edition:
Associated Music Publishers

Bibliography:
Publisher's page for David Baker, Accessed August 4, 2023, https://keisersouthernmusic.com/composers/david-baker.

Recordings:
One commercial recording is available by Janos Starker Laurel Records, 2007.

James Balentine (b. 1947) — a wiser man: 6 short songs for cello & piano

Date of Composition: 1995
Date of Premiere: 1995
Premiered by: Brian Hodges, cello, and Kristin Roach, piano
Approximate Length: 18 min.

> I. a quiet time or two (3 min)
> II. brian (4 min)
> III. ludwig (4 min)
> IV. tennis anyone? (2 min)
> V. kathy (4 min)
> VI. the brain (1 min)

Background Information:

James Balentine is Professor Emeritus of Music Theory and Composition at the University of Texas at San Antonio. His compositions and arrangements have been performed by the San Antonio Symphony, the Flint Symphony, the Phoenix Symphony, and the Mid-Texas Symphony among others.

This song cycle for cello and piano was commissioned by Kathryn Hodges in honor of Donald A. Hodges (the author's father) on the occasion of his 50th birthday. Each of the six songs is accompanied by a short poem written by Balentine himself.

> *a quiet time or two*
> *don, a thoughtful man, reads and ponders;*
> *thinks and wonders;*
> *a wiser man than most*
> *resides in the brightness of the shadow of God.*
>
> *brian*
> *the son of his mother and father; her hands, his voice;*
> *their music; himself a wiser man to be ...*
>
> *ludwig*
> *the Dog; I remember him as a puppy;*
> *as elegant a dog as a dog could be*
> *and still be a dog, although a dog of musicians*
> *does sometimes wear the cloak of his namesake.*
>
> *tennis anyone?*
> *competent and aggressive, he plays the game to win, not to beat;*
> *for fun, not defeat.*
>
> *kathy*
> *more than a wife, more than a companion, she herself wiser than most;*
> *the counterpart, the matching page in a book*
> *that explains why, and why not.*
>
> *the brain*
> *ah, the mystery; a life's work, the source of a thoughtful man;*

James Balentine (b. 1947) — a wiser man: 6 short songs for cello & piano

it thinks and wonders; it hides in the shadow
more than a few of his questions;
it is the quest of a wiser man.

Edition:
Southern Music

Bibliography:
Official website of the composer, Accessed November 1, 2022, https://www.jamesbalentine.com/writings.

Recordings:
No commercial recording exists.

Samuel Barber (1910-1981) — Cello Concerto, Op. 22

Date of Composition: 1945
Date of Premiere: April 5, 1946
Premiered by: Raya Garbousova, with Serge Koussivitsky conducting the Boston Symphony Orchestra
Approximate Length: 30 mins. 13 sec.

I. Allegro moderato (12'48)
II. Andante sostenuto (7'19)
III. Molto allegro ed appassionato (10.06)

Background Information:

    Samuel Barber is one of the most well-known American composers of the twentieth century. However, his musical language and style differed greatly from his contemporaries, who more and more were moving further into atonality and experimental music. Barber stayed, for the most part, on solid tonal grounding and dared to write traditional pieces with melodies, something he received a fair amount of derision for. Knowing his neo-Romantic sensibilities set him apart, he referred to himself as a "living dead" composer.

    Born in West Chester, Pennsylvania, he went on to study at the Curtis Institute, attracting a lot of attention for his compositions. He was already writing mature works (his one and only Sonata for Cello and Piano was written just as he was finishing his degree (see other entry)) at this point. After winning a few prestigious awards, his works began to be performed by major orchestras and artists.

    When World War II broke out, Barber served in the Army corps. During this time, the Boston Symphony commissioned a cello concerto from him for the great cellist, Raya Garbousova. He finished the work just as he was discharged from the army and the premiere with Garbousova and the Boston Symphony took place a few months later.

    The work is lavish and highly lyrical, and is arranged in a standard concerto three-movement format. The first movement begins with a lopsided rhythm in the orchestra, before the cello comes in with its sweeping melody. The lyricism gives way to some spiky and syncopated rhythms, but never goes away for long, Barber leaning into the cello's singing capabilities heavily.

A tender oboe solo opens the second movement, eventually becoming somewhat of a duet between the two instruments. It's a plaintive, moody and introspective movement that makes good use of the cello's dark inner and lower registers.

    The last movement's overall mood is generally upbeat (after an intense and tragic orchestral introduction). There are delightful back and forths between the cello and orchestra, trading fun and witty banter throughout. The cello charges to the finish line, flying all the way to the top of its register for one last anguished statement of the theme, before the orchestra ends the work in a dramatic and bombastic final cadence. It's a tremendous work.

    Despite Barber's Violin Concerto being a standard concerto in the violin canon, his cello concerto has failed to catch on in the same way. Citing the intensely difficult passages throughout, many cellists have largely stayed away from it. Plenty of other demanding concerti for cello have become staples of the repertoire, so, hopefully, this will find its way back into the pantheon of cello concerti.

Edition:
G. Schirmer

Samuel Barber (1910-1981) — Cello Concerto, Op. 22

Bibliography:
Davies, Daniel Edward An analytical, historical and pedagogical overview of Samuel Barber's Cello Concerto, Dmitri Shostakovich's Cello Concerto #1, and William Walton's Cello Concerto dissertation Northwestern University, 1999.
Publisher page on Samuel Barber, Accessed August 14, 2023, https://www.wisemusicclassical.com/composer/72/Samuel-Barber/.
Whitehouse, Richard, Liner notes, Barber Samuel, Orchestral Music, Volume 2, Wendy Warner, cello, Royal Scottish National Orchestra, cond. Marin Alsop, Naxos, 2001.

Recordings:
There are quite a few commercial recordings available.

Samuel Barber (1910-1981) — Sonata in C Minor for Cello & Piano, Op. 6

Date of Composition: 1932
Date of Premiere: March 5, 1933
Premiered by: Orlando Cole, cello, and Samuel Barber, piano
Approximate Length: 18 min.

I. Allegro ma non troppo (8 min)
II. Adagio (4 min)
III. Allegro appassionato (6 min)

Background Information:

Samuel Barber achieved a high amount of fame and recognition during his career, in spite of the critical attacks against his music. At a time when music was expected to be experimental and free of tonal attachment, Barber dared to do the opposite, preferring plenty of melody and tonal centering.

As a student at the Curtis Institute, he was already receiving quite a bit of attention for his compositions. It was there, toward the end of his studies, that he composed his one and only sonata for cello and piano. The sonata is dedicated to his teacher, Rosario Scalero.

Barber had a bit of experience playing the cello—he studied it in his youth—and seemed to have a full understanding of the instrument based on the scope and content of the sonata. It is an unabashedly Romantic sonata, overflowing with long, lyrical lines and dark harmonies. While nowhere near as difficult as his Cello Concerto (see other entry), there are some passages of virtuosity sprinkled throughout.

The outer two movements are intense and melodramatic, spanning the extreme ranges of the two instruments. The slow movement is quintessential Barber, with an achingly beautiful melody, broken up by a jaunty and loping scherzo, only to be brought back to the opening slow material.

This sonata factored heavily into critics referring to him as a NeoRomantic, given its passionate and emotional nature.

Edition:
G. Schirmer

Bibliography:
Berger, Melvin. Guide to Sonatas: Music for One or Two Instruments (Achor Books, New York, 1991).
Publisher page on Samuel Barber, Accessed November 1, 2022, https://www.wisemusicclassical.com/composer/72/Samuel-Barber/.

Recordings:
There are a number of commercial recordings available.

Jean-Baptiste Barrière (1707-1747)   Sonatas for Cello & Basso Continuo

Date of Compositions: 1733-1740
Date of Premieres: Unknown
Premiered by: Unknown, but presumably Barrière himself
Approximate Length: 10 min.

Background Information:

Jean-Baptiste Barrière was one of the leading cellists in France at a time when the cello was relatively new. The viola da gamba family had been the reigning family of stringed instruments across Europe for some time, and the French, in particular, were reluctant to entertain the newer modern string instruments (violin, viola and cello), when places like Italy had all but abandoned the gamba. While information about Barrière's early life and education is thin, he does show up in Paris in the early 1700's as a member of the orchestra of the Royal Opera. He eventually earned the favor of the monarch, as King Louis XV granted him the privilege to compose and publish his own instrumental music.

His first volume (Livre I) of sonatas for cello and basso continuo appeared in 1733, and consisted of six sonatas. Over the next several years, three more volumes of sonatas for cello were published (Livres II-IV), each containing six sonatas as well. Each sonata typically has four movements, although some only have three; the sonatas range from 9 minutes to 12 minutes. The style of the sonatas tends to veer more toward the Italian style, rather than the French style, influenced no doubt by the year or so he spent in Italy studying the cello.

Despite not having a wealth of personal information on Barrière, what is clear is how skilled he was at the cello. Judging by the content of his sonatas, many of them have quite demanding solo parts, which shows he must have been a cellist of considerable talent. They are wonderful works and display a wide range of techniques and affekts for the cellist. Barrière played a huge part in the cello's acceptance and success in France, and helped pave the way for future French cello virtuosos such as Brèval and Duport.

Selected Editions:
Anne Fuzeau Productions and the Grancino Editions offer facsimile and parts based off of the manuscript.
Modern editions, such as International, are available with realized continuo parts.

Bibliography:
Kocevar, Erik, "The Art of Adding a French Touch to a Italian Style", Liner notes for Barrière, Jean "Sonates pour le violoncelle avec la basse continue", Bruno Cocset, cello, Les Basses Réunies, Alpha Classics, 2001.
Walden, Valerie One Hundred Years of Violoncello: A History of Technique and Performance Practice (1740-1840) (Cambridge University Press, Cambridge, 2004)

Recordings:
There are a few commercial available recordings available of these sonatas.

Mason Bates (b. 1977) — Cello Concerto

Date of Composition: 2014
Date of Premiere: December 11, 2014
Premiered by: Joshua Roman, cello; Mirga Gražinytė-Tyla, conductor; Seattle Symphony
Approximate Complete Length: 25 min.

> I. Con moto--Grazioso--con moto
> II. Serene
> III. Léger

Background Information:

The pairing of Mason Bates, one of the twenty-first century's composers du jour, and Joshua Roman, the wunderkind former youngest principal cellist of the Seattle Symphony and youtube star, was a dream pairing that led to the creation of a new and modern cello concerto. Bates, a Grammy-winning composer and DJ and Roman had collaborated on a few projects which eventually led to the commission of this concerto, with additional support from the Seattle Symphony, Los Angeles Chamber Orchestra, and the Columbus Symphony Orchestra.

From Bates' own program notes:

This cello concerto began with a friendship. Josh Roman is beloved by just about everyone who meets him, and I am no exception. Immediately apparent is…his unmatched musicianship and technique, and soon I was composing a fiendishly difficult solo work for him to premiere on his series at Town Hall…That experience proved to be a great warm-up for this concerto. The piece begins plaintively, with Josh floating over a restless orchestra, and the lyricism only expands in the central slow movement. But by the final movement the rhythmic energy wins the day, and at one point Josh even plays with a guitar pick. This is, after all, the same fellow who played arrangements of Led Zeppelin at Town Hall, so I had to send him out with a bang.

Roman has performed it with a variety of different orchestras, but to date, has yet to record it.

Edition:
Aphra Music (Study Score for purchase, parts for rental only as of press time)

Bibliography:
Composer's page on the piece, Accessed November 17, 2020, https://www.masonbates.com/cello-concerto/

Recordings:
None, but excerpts can be found on youtube.

Armando Bayolo (b. 1973) — Orfei Mors for Cello & Orchestra

Date of Composition: 2009
Date of Premiere: March 11, 2010
Premiered by: Philip von Maltzahn, cello and The Society for New Music in Syracuse, New York
Approximate Length: 20 min.

I. Clutching Vain Shadows, yearning
II. Baccantes
(played without pause)

Background Information:
Armando Bayolo is a Puerto-Rican composer who studied at Interlochen, the Eastman School of Music, Yale School of Music, and the University of Michigan.

His notes on his work Orfei Mors for Cello and Orchestra:

The story of Orpheus is a sort of foundational myth for Western musicians and the hero's exploits as a master songsmith whose gifts could "tame the savage breast" (or beasts, depending on which version one follows), his ill-fated love for Euridice and his subsequent travels to the underworld to secure her return to life have inspired composers from Peri to Stravinsky…The original myth, however, is far more tragic and it is this less often told part of the story that interested me when I set out to write my cello concerto, Orfei Mors. Orfei Mors ("The Death of Orpheus") is cast in two movements (performed without pause) each itself a kind of nesting doll enclosing several shorter pieces within its structure…Orfei Mors was commissioned by the Western Piedmont Symphony, John Gordon Ross, Music Director and the Syracuse Society for New Music, Neva Pilgrim, Artistic Director for Cellist Philip von Maltzahn. It was written in the winter and spring, 2009 in Alexandria, Virginia.

Edition:
Olibel Music

Bibliography:
Official website of Armando Bayolo, Accessed November 18, 2020, www.armandobayolo.com

Recordings:
No commercial recording as of yet, but a live recording of von Maltzahn and the Great Noise Ensemble, conducted by Armando Bayolo is available on the composer's website and Soundcloud

Amy Beach (1867-1944) — Five Compositions for Cello & Piano

Date of Composition: 1903 (original version for violin written in 1898)
Date of Premiere: Unknown
Premiered by: Unknown
Approximate Length: 17 mins

> La Captive (4 min)
> Berceuse (3 min)
> Mazurka (3 min)

Background Information:

Amy Marcy Beach was a child prodigy who persevered in music at a time when women were actively discouraged from having a career in music. She had an auspicious debut as a piano soloist and kept her studies in America, despite the allure of studying in Europe, a fashionable and serious thing to do at the time. A performance of her Mass in E-flat by the Handel and Haydn Society in 1892 brought her widespread attention and brought her music to a wider audience. The Boston Symphony performed her Gaelic Symphony, which has the distinction of being the first symphony by a woman composer performed by an American orchestra.

In 1898 she published a collection of shorter violin pieces for the violinist Maud Powell. Six years later, she transcribed them for cello, the impetus for which is not known, although it might have been requested by her publisher.

The original Op. 40 contained just the three works: La Captive, Berceuse and Mazurka, however later publications have added in two more works: Dreaming and Pastorale.

Edition:
Hildegard Publishing

Bibliography:
Block, Adrienne Fried. Liner notes, Beach, Amy and Clarke, Rebecca "Sonata for Cello and Piano", Pamela Frame, cello, Barry Snyder, piano, Robert Weirich, piano, Koch Classics, 1994.
Official website for Amy Beach, Accessed August 9, 2023, https://www.amybeach.org/

Recordings:
There are a number of commercial recordings made by cellists of these wonderful pieces, including Pamela Frame (the author's former teacher), on Koch Classics.

Sally Beamish (b. 1956) — Sonata for Cello & Piano

Date of Composition: 1999
Date of Premiere: May 20, 2000
Premiered by: Robert Irvine, cello and Sally Beamish, piano
Approximate Length: 20 min.

> 1. Prelude: Allegro moderato (3 min)
> 2. Scherzo. Allegro (4 min)
> 3. Ballad. Lento (6 min)
> 4. Theme-Variations 1-7 (7 min)

Background Information:

Sally Beamish is a British composer who performed for years as a violist with the Academy of Saint-Martin-in-the-Fields, the London Sinfonietta, the London Mozart Players and the Scottish Chamber Orchestra (the latter two as principal violist). She currently resides in Scotland, which permeates and inspires her compositions.

She has written several works for cello, the sonata being one of her more substantial works.

On the sonata, she writes:

This sonata was commissioned in 1999 By Beryl Calver-Jones and Gerry Mattock, and is the second in a series of commissions reflecting their support for and encouragement of my work. They asked me to create individual portraits of four friends: themselves and the first performers, the cellist Robert Irvine and myself.

The first movement, dedicated to Gerry, takes a decisive theme and explores it in detail, with a ruminating quaver accompanying motive.

This leads to the second movement; a restless scherzo with a central section reflecting my admiration of Thelonius Monk.

The third movement is for Beryl, and is a gentle pastorale, laced with birdsong.

The final movement, for Robert, is a set of variations, and shows its theme in different lights–playful, declamatory, virtuosic, expressive.

Edition:
Peters Edition

Bibliography:
Composer's page on the piece, Accessed July 21, 2023, https://www.sallybeamish.com/single-post/2019/04/12/sonata-for-cello-and-piano.

Recordings:
Cellist Robert Irvine and Sally Beamish released a recording of this and other of her cello works on the BIS label in 2001.

Ludwig van Beethoven (1770-1827) Sonata for Cello and Piano in A Major, Op. 69

Date of Composition: 1808
Date of Premiere: March 1809
Premiered by: Nikolaus Kraft, cello and Baroness Dorothea von Ertmann, piano
Approximate Complete Length: 27 min.

> I. Allegro, ma non tanto (13 min)
> II. Scherzo--Allegro molto (5 min)
> III. Andante cantabile--Allegro vivace (9 min)

Background Information:

Emerging within Beethoven's Middle Period, the Sonata in A Major is markedly different from its predecessors, the two Opus 5 Sonatas (Sonatas Op. 5, No 1 and No. 2), in many ways. Whereas Beethoven had in the previous sonatas listed the piano first and the cello second, in the A Major Sonata, the cello gets top billing, reflecting a change in how the cello part is treated in these duo sonatas.

The same year that Beethoven wrote this sonata, he also composed his Fifth and Sixth Symphonies, as well as the Choral Fantasy and a pair of piano trios, making this third cello sonata of his landing squarely in the so-called Middle Period of his career. Rather than being effused with the triumphant, victorious spirit of the majority of other pieces from this period, the sonata carries a noble quality that suits the cello very well.

The opening of the sonata is one of the most notorious out of all the standard cello sonatas. It begins with the cello intoning the melody completely by itself, creating a lonely, yet noble and regal mood. At once simple, but enormously complex and daunting, the melody has given many cellists pause in regards to interpretation and fluid technical execution. A fiendishly tricky and impish scherzo and a rousing final movement round out the work.

Premiering the work was Nikolaus Kraft, son of Antonín Kraft, the principal cellist in the Esterhazy Orchestra under the direction of Haydn (see entries on Haydn's two cello concerti, as well as the entry on Kraft's concerto). Nikolaus was friendly with the major composers of the Classical period, reportedly performing chamber music with Mozart and premiering several of Beethoven's works. Joining him in the premier was Dorothea von Ertmann, a student of Beethoven's who premiered many of his works as well.

Selected Editions:
Bärenreiter (Urtext)
G. Henle Verlag (Urtext)

Bibliography:
Moskovitz, Marc D. and R. Larry Todd. Beethoven's Cello: Five Revolutionary Sonatas and Their World (Boydell Press, Suffolk, UK, 2017).

Recordings:
Numerous recordings have been made of this sonata, both on modern and period setup.

Ludwig van Beethoven (1770-1827) — Sonatas for Piano & Cello, Op. 5, No. 1 and No. 2

Date of Composition: 1796
Date of Premiere: 1796
Premiered by: Jean-Louis Duport, cello with Beethoven, piano
Approximate Length: 24 min.

Sonata No. 1 in F Major for Piano and Cello, Op. 5, No. 1
I. Adagio sostenuto - Allegro (17 min)
II. Rondo: Allegro vivace (7 min)

Sonata No. 2 in G Minor for Piano and Cello, Op. 5, No. 2
I. Adagio sostenuto e espressivo - Allegro molto più tosto presto
(13 min)
II. Rondo: Allegro (11 min)

Background Information:

Ludwig van Beethoven, ever the innovator, can be credited with writing the first sonatas for cello and piano. Of course, there were numerous other sonatas for cello prior to Beethoven's, but they were only for cello and continuo. Here we have a cello and keyboard (a fortepiano specifically), and by the middle sonata, Op. 69, the instruments were on equal footing, paving the way for duo sonatas to come.

The cello sonatas, much like his solo keyboard music, symphonies and string quartets, span across the three periods of this compositional career. Thus, one can certainly hear the progression and development of his ideas through these five sonatas.

The first two, which make up his Opus 5 are early works and while steeped in the Classical style, his uniqueness was already present. Written while Beethoven was on tour, he was no doubt inspired to compose them when meeting King Friedrich Wilhelm II, the King of Prussia. Friedrich was a cellist, and the fact that the cellist Duport brothers were there at Friedrich's court, made the perfect opportunity for Beethoven to write some cello works. He had already written an early set of variations (see other entry), which may have been a way of him winding up to tackle the sonata.

These two sonatas are effectively piano sonatas with cello; note the listing Sonata for Piano and Cello, with 'Cello' listed second. As would be expected from a prodigious pianist such as Bethoven, the piano part is considerable, much bigger and substantive than the cello part. However, like the early variations, the cello part does contain some disproportionately tricky passages compared to the rest of the part.

Both of these pieces are similar in their design, each with two larger movements; both have a slow introduction to the first movement, and a rondo for the last movement. There's a certain sense of formality and grandeur to these two sonatas, reflecting the royal dedicatee.

Selected Editions:
Barenreiter (Urtext)
G. Henle Verlag (Urtext)

Ludwig van Beethoven (1770-1827) — Sonatas for Piano & Cello, Op. 5, No. 1 and No. 2

Bibliography:
Cooper, Barry, Preface, Beethoven, Ludwig van. "Sonatas for Cello and Piano", Kassel: Barenreiter, 2004. Moskovitz, Marc D. and R. Larry Todd. Beethoven's Cello: Five Revolutionary Sonatas and Their World (The Boydell Press, Woodbridge, 2017).
Steinberg, Michael, Liner notes, Beethoven, Ludwig van, "Sonatas for Fortepiano and Cello", Anner Bylsma, cello, Malcolm Bilson, fortepiano, Elektra Nonesuch, 1987.

Recordings:
Many cellists have recorded these sonatas, both on period and modern instruments.

Ludwig van Beethoven (1770-1827)   Sonatas for Cello & Piano, Op. 102, No. 1 and No. 2

Date of Composition: 1815
Date of Premiere: 1816
Premiered by: Op. 5, No. 1: Joseph Linke, cello with Countess Marie von Erdödy, piano/ Op. 5, No. 2: Joseph Linke, cello and Carl Czerny, piano (?)
Approximate Length: 16 min.

Sonata for Cello and Piano in C Major, Op. 102 No. 1 (14 min)
I. Andante – Allegro vivace (7 min)
II. Adagio – Tempo d'andante – Allegro vivace (7 min)

Sonata for Cello and Piano in D Major, Op. 102 No. 2 (18 min)
I. Allegro con brio (7 min)
II. Adagio con molto sentimento d'affetto (7 min)
III. Allegro - Allegro fugato (4 min)

Background Information:

    Roughly seven years had passed between the writing of the Cello Sonata in A Major, op. 69 and these last two cello sonatas Beethoven would compose. They were very eventful seven years; by now, he was completely deaf, he had composed the major works from the Middle Period (5th Symphony, Emperor Piano Concerto, etc.), and he had just lost his younger brother, Carl, and was about to enter into a custody battle for his nephew that would drag on for years on end.

    As he wrote these two sonatas, he was almost a completely different person. Of course, his deafness loomed large over his entire existence, understandably so, but he had a host of other maladies which caused him great discomfort, affecting his mood and ability to interact with others. The two cello sonatas Op. 102 were written at the cusp of what would be known as his Late Period, a time of composing where he retreated further into his interior world and crafted works of such sublime beauty and imagination. They were so ahead of their time that audiences (and performers) found them curious, odd, yet fascinating and compelling.

    Around this time, Beethoven became connected with the cellist Joseph Linke. Linke was based in Vienna and was a part of the Schuppanzigh String Quartet, which premiered a number of Beethoven's chamber works. Beethoven became fond of Linke and his talent, most likely composing these last two sonatas with him in mind.

    The Sonata in C Major, Op. 102, No. 1 (his fourth sonata) was originally subtitled a frei or 'free' sonata, most likely referring to the structure and form. The shortest of his cello sonatas, it's a paradigm of brevity and mastery of thematic organization. It is cyclical: the introductory opening material returns at the end of the sonata, bringing it full circle, and tying the sonata together in a thematic arc. Much like the A Major sonata before it, the cello begins the whole piece alone, singing a wistful melody, sounding quite desolate for C Major. The piano joins in and the two instruments exchange beautiful lines that wind around listfully, meandering and searching. A small piano cadenza and the mood abruptly changes into ferocious energy in the form of terse dotted rhythms. The turbulence is not consistent, it melts into beautiful cantabile lines before charging ahead again.

    The Adagio that opens the second movement is graceful and elegant, with long strands of ornamented filigree. After some sinister music, a melody emerges that is incredibly tender and heartful, before ushering in the opening theme from the first movement making an appearance again. We then move quickly into the Allegro section which is jolly and raucous. And with a rush of energy, it's all done. Beethoven certainly doesn't overstate his welcome in this sonata, but makes the most out of every moment.

Ludwig van Beethoven (1770-1827)   Sonatas for Cello & Piano, Op. 102, No. 1 and No. 2

In many ways, the Sonata in D Major, Op. 102, No. 2 (his fifth sonata) feels like it's more extroverted and on a grander scale. A fanfare opening in the piano introduces the cello, which launches, aggressively into a D Major arpeggio full steam ahead before suddenly relenting into a operatic melody, serene and warmhearted (this huge buildup in energy which suddenly evaporates just before the peak is a similar trick he did to great effect in the opening of the 5th Symphony). Like many of his pieces in the Late Period the extremes between forte and piano dynamics, characters, moods, and textures is pushed as far as he can take it in this sonata.

The Adagio con molto sentimento d'affetto (to be played with much affectionate emotion) movement that follows is one of those transcendent movements that defy earthly definition, like many movements from his late string quartets. It begins like a chorale, cello and piano in unison in bare, funeral-march chords. It's somber, operatic, melodramatic, and profound. The vulnerability of the opening evolves into the cello playing long, drawn-out lines of utmost beauty (reminiscent of the slow theme from his Ghost Piano Trio), the piano prodding and urging underneath. However, Beethoven can't stay away from the opening mournful chorale for long, which keeps returning. Upon its third appearance, it gradually (and extremely slowly) dissipates into the final movement.

The third movement starts with the cello and piano tentatively and hesitatingly playing the theme to the forthcoming fugue, which then quickly gets underway. It's a rowdy fugue that is the complete antithesis of the adagio movement that preceded it. Beethoven keeps up the energy and polyphonic interplay going for a considerable amount of time before bringing it all to a triumphant close.

Selected Editions:
Barenreiter (Urtext)
G.. Henle Verlag (Urtext)

Bibliography:
Dufner, Jens, 2008, Preface. In Beethoven "Sonatas for Piano and Cello", Munich: G. Henle Verlag.
Moskovitz, Marc D. and R. Larry Todd. Beethoven's Cello: Five Revolutionary Sonatas and Their World (The Boydell Press, Woodbridge, 2017).
Steinberg, Michael, Liner notes, Beethoven, Ludwig van, "Sonatas for Fortepiano and Cello", Anner Bylsma, cello, Malcolm Bilson, fortepiano, Elektra Nonesuch, 1987.

Recordings:
Many cellists have recorded these sonatas, both on period and modern instruments.

Ludwig van Beethoven (1770-1827) — Three Sets of Variations for Piano & Cello, WoO

Date of Composition: 1796-1801
Date of Premiere: Unknown
Premiered by: Unknown
Approximate Length: 9 min. average

Background Information:

Beethoven's relationship with the cello spans his entire career through 5 sonatas with piano (see other entries), a triple concerto with piano, violin and cello (see other entry), and three sets of variations for cello and piano. The variations all come from his earliest forays into composition.

Variations on opera themes for instruments were very popular in those days (extending into its peak popularity in the nineteenth century). It was a way for an opera composer to extend the brand of their opera to more people. Not much is known about the impetus behind Beethoven writing these three sets of variations, although he was friendly with the Duport brothers around this time, which may have served as the catalyst.

It's worth noting that the variations are listed as being for 'Piano and Cello', not the other way around. This gives some insight into his mindset, Beethoven was a brilliant pianist, after all; instrumental sonatas in those days were mostly written for the keyboard with obbligato instruments, something that Beethoven himself had a hand in changing (see the entry on his Cello Sonata in A Major, Op. 69).

Indeed, the piano takes on the lion's share of introducing the themes or the variations, the cello offering up commentary; there are entire variations, in fact, where the piano plays entirely on its own without the cello. Interestingly enough, although the cello part is typically only one level higher than mere accompaniment, there are spots where it suddenly (and with little warning) launches into some fiendishly tricky passage way up in thumb position, vulnerable and exposed. It makes for an interesting experience to play these pieces; navigating the disparity in difficulty is significant. The first set of variations is based on the "See the conquering hero come" from Handel's oratorio Judas Maccabbeus. He turns to two arias from Mozart's fantasy opera Die Zauberflöte for the next two sets: Ein Mädchen oder Weibchen and Bei Männern, welche Liebe fühlen. Each set of variations is charming and full of invention. His first two sonatas for cello were just around the corner, and it's hard not to see him using these variations as a warm up to the main event. These are delightful and charming works from a young Beethoven, still finding his voice.

Selected Editions:
Barenreiter (Urtext)
G. Henle Verlag (Urtext)

Bibliography:
Dufner, Jens, 2010, Preface, Beethoven "Variations for Piano and Cello", Munich: G. Henle Verlag. Moskovitz, Marc D. and R. Larry Todd. Beethoven's Cello: Five Revolutionary Sonatas and Their World (The Boydell Press, Woodbridge, 2017).

Recordings:
Many recordings have been released both on period and modern instruments.

Ludwig van Beethoven (1770-1827) Triple Concerto in C Major for Piano, Violin and Cello, Op. 56

Date of Composition: 1804; published in 1807
Date of Premier: May 1808
Premiered by: Archduke Rudolph, piano; Ferdinand August Seidler, violin; Anton Kraft, cello, with the court orchestra of Archduke Rudolf
Approximate Length: 35 min.

> I. Allegro (16 min)
> II. Largo-- (4 min)
> III. Rondo alla polacca (15 min)

Background Information:
    Coming in the midst of an enormous outburst of creativity, the Triple Concerto is a unique work, both in the context of Beethoven's oeuvre, but in the scope of music history as well. Essentially an amplified piano trio, in other words, a piano trio with orchestral accompaniment, the work was somewhat lost in the shadow of the other works that were completed around it, namely, the watershed Eroica symphony.

    There is some confusion as to who actually premiered the work. The piece was written for Archduke Rudolf, friend, patron and piano student of Beethoven's, with a later dedication to Prince Lobkowitz. The Archduke is thought to have premiered the piece with his court violinist and cellist, Siedler and Kraft respectively, and his court orchestra accompanying, however, reports are murky and unverified.

    There is a strong case for it being for the Archduke, as he was somewhat of an amateur pianist, and the piano part for the concerto is not up to the usual level of difficulty that Beethoven crafts. Conversely, the cello part is quite challenging, with many passages way up in the upper reaches of the instrument, appropriate for the skill level of Kraft, who was the dedicatee of Haydn's notoriously difficult Cello Concerto in D Major (see entry).

    Indeed the cello gets plenty of spotlight moments, the tender, yet soaring opening theme of the Largo movement a highlight. For the most part, the material is balanced across the three soloists well, with the cello managing to resist burial in the texture for the majority of the piece.

    What possessed Beethoven to compose a work of this nature for that specific instrumentation remains a mystery. It is thought that the Archduke himself requested it, but again, there is no specific evidence for support. Taking its cue from the concerti grossi of the Baroque era, and Mozart's famous Symphonie Concertante, there aren't any triple concerti for piano, violin and cello before it, and very few following. Since Beethoven was never to write a dedicated cello concerto, this mighty triple concerto will have to fill that space.

Selected Editions:
Bärenreiter (Urtext)
G. Henle Verlag (Urtext)

Bibliography:
Program Notes from the Chicago Symphony, Accessed September 12, 2020, https://cso.org/uploadedFiles/1_Tickets_and_Events/Program_Notes/ProgramNotes_Beethoven_Triple_Concerto.pdf.
Steinberg, Michael. The Concerto: A Listener's Guide (Oxford University Press, London, 1998)
Swafford, Jan. Beethoven: Anguish and Triumph (Houghton Mifflin Harcourt, New York, 2014)

Recordings:
Many commercial recordings are available.

Leonard Bernstein (1918-1990)
Three Meditations from 'The Mass' for Cello & Orchestra

Date of Composition: 1977
Date of Premiere: October 11, 1977
Premiered by: Mstislav Rostropovich, cello; Leonard Bernstein, conductor; National Symphony Orchestra
Approximate Length: 17 min.

I. Lento assai, molto sostenuto (5 min)
II. Andante sostenuto (4 min)
III. Presto - Fast and Primitive - Molto adagio (8 min)

Background Information:

Leonard Bernstein was known for many things throughout his life as a celebrity—a conductor, a pianist, a lecturer, an author, a TV personality—that it's easy to overlook his strengths as a composer. While his most successful work is the enduringly popular Broadway musical West Side Story, most of his music tends to be more serious, leaning more towards contemporary music practices for the concert hall.

In 1971, Jackie Kennedy commissioned a Mass from Bernstein for the grand opening of the John F. Kennedy Center for the Performing Arts. He obliged, creating a liturgical work incorporating dance and theater. Several years later, he extracted passages from the Mass and fashioned them into three Meditations for cello and orchestra for his friend, Mstistlav Rostropovich. The work premiered at the Kennedy Center with Bernstein conducting the National Symphony Orchestra.

The name Meditation is appropriate for the titles, as the music oscillates between thoughtful searching, yearning, and ferocious intensity. The cello part weaves in and out of the orchestral texture, driving the ideas, but also providing commentary as well.

There is also a version for cello and piano.

Edition:
Boosey & Hawkes

Bibliography:
Official page on this piece, Accessed July 6, 2023, https://leonardbernstein.com/works/view/76/three-meditations-from-mass.

Recordings:
A few commercial recordings are available, both in orchestra and piano accompaniment versions.

David Biedenbender (b. 1984)   Light Over Mountains for Cello & Piano

Date of Composition: 2016
Date of Premiere: September 16, 2016
Premiered by: Brian Hodges, cello; Betsi Hodges, piano
Approximate Length: 8 min.

Background Information:

David Biedenbender is an award-winning composer, conductor, and educator, who performs and collaborates with all varieties of artists and performers. He is currently Associate Professor of Composition at Michigan State University. He was formerly on the faculties at Boise State University and Eastern Michigan University, and in the summers has taught at Interlochen Arts Camp. Biedenbender has collaborated with Alarm Will Sound, the PRISM Saxophone Quartet, the United States Navy Band and the Eastman Wind Ensemble among others.

Light Over Mountains was commissioned by the Idaho Music Teachers Association. Biedenbender's program notes on the piece:

I grew up mostly in Michigan, far from the beautiful mountains and varied topography of the western United States. When I moved to Boise in 2014, I was overwhelmed by the effect the foothills (they're mountains, for me!) had on me. Their immense size and beauty captivated my thoughts daily, reminding me of the awesome size of this planet and my relative insignificance, but also providing a center and stability that made me feel content and secure. And the mountains are also dynamic, bearing the colors, marks, and bruises of the changing seasons – green in the spring, yellow and brown in the hot, dry summer, speckled with white snow in the winter, and sometimes black and gray with ash and smoke from fire. I remember many beautiful sunrises over the mountains in Boise, the light accentuating the boundary between earth and sky as glowing streaks of yellow and crimson bled into the deep cerulean of the night. I am grateful for this place and for the time I spent here. This piece is for Boise, for the mountains, and for the friends I made while here, including Brian and Betsi Hodges, to whom I would like to offer my profound gratitude for bringing this music to life.

"Mountains seem to answer an increasing imaginative need in the West. More and more people are discovering a desire for them, and a powerful solace in them. At bottom, mountains, like all wildernesses, challenge our complacent conviction - so easy to lapse into - that the world has been made for humans by humans. Most of us exist for most of the time in worlds which are humanly arranged, themed and controlled. One forgets that there are environments which do not respond to the flick of a switch or the twist of a dial, and which have their own rhythms and orders of existence. Mountains correct this amnesia. By speaking of greater forces than we can possibly invoke, and by confronting us with greater spans of time than we can possibly envisage, mountains refute our excessive trust in the man-made. They pose profound questions about our durability and the importance of our schemes. They induce, I suppose, a modesty in us."

— Robert Macfarlane, Mountains of the Mind: Adventures in Reaching the Summit

Edition:
Available directly from the composer

Bibliography:
Official website of the composer, Accessed August 31, 2023, https://davidbiedenbender.com/
Program notes used by permission of the composer.

Recordings:
No commercial recording available.

Ernest Bloch (1880-1959)
From a Jewish Life (Prayer, Supplication & Jewish Song) for Cello & Orchestra

Date of Composition: 1924
Date of Premiere: 1924
Premiered by: Hans Kindler, cello
Approximate Length: 9 min.

> I. Prayer: Andante moderato (4 min)
> II. Supplication: Allegro non troppo (2 min)
> III. Jewish Song: Moderato (2 min)

Background Information:

There was a particular section of Ernest Bloch's life and career that is known as "The Jewish Cycle" where he wrote music based on Jewish themes. These include the Israel Symphony, the Baal Shem Suite, and Schelomo for cello and orchestra (see other entry). Written after Schelomo, this set of three pieces called From a Jewish Life further explores Bloch's heritage.

While Jewish songs are quoted faintly throughout, these pieces actually contain more impressions on the Jewish experience, rather than overt quotes, aiming to capture, as Bloch wrote, "the soul of the Jewish people".

Prayer, the opening piece is a slow, contemplative movement. The cello, at times, seems to be weeping, while the accompaniment tries to offer consolation.

Supplication, the act of pleading with humility, has a sense of urgency to it, insistent yet resigned. The orchestra once again lends comfort to the pained soul of the cello.

Jewish Song is a solemn piece that has the cello bearing its soul. Bloch makes good use of close intervals and slides, giving the cellist's anguish a voice. Ultimately, the piece ends quietly, its soul, at least for now, at rest.

Edition:
Carl Fischer

Bibliography:
Dubal, David The Essential Canon of Classical Music (North Point Press, New York, 2001).
Page on Bloch's From a Jewish Life, Accessed August 16, 2023, https://www.milkenarchive.org/music/volumes/view/intimate-voices/work/from-jewish-life/#:~:text=Ernest%20Bloch's%20From%20Jewish%20Life,in%20a%20traditional%20Ashkenazi%20synagogue.
Knapp, Alexander, Liner notes for Bloch, Ernest "From Jewish Life", Natalie Clein, cello, Hyperion, 2021.

Recordings:
Many cellists have recorded this set of pieces.

Ernest Bloch (1880-1959)
Schelomo: Rhapsodie hébraïque for Cello & Orchestra

Date of Composition: 1915-1916
Date of Premiere: May 13, 1917
Premiered by: Hans Kindler, cello; Artur Bodanzky conductor.
Approximate Length: 21 min.

Background Information:

"It is the Jewish soul that interests me," Ernest Bloch once wrote, "the complex, glowing, agitated soul that I feel vibrating throughout the Bible…the sacred emotion of the race that slumbers far down in our soul." Bloch's Jewish heritage was something he cared very deeply about and let it infuse his music. Some of his best-known works are based on Jewish songs or themes.

Schelomo:Rhapsodie hébraïque, from the Hebrew word for Solomon, is a twenty minute work that casts the cello as the voice of Solomon, typically associated with wisdom. Initially, Bloch had been mulling over setting verses from the book Ecclesiastes in a vocal work, but after meeting cellist Alexandre Barjansky, he changed the course of the piece into a work for cello and orchestra.

There is an intensity that runs through the piece, with cello doing its best to stay above the fray. The orchestra plays the part of the chaotic world, often at odds with the cello line. The piece ends defiantly on a low D, however the whole piece feels rather unresolved. Perhaps this is Bloch's way of musically interpreting the opening and closing of Ecclesiastes which says, "Everything is meaningless". Whatever Bloch's intention, Schelomo is a powerful work that stays with the listener long after the last note has died away.

Selected Editions:
Carl Fischer
G. Schirmer

Bibliography:
Dubal, David The Essential Canon of Classical Music (North Point Press, New York, 2001).
Program notes from the Boston Symphony, Accessed August 16, 2023, https://www.bso.org/works/schelomo-rhapsody-hebraique-for-cello-and-orchestra.

Recordings:
There are many commercial recordings of this work available.

Luigi Boccherini (1743-1805) — Sonatas for Cello & Basso Continuo

Date of Composition: Unknown
Date of Premiere: Unknown
Premiered by: Unknown, but most likely Boccherini
Approximate Length: 15 min. (average)

Background Information:
    Luigi Boccherini was a cello prodigy, who dramatically moved the cello forward as a solo instrument into the 19th century. The son of a double-bassist, he moved around to various courts in Spain and his home country of Italy, carving an internationally renown career in the process. His composition style sits very well alongside that of Haydn and Mozart in a very elegant, Classical manner. He made full use of the range of the cello, extending the acceptable range considerably, often placing lengthy passages at the end of the fingerboard. This necessitated the use of thumb position, a technique that had been around before, but hadn't been put into standardized use.
    Most of his writing tends to be florid and rhapsodic, interjected by sections of double-stops.
    Boccherini contributed numerous compositions to the solo cello repertoire with a dozen or so concertos (see entry on Boccherini Concertos) and approximately 34 sonatas for cello and continuo. Unfortunately, there is no concrete evidence regarding the dates of composition or premieres of these works.
    Only six sonatas were collected and published in 1772; the rest of them were discovered here and there afterwards, with some found as recently as 1987. As is typical of Boccherini's cello music, there are alterations and differing versions that exist for certain sonatas, in some cases making the act of performing his authentic, original sonatas somewhat of a moving target.
    The majority of the sonatas are in a three-movement format, alternating between slow tempi and fast. The accompaniment is for a second cello part, or more specifically, a double-bass, which his father would have played. Modern keyboard realizations do exist, however.

Selected Editions:
Musedita
Ricordi

Bibliography:
Bylsma, Anner, Liner notes, Boccherini, Luigi "Boccherini Cello Sonatas", Anner Bylsma, cello, Ken Slowik, cello, Bob van Asperen, fortepiano, Sony Classics, 1993.
Le Guin, Elisabeth. Boccherini's Body: An Essay in Carnal Musicology (University of California Press, Berkely, 2006).

Recordings:
Various commercial recordings are in print.

Boccherini, Luigi (1743-1805) — Concerti for Cello and Orchestra

Date of Composition: Unknown
Date of Premier: Unknown
Premiered by: Unknown, but most likely by Boccherini
Approximate Length: 16 min. (average)

Concerto No. 1 in E-flat Major, G. 474
Concerto No. 2 in A Major, G. 475
Concerto No. 3 in D Major, G. 476
Concerto No. 4 in C Major, G. 477
Concerto No. 5 in D Major, G. 478
Concerto No. 6 in D Major, G. 479
Concerto No. 7 in G major, G. 480
Concerto No. 8 in C Major, G. 481
Concerto No. 9 in B-flat Major, G. 482
Concerto No. 10 in D Major, G. 483
Concerto No. 11 in C Major, G. 573
Concerto No. 12 in E-flat Major (not included in Gérard's catalog)

Background Information:

"When asked whom he considered the best cellist of the past, Piatigorsky said: 'For me there was only one supremely great cellist of early times and, in the same person, a great composer for the instrument. This was Boccherini.'" (Ginsburg, p. 258)

Luigi Boccherini is often considered the first, great cello virtuoso. He is credited with expanding the cello technique (thumb position, extended passages of double-stops) and bringing it more into the standard way of playing the cello. In his own time, he was well known for his prodigious playing, as well as his compositions.

The lion's share of his compositional output centered around chamber music (string duos, trios, quartets, quintets, sextets, as well as chamber music with keyboard and winds), which often featured the cello in a melodic capacity—something that was not so common at the time. He also composed symphonies and some liturgical works, but in this category of large-scale works, he is mostly known for his cello concerti.

Correction: he is mostly known for one cello concerto out of his twelve cello concerti: his infamous Concerto No. 9 in B-flat major. In the late 19th century, famed cellist Friedrich Grützmacher (1832-1903) (a major performer, and composer himself, but not above adapting other composer's works) felt that he could improve upon this piece by adapting it for the style of the period. He made huge changes, taking out whole sections, rearranging material, and replacing the entire second movement with a movement from one of Boccherini's cello sonatas. Because this version was widely published, and notably recorded by some of the most famous cellists of the 20th century (duPre, Starker, etc.), this became the version that everyone knew—many not realizing it wasn't the original version. Thankfully, Boccherini's original has survived and is available in printed editions as well as recordings.

As it stands, the B-flat concerto tends to be the sole representation of his concerti, with the other eleven works largely unknown. They are well worth seeking out, however, offering a rich experience for cellists and listeners.

Like his sonatas, Boccherini doesn't hold back in technical difficulty for the soloist. There are lengthy passages in very high registers, necessitating the use of thumb position, not to mention extensive use of double stops. But even with the technical demands, Boccherini never fails to bring out the melodic qualities, infusing the music with personality and beauty. All of his concerti are virtuosic, for sure, but also sublimely beautiful and charming.

Boccherini, Luigi (1743-1805) — Concerti for Cello and Orchestra

Selected Editions:
Musedita
Ricordi

Bibliography:
Ginsburg, Lev. History of the Violoncello (Paganiniana Publishing, New Jersey, 1983)
Le Guin, Elisabeth. Boccherini's Body: An Essay in Carnal Musicology (University of California Press, Berkely, 2006)

Recordings:
Various commercial recordings are available, mostly on period instruments, but some on modern

Léon Boëllmann (1862-1897) — Variations symphoniques, Op. 23 for Cello & Orchestra

Date of Composition: 1892
Date of Premiere: November 27, 1892
Premiered by: Joseph Salmon, cello; with Charles Lamoureux conducting the Orchestre des concerts Lamoureux
Approximate Length: 12 min

Background Information:

Léon Boëllmann is perhaps not as well known these days as he once was; that might have had to do with his untimely death at the age of 35. He was poised for a great and long-standing career, alongside the likes of Camille Saint-Saëns, César Frank and Jules Massanet. Boëllmann rose to prominence thanks to his early organ works. He worked most of his life as a church organist, teacher and composer. His works are mostly keyboard (organ and piano), chamber and a few orchestral works. His final work was his Sonata in A Minor for Cello and Piano.

His Variations symphoniques for Cello and Orchestra was, for a time, one of his more popular works, but in the early part of the twentieth century, it fell out of favor, being replaced by some of the other big cello concerti of the time.

As expected, the variations are a vehicle for showing off the cello, mostly in long melodic lines. The heroic cello line reveals Boëllmann's gift for melody as the tune the variations are based on is incredibly catchy. A fun, beautiful crowd-pleasing work, hopefully it will find its place again on concert stages more often.

Selected Editions:
Durand
International Music

Bibliography:
https://www.editionsilvertrust.com/boellmann-variations.htm
Tchamkerten, Jacques, Liner notes, Boellmann, Ludwig "Orchestral Works", Henri Demarquette, cello, Orchestre symphonique de Mulhouse, Patrick Devon, cond., Outhere Music, 2021.

Recordings:
There are a handful of commercial recordings of this work, as well as live performances on youtube.

Mélanie Hélène Bonis (1858-1937) — Sonata for Cello & Piano in F Major, Op. 67

Date of Composition: 1905
Date of Premiere: Unknown
Premiered by: Unknown, but dedicated to Maurice Demaison
Approximate Length: 19 min.

> I. Moderato, quasi andante (7:38 min)
> II. Trés lent (4:38 min)
> III. Moderato molto (6:35 min)

Background Information:

    Mélanie Hélène Bonis was a French Romantic composer who composed over 300 works over her lifetime. She was a student of Cesar Franck, eventually formally studying with him at the Paris Conservatoire (Claude Debussy was a student there at the same time).

    She weathered a host of personal problems, including an arranged marriage and a secret child out of wedlock which she was separated from, but managed to get her music published and publicized at a time when this proved difficult for women. She amended her name to Mel on her compositions as it sounded more masculine and didn't immediately sound like a female name.

    The cello sonata is in three movements, and is highly lyrical, showcasing both instruments.

Edition:

E. Demets

Bibliography:

Web page on Bonis and the cello sonata, Accessed June, 8, 2023, https://www.soundgardenclassical.com/post/mel-bonis-cello-sonata

Recordings:

A commercial recording is available, plus live recordings on youtube.

Lili Boulanger (1893-1918)

Nocturne for Cello & Piano
(transcription by Paul R. van der Reidjen)

Date of Composition: 1911-1914
Date of Premiere: Unknown
Premiered by: Unknown
Approximate Length: 3 min.

Background Information:

Lili Boulanger, the younger sister of Nadia Boulanger, the famed composer and teacher, had an all-too-brief career, which was tragically cut short due to tuberculosis. The first female to win the prestigious Prix de Rome prize, she began her career incredibly young.

This Nocturne, a lovely little gem taken from her Deux Morceaux (Two Pieces) for Violin and Piano, is one of her earliest works. Sweet, tender and reminiscent of French Impressionism, it is an exquisite, ethereal character piece.

Edition:
Transcription by Paul R. van der Reijden, Musica Deliberata (free download on IMSLP)

Bibliography:
Rosenstiel, Léonie. The Life and Works of Lili Boulanger (Fairleigh Dickinson University Press, 1978).
Program notes from the Left Coast Ensemble, Accessed November 18, 2020, https://www.leftcoastensemble.org/french

Recordings:
No commercial recording exists of the cello version

Nadia Boulanger (1887-1979) — Trois Pièces for Cello & Piano

Date of Composition: 1914
Date of Premiere: Unknown
Premiered by: Unknown
Approximate Length: 8 min.

>   I. Modéré (3 min)
>   II. Sans vitesse et á l'aise (2 min)
>   III. Vite et nerveusement rythmé (3 min)

Background Information:
   Nadia Boulanger was one of the most important composition teachers of the twentieth century. Her students included Elliott Carter, Aaron Copland, Astor Piazzolla and Philip Glass. Starting out, she focused mainly on composition, along with her younger sister Lili Boulanger, creating a catalog of music that encompassed vocal, orchestral and some chamber works. After her sister died unexpectedly at the age of 24, Nadia moved from composing to teaching.
   Troi Pièces for Cello and Piano was adapted by Boulanger herself from her same work for organ.

Edition:
Leduc (of the original Hegel printed edition)--sold as three separate pieces.

Bibliography:
Rosenstiel, Léonie. Nadia Boulanger: A Life in Music (W. W. Norton, New York, 1982).

Recordings:
There are a few commercial recordings available.

Johannes Brahms (1833-1897) — Concerto in A Minor for Violin and Cello, Op. 102

Date of Composition: 1887; published in 1888
Date of Premiere: October 18, 1887 (public)
Premiered by: Joseph Joachim, violin and Robert Hausmann, cello; Johannes Brahms, conductor; Gürzenich Orchestra of Cologne
Approximate Length: 35 min.

> I. Allegro (18 min)
> II. Andante (8 min)
> III. Vivace non troppo (9 min)

Background Information:

Concertos for more than one instrument have been around since the creation of the concerto format, actually predating concertos for a single solo instrument. Corelli started the trend with his numerous concerti grossi, followed by Vivaldi with his numerous concertos for two violins, or even four violins. Although multi-instrument concerti were popular during the Baroque, barely any featured the cello (a notable example being the Vivaldi Concerto in G Minor for 2 Cellos. In the Classical period, the focus shifted much more towards single instrument concerti, with the stand-out exceptions being Mozart's Sinfonia Concertante and Beethoven's Triple Concerto (see entry).

By the time of the late 19th-century when Brahms was in the peak of his career, double and triple concerti were a rare commodity. Unfortunately, Brahms never wrote a proper solo cello concerto; after hearing cellist Robert Hausmann play the Dvorak Concerto, he was reported to have lamented that if he had known it was possible to write a concerto like that for cello, he would've done it. The Double Concerto might have been a conciliatory gesture towards Hausmann for not writing a cello concerto, but more importantly as a peace offering to his old friend, violinist Joseph Joachim.

Brahms' and Joachim's long-standing friendship had been damaged due to Brahms rather awkwardly siding with Joachim's estranged wife during their divorce proceedings. Joachim, incensed and hurt, effectively broke off communication with Brahms for some time. After several attempts at mending the relationship, Brahms crafted this work as a bigger gesture towards restoration (Clara Schumann referred to it as the "Reconciliation Concerto"). Joachim was obviously appeased and agreed to take on the work. They resumed their cordiality as Brahms' offering seemed to have done the trick.

The piece upon completion and performance was met with a rather reserved response, but in the years since, has gained in importance and esteem, to the point where it now sits as a masterpiece, beloved by performers and audiences. However, Brahms, ever the master of self-depreciation, was insecure about his writing for strings. In a letter to Clara, he said, "I really should've passed the idea on to someone who knows strings better than I…Well, we'll wait and see. Joachim and Hausmann are going to try it." (Avins, p. 649) He needn't have worried. Although the work is difficult for sure, it is well-written for both instruments.

Not simply because it's a piece by Brahms, who, by this point in his career was firmly out of Beethoven's shadow and ensconced as a great composer in his own right, the concerto is significant for the equal footing he gives the two soloists. Naturally, in a piece of this type, there is dazzling virtuosity on display throughout from both instruments, but what really stands out is the conversational aspect to the two solo lines, almost chamber-music-like.

The first movement opens with a terse, yet bold and impassioned opening statement from the orchestra, before giving way to a cello cadenza, a gorgeous soliloquy that encompasses the entire range of the cello. The dialogue between the two soloists commences throughout the first movement, matching each other statement to statement.

Johannes Brahms (1833-1897) — Concerto in A Minor for Violin and Cello, Op. 102

The third movement rondo is a rousing and invigorating finale, infused with Hungarian and gypsy-like flavorings, no doubt in homage to Joachim's heritage, but it's the second movement, the gentle and tender Andante which contains the beating heart of the piece. Across the entire movement, the two soloists play together in lyrical tandem, with the orchestra dovetailing in and out of the conversation. It's not hard to imagine this is where Brahms is offering his true atonement to Joachim; it would be difficult for anyone not to be swayed by this beautiful and adoring music.

Taken as a whole, this work can be seen as a synthesis of all of Brahms' considerable talents as a composer. What would end up being his last large-scale orchestral work contains an amalgam of his skills: the thoughtful inclusion of form and order, the power and might of the orchestration, the lyrical, almost folk-like rhythms, and the expansive scale and scope of his emotional range.

Brahms once said, "Straight-away the ideas flow in upon me, directly from God, and not only do I see the distinct themes in my mind's eye, but they are clothed in the right forms, harmonies, and orchestrations." All that is laid out for the listener in this landmark work--a gift, initially to his two musician friends, but for us as well.

Selected Edition:
Breitkopf und Härtel (Urtext)

Bibliography:
Avins, Styra, ed. Johannes Brahms: Life and Letters (Oxford University Press, London, 2004)
Botstein, Leon, ed. The Compleat Brahms: A Guide to the Musical Works of Johannes Brahms. (W.W. Norton & Company, New York, 1999)
Geiringer, Karl. On Brahms and His Circle, revised by George S. Bozarth (Harmonie Park Press, Michigan, 2006)
Musgrave, Michael. The Music of Brahms (Routledge & Kagan Paul, London, 1985)
Steinberg, Michael. The Concerto: A Listener's Guide (Oxford University Press, London, 1998)

Recordings:
Many recordings by some of the great cellists are available.

Johannes Brahms (1833-1897) Sonata for Cello and Piano No. 1 in E Minor, Op. 38

Date of Composition: 1862-65; published 1866
Date of Premiere: May 3, 1866
Premiered by: Ferdinand Thieriot, cello and Theodore Billroth, piano
Approximate Length: 26 min.

I. Allegro non troppo (12 min)
II. Allegretto quasi Menuetto. Trio (6 min)
III. Allegro (8 min)

Background Information:

The first of two sonatas Brahms wrote for the cello came reportedly after he had made a couple of attempts at a piece for cello early on in his compositional career before ultimately destroying them. Like many of Brahms' works, the sonata went through a number of revisions, with Brahms originally envisioning it to have four movements, but changing his mind later, excised the slow movement.

Brahms had mild experience on the cello from studying it in his youth from his father, an amateur cellist, which is reflected in the thoughtful manner he approached the cello line throughout. The work exploits the full range of the cello, with a good portion of the musical material making good use of the lower strings, something he was later criticized for.

The first movement is soulful and reflective, mostly contemplative with a fiery development. The second movement is a nod to sonatas (or suites) from the past, with a contrasting minuet and trio. The third is an epic finale with a fugal dialogue between the two instruments. Being a fervent musicologist and student of music history, he includes homages to Bach in this work, basing themes from the first and third movements from Contrapunctus 4 and 13 from The Art of the Fugue respectively.

The work was brought out slowly, with it receiving a handful of performances before it was officially published. Cellist Ferdinand Theiriot and Brahms' good friend, surgeon and amateur pianist, Theodor Billroth are thought to have performed it for the first time. In a letter to Brahms, Billroth says, "I also played your new cello sonata with Thieriot; a delicate little jewel, both as regards the invention and the secure, definite, yet delicate architecture of all the details." (Barkan, p. 5)

For the next few years, it was performed by a various group of cellists and pianists, namely the imminent 19th-century cellist David Popper. Brahms dedicated the piece to his friend, Josef Gansbacker, an amateur cellist. There is an amusing anecdote which describes a private performance Gansbacker gave of the sonata with Brahms at the piano. After the performance, Gansbacker was said to have groused that Brahms played too loudly, that the audience couldn't hear his cello playing. Brahms was said to have retorted, "lucky for you."

It was cellist Robert Hausmann who championed the work performing it a number of times towards the close of the 19th century, earning its well-deserved reputation. This sonata remains one of the more important entries in the sonata repertoire for cello since Beethoven.

Selected Editions:
Barenreiter (Urtext)
G. Henle Verlag (Urtext)

Johannes Brahms (1833-1897) — Sonata for Cello and Piano No. 1 in E Minor, Op. 38

Bibliography:

Barkan, Hans, ed. Johannes Brahms & Theodor Billroth: Letters from a Musical Friendship. (University of Oklahoma Press, Norman, 1957).

Brown, Clive. Preface notes to Sonata in E Minor, Op. 38 (Barenreiter, Kassel, Germany, 2015)

Drinker, Henry S. Chamber Music of Johannes Brahms. (Greenwood Press Publishers, Westport, Connecticut, 1976.

Recordings:

Many commercial recordings are available.

Johannes Brahms (1833-1897) — Sonata for Cello and Piano No. 2 in F Major, Op. 99

Date of Composition: 1886; published in 1887
Date of Premiere: October 29, 1886 (private); November 24, 1886 (public)
Premiered by: Robert Hausmann, cello and Johannes Brahms, piano
Approximate Length: 28 min.

>   I. Allegro vivace (7 min)
>   II. Adagio affettuoso (8 min)
> III. Allegro passionato (7 min)
>   IV. Allegro molto (6 min)

Background Information:

Whereas Brahms' first sonata for the cello has a more twilight mood to it, more austere and formal, this second sonata, written about two decades later, is bursting with unbridled energy and power. Composed during a fruitful summer in Switzerland, the cello sonata emerged alongside the A Major Violin Sonata, the D Minor Violin Sonata and the Piano Trio in C Minor. Written presumably with the cellist Robert Hausmann's technique in mind, the sonata is a major step up in terms of scope and difficulty from his first cello sonata, Op. 33.

The first movement bursts into existence with a ferocious oscillating pattern rumbling from the piano (which the cello answers later in bariolage), the cello piecing together an arching melody from tiny jagged fragments climbing up to the highest reach of the instrument, no doubt mirroring the mountain peaks around the lake where Brahms was summering.

In a letter to Brahms, Theodor Billroth, Brahms' good friend and amateur musician, describes his impression of the sonata after Brahms had sent him the score for feedback:

The beginning of the cello sonata is almost dangerously á la Rubenstein. But the danger is not great for you! In what follows, you understand even more how to captivate through quiet beauty than through the passionate excitement of the opening. I confess that previously I found the first movement somewhat serious, to the extent that I wondered: how should it go on like this? But you always know how to find the right way to the purely musical…The piece seems difficult at first glance; but once it has been grasped, it should soon succeed in an effective performance. (Brown, p. III)

The second movement, perhaps originally intended for the E Minor sonata, is a tender and heartfelt movement in the unusual key of F# Major, with Brahms giving a clue to the emotional content of the movement by labeling it Allegro affettuoso.

The third movement, ostensibly a Scherzo, is a spiky and punchy movement contrasted with a smooth and lush trio section. In a letter to Brahms, Elisabeth von Herzogenberg, a pianist and friend, cheekily stated that she couldn't wait to hear Brahms perform this scherzo so that she could hear him "snort" and "puff" throughout as he played.
The fourth, as Billroth described, is comfortable and reassuring in its character, although certainly not in the technical aspect, the opening melody slightly awkward with its leaps and expanded phrase length. Indeed, the song-like themes envelop and comfort from the raw energy from the former movements. It ends with the main theme impishly played in pizzicato before a flourishing conclusion.

Whether he had taken the critical opinions of his first cello sonata to heart is unclear; Brahms was generally loath to take advice from others. But certainly, the F Major Sonata raises the game in almost every aspect, both emotionally and technically, largely doing away with the balance issues between the cello and piano that plagued the earlier work. It creates an interesting counterpoint to the more earthbound, sage-like, but no less potent, E Minor Sonata. Taken together, they form a full and complete universe that only Brahms could conceive.

Johannes Brahms (1833-1897)
Sonata for Cello and Piano No. 2 in F Major, Op. 99

Selected Editions:
Barenreiter (Urtext)
G. Henle Verlag (Urtext)

Bibliography:
Barkan, Hans, ed. Johannes Brahms & Theodor Billroth: Letters from a Musical Friendship. (University of Oklahoma Press, Norman, 1957).
Botstein, Leon, ed. The Compleat Brahms: A Guide to the Musical Works of Johannes Brahms. (W.W. Norton & Company, New York, 1999)
Brown, Clive. Preface notes to Sonata in F Major, Op. 99 (Barenreiter, Kassel, Germany, 2015)
Drinker, Henry S. Chamber Music of Johannes Brahms. (Greenwood Press Publishers, Westport, Connecticut, 1976.
Gottlieb-Billroth, Otto. Billroth und Brahms im Briefwechsel (Urban and Schwarzenberg, Berlin, Germany, 1935)

Recordings:
Most of the major cellists have recorded and released the two sonatas commercially.

Frank Bridge (1879-1941) — Sonata for Cello & Piano

Date of Composition: 1913-1917
Date of Premiere: 1917
Premiered by: Felix Salmond, cello, and Harold Samuel, piano
Approximate Length: 23 min.

I. Allegro ben moderato (10 min)
II. Adagio ma non troppo - Molto allegro e agitato - Adagio ma non troppo - Allegro ma non troppo - (13 min)

Background Information:

Frank Bridge, one of the preeminent British composers of the early twentieth century, composed music that was both forward and backward looking. He was inspired by forms of the past, especially those of Renaissance and Baroque England, infusing his music with Romantic melodies, all with a more modern harmonic underlay, which grew increasingly more adventurous especially after World War I.

The Cello Sonata bears the weight of the war, as it was written before and throughout, taking him four years to ultimately complete. Bridge's anguish can be felt throughout the sonata. The cellist, Antonia Butler, who gave the initial performance in France, wrote, "I first played the sonata with a contemporary pianist of his called Ada May Thomas. She told me that during the First World War, when Bridge was writing the slow movement, he was in utter despair over the futility of war and the state of the world generally and would walk around Kensington in the early hours of the morning unable to get any rest or sleep, and that the idea of the slow movement really came into being during that time." (Hindmarsh, p. 6)

The first movement moves along in long, sinewy, heartfelt lines, passionate and surging. The second movement can be seen as a second and third movement compacted together. The cello intones its mournful material, the piano a graceful support underneath, before exploding in a fit of nervous energy in the 'Molto allegro' section. The opening slow section returns, in another example of the 'phantasy'-cyclical form he favored so much.

Like so many people, Bridge was forever changed by the war, which of course, cast a major shadow over his music. Whereas his cello concerto "Oration" (see other entry) was a caustic and unflinching look on war, the earlier Cello Sonata takes the route of despair more than anger. It's a beautiful work, fringed with echoes of lament for the loss of innocence.

Edition:
Boosey & Hawkes

Bibliography:
Dubal, David The Essential Canon of Classical Music (North Point Press, New York, 2001)
Hindmarsh, Paul, Liner notes Bridge, Frank "Phantasy Quartet and & Sonatas", The Nash Ensemble, Hyperion Records, 2013.

Recordings:
There are numerous commercial recordings available.

Frank Bridge (1879-1941)   Oration (Concerto elegiaco) for Cello and Orchestra

Date of Composition: 1929
Date of Premiere: January 16, 1936
Premiered by: Florence Hooten, cello; Frank Bridge, conductor; BBC Symphony Orchestra
Approximate Length: 30 min.

Poco lento--Allegro--Ben moderato (poco lento)--Allegro giusto--Ben moderato mesto e tranquillo--Cadenza--Allegro--Lento--Epilogue: Andante tranquillo

Background Information:
    At the turn of the twentieth century, an amateur musician and philanthropist named W.W. Cobbett started a competition for British composers. Cobbett felt that the English National Identity had been lost, in favor of more Central Europe styles and composers. He wanted to inspire and give attention to British composers, something he felt was sorely lacking. One of the main criteria for the competition was that each submitted piece had to be in the form of a Fantasy, an earlier style made famous by the likes of Purcell. The Fantasy was a single movement work that was broken up into smaller, contrasting sections, coming full circle back to the opening to conclude. Frank Bridge entered and won the competition in 1906 with his Phantasie Piano Trio, and it would be a form he would return to again and again, including his epic cello concerto called "Oration (concerto elegiaco)".
    Between the completion of the work and the premiere was a period of almost seven years. Bridge tried unsuccessfully to procure cellists who would play the work, starting with Felix Salmond, the famed British cellist who premiered the Elgar Cello Concerto and Bridge's own cello sonata about twenty years earlier. Finally, he turned to a cellist who he heard perform one of his chamber works, Florence Hooten, who agreed to take on the work.
    The piece is structured in a palindromic fashion. Beginning in a whisper, the piece churns through emotions, turbulent to anguished. It is a tough piece to be immune to; Bridge was not tentative with his feelings toward war in this piece whatsoever. "Oration" was not the first time Bridge had written a piece as a statement about war, but it's one of his more confronting, therefore being somewhat of a tough pill to swallow for audiences. The response to the premiere was polite, but tepid. The piece languished in near obscurity for the next couple of decades--the score not being available in published form until 1979--until Julian Lloyd Webber made the inaugural recording of the work.
    It is a mournful work with the cello layered on top of the orchestration, not simply as a vehicle for virtuosity. The cello perhaps represents Bridge and his futile outrage and grief at so much loss. It's a powerful work that doesn't shy away from its emotions, refusing to coddle the listener. It's a blunt work, but necessary nonetheless. Hopefully it will continue to find more cellists to take it on.

Edition:
Faber Music

Bibliography:
Hodges, Betsi. W.W. Cobbett's Phantasy: A Legacy of Chamber Music in the British Musical Renaissance (VDM Verlag Dr. Müller, 2009)
Steinberg, Michael. The Concerto: A Listener's Guide (Oxford University Press, London, 1998)

Recordings:
There are several commercial recordings of this available.

Benjamin Britten (1913-1976) — Three Suites for Solo Cello

Dates of Compositions: Suite No. 1, Op. 72 - 1964; Suite No. 2, Op. 80 - 1967; Suite no. 3 , Op. 87 - 1971
Date of Premieres: 1965, 1968, 1974
Premiered by: Mstislav Rostropovich, cello
Approximate Lengths:

Cello Suite No. 1, Op. 72 (25 min)
Canto primo: Sostenuto e largamente
Fuga: Andante moderato
Lamento: Lento rubato
Canto secondo: Sostenuto
Serenata: Allegretto (pizzicato)
Marcia: Alla marcia moderato
Canto tero: Sostenuto
Bordone: Moderato quasi recitato
Moto perpetuo e Canto quarto: Presto

Cello Suite No. 2, Op. 80 (22 min)
Declamato: Largo
Fuga: Andante
Scherzo: Allegro molto
Andante lento
Ciaccona: Allegro

Cello Suite No. 3, Op. 87 (23 min)
Introduzione: Lento
Marcia: Allegro
Canto: Con moto
Barcarolla: Lento
Dialogo: Allegretto
Fuga: Andante espressivo
Recitativo: Fantastico
Moto perpetuo: Presto
Passacaglia: Lento solenne

Background Information:

Widely regarded as one of the most important British composers of the twentieth-century, Benjamin Britten had a long and distinguished career, whether as a composer, conductor, or pianist. Getting his start composing at an early age, he would go on to study with Frank Bridge and John Ireland (who both wrote fantastic works for cello–see their entries). His large-scale works brought him fame and recognition, from his operas Peter Grimes, Turn of the Screw, and Billy Budd, to his War Requiem. He wrote pieces for many of the world's leading musicians, including Janet Baker, Peter Pears–who was his partner privately and professionally, Dietrich Fischer-Dieskau, and Mstislav Rostropovich.

It was his connection with Rostropovich that produced the three Solo Suites for Cello, which many consider the greatest set of unaccompanied works for solo cello since the Bach Suites. The two met after a performance of Shostakovich's Cello Concerto No. 1 given by Rostropovich. Britten was so inspired, not only by Rostropovich's playing, but by his personality, that he ended up writing five works for cello: the three solo suites, a Cello Symphony, and a sonata for cello and piano (see other entry).

Benjamin Britten (1913-1976) — Three Suites for Solo Cello

The Suites of Bach (not to mention Rostropovich's interpretation of them) provide a backdrop for Britten's Suites. Even as Britten is exploring for himself the depths of the cello, Bach's Suites are never far off.

The Suites are towering works, both incredibly difficult technically, pushing the boundaries of cello technique, and emotionally rich. From the cathedral-like architecture of the opening chords of Suite 1 to the monk-like hush of the ending of Suite III, these works cover the entire spectrum of cello playing.

It is hard to separate Rostropovich's influence from the suites. While not directly involved in the writing that we know of, his indelible style and persona is embedded throughout. In what appears to be a personal nod to both Rostropovich and Shostakovich, Britten quotes a few Russian folk songs in the third suite. A moving tribute to both of his friends. Rostropovich was deeply moved as well, refusing to perform the third suite after Britten's death, finding it unbearable.

Edition:
Faber Music, Ltd.

Bibliography:
Brett, Philip, Liner notes, Britten, Benjamin, "Cello Suites 1 & 2", Mstislav Rostropovich, London Records, 1968.
Publisher's page on Britten, Accessed August 13, 2023, https://www.boosey.com/pages/cr/composer/composer_main?composerid=2770&ttype=BIOGRAPHY

Recordings:
There are many recordings available made by the world's top cellists, but one should absolutely start with Rostropovich's iconic recordings of the first two suites.

Benjamin Britten (1913-1976) — Sonata in for Cello & Piano, Op. 65

Date of Composition: 1961
Date of Premiere: July 7, 1961
Premiered by: Mstislav Rostropovich, cello with Benjamin Britten, piano
Approximate Length: 24 min

I. Dialogo. Allegro (7 min)
II. Scherzo-Pizzicato. Allegretto (2 min)
III. Elegia. Lento (6 min)
IV. Marcia. Energico (2 min)
V. Moto perpetuo. Presto (7 min)

Background Information:

When one of the greatest cellists of the twentieth century meets one of the greatest English composers of the twentieth century, magic can happen. Mstislav Rostropovich and Benjamin Britten met in 1960 after Rostropovich performed Shostakovich's Cello Concerto No. 1. Britten was so impressed by him, both as a player and a person, that he proceeded to compose five masterful works over the next ten years for the cellist: three unaccompanied suites (see other entry), a Cello Symphony, and a Sonata for Cello and Piano.

The Sonata begins in halting, almost hesitant phrases from the cello based on a minor second (up or down), the piano patiently answering. Buildups to huge outbursts from both instruments immediately follow and a naive and innocent melody from the cello to calm things down. The rest of the movement weaves its way into different textures, restless and searching.

The second movement is all pizzicato for the cello, some points imitating the sound of a guitar, others slinking around mischievously. In addition to pizzicato, the cellist is called upon to hammer the fingers upon the fingerboard percussively. It's a brisk and impish movement.

The third movement Elegia is as moving as the title suggests. The piano intones almost dirge-like chords underneath a somber cello melody. It gradually builds in intensity before coming back down into ethereal harmonics and a muted ending.

The Marcia is a robust and confrontational march, all gruff and bravado. Glissandi harmonics close off the movement, as if the march evaporates off into the distance.

The Moto perpetuo with its persistent ricochet in the cello, and sinister, subterranean piano line gives it a propulsive energy. The movement charges forward, with a few diversions, before the music breaks wide open as the two instruments play in unison, crashing into its final cadence.

This sonata, being the first of the cello works that Britten wrote for Rostropovich, was an auspicious beginning to their partnership. It's a phenomenal work.

Edition:
Boosey & Hawkes

Bibliography:
Britten, Benjamin, Liner notes, Britten, Benjamin "Cello Suites 1 & 2", Mstislav Rostropovich, cello, Benjamin Britten, piano, London Records, 1961.

Recordings:
Many cellists have recorded this work, although the most iconic recording is the aforementioned one made by Rostropovich with Britten on the piano.

Max Bruch (1838-1920) — Kol Nidrei, Op. 47 for Cello & Orchestra

Date of Composition: 1880
Date of Premiere: November 2, 1880
Premiered by: Joseph Hollmann, cello, in Liverpool, England
Approximate Length: 10 min.

Background Information:

Despite being known today primarily for his violin concerto, and this Kol Nidrei for Cello and Orchestra, Max Bruch was one of the more prominent German composers of the Romantic period. He was good friends with famed Hungarian violinist Joseph Joachim, who solicited the violin concerto from him, and after receiving it, declared it one of the four greatest violin concertos of all time–next to Beethoven, Brahms and Mendelssohn (exalted company, indeed).

Cellist Robert Hausmann, who was also good friends with Brahms–he premiered his second cello sonata–approached Bruch about writing a piece for cello. Like his Scottish Fantasy for Violin and Orchestra, Bruch used melodies from other sources to base his piece on. For the Kol Nidrei these would be two Hebrew tunes, one a song of penitence, the other a song of weeping. He claimed he learned of these melodies from acquaintances of his when he was in Berlin.

Due to the popularity of this work, and of course, because of the use of Hebrew themes, it was largely assumed that Bruch himself was Jewish. He was, in fact, Protestant, but didn't mind that people thought that. To him, he felt that "Although I am a Protestant, as an artist, I felt the extraordinary beauty of these melodies very deeply, and have been happy to disseminate them through my arrangements."(Oppermann, iv)

Kol Nidrei is in two parts–one minor, one major. In a halting melody at the opening, the cello seems to be lamenting, with the accompaniment gently urging it on offering support. Eventually, the cello line opens up and spins long lines, taking it higher and higher in its range. The return of the opening material closes the first section. The second part flows seamlessly after the first, and it's as if the clouds have parted, the warmth of the major key glowing through in the orchestral interlude. The cello takes up the new theme emerging victorious after the sorrow of the first section. The piece ends with the cello ascending to heavenly heights and all is well.

Selected Editions:
G. Henle Verlag (Urtext)
International

Bibliography:
Dubal, David The Essential Canon of Classical Music (North Point Press, New York, 2001)
Oppermann, Annette, Preface, "Kol Nidrei", Munich: Henle, 2019.

Recordings:
Numerous commercial recordings of this work have been released.

Kenji Bunch (b. 1973) — Broken Music for Cello & Piano

Date of Composition: 2002
Date of Premiere: February 2003
Premiered by: Clancy Newman, cello and Noreen Cassidy-Polera, piano
Approximate Length: 19 min.

> I. Broken Voice (5 min)
> II. Broken Chord (4 min)
> III. Broken Verse (7 min)
> IV. Broken Music (3 min)

Background Information:

Violist and composer, Kenji Bunch is originally from Portland, Oregon. After studying at the Juilliard School, he returned to Portland where he currently teaches at Portland State University. Known for his clever meshing of traditional and modern vernacular music styles, he is an increasingly favorite composer for performers and audiences alike. Violists like to claim him for themselves, since he is a violist, and music for viola makes up the majority of his oeuvre. However, more and more, his music for other instruments, and especially orchestra, is gaining more attention.

His piece Broken Music for Cello and Piano came from a commission from the Naumburg Foundation. The piece was one element of the prize for winning their competition, the winner premiering it on their debut recital in Alice Tully Hall. Cellist Clancy Newman was the awarded recipient that year, and coincidentally had known Kenji Bunch back from their schooling days.

In a video recorded interview, Newman talks about the work:

"This piece is just an amazing, amazing work. It's four movements long; every movement is very different, but there is a thread, I think, that keeps them all together. A lot of Kenji's music is happy or has a lightness to it, but this piece is more dark and brooding…One thing that has always amazed me about this piece is how it speaks to an audience. Every time I've played it, the audience just loves it, and I think that there is this immediacy to the music and a directness that speaks to people. Beautiful melodies, great dance rhythms, it's just so well conceived from beginning to end…"--Newman, Kingston Chamber Music Festival, Oct. 26, 2020

Edition:
Bill Holab Music

Bibliography:
Official website for the composer, Accessed November 18, 2020, www.kenjibunch.net.
Clancy Newman interview, Accessed November 18, 20202, https://www.youtube.com/watch?v=voD0GxOX4m0&feature=share

Recordings:
Clancy Newman has recorded the work on his album "From Method to Madness" on Albany Records, 2023.

Nicola Saraceni Canzano (b. 1991) — Partita per Violoncello Solo

Date of Composition: December, 2022
Date of Premiere: 2023
Premiered by: Brian Hodges: Red Lodge Music Festival, Red Lodge, Montana, June 3, 2023
Approximate Length: 12 min.

> I. Prelude (4 min)
> II. Allemande (3 min)
> III. Sarabande (3 min)
> IV. Allegro (2 min)

Background Information:

Nicola Canzano is a harpsichordist and composer who specializes in the art of Baroque improvisation and composition. Although written in the 21st century, they are of a sound world very much at home in the 18th century.

His Partita per Violoncello Solo was completed in December of 2022. It follows a scheme similar to the suites of Bach, but takes some new and fresh twists and turns, without ever betraying its modern creation. Written in the key of G Major, the Prelude exploits the key and the range of the cello, with arpeggiated figures bouncing across the four strings in addition to huge leaps and skips. The Allemande, also in G Major, is a dreamy rumination, flirting with melancholy, but never falling completely into a darker affekt. The Sarabande does go to a dark place–the key of G Minor, and is a mediation on sorrow, with chords and melismas inviting the listener to share in the poignancy. The Allegro completes the Suite, back in the sunny warmth of G major, with running passages all through, punctuated by three short double stops throughout.

Edition:
Personal edition by the composer, found on imslp.

Bibliography:
Official website of the composer, Accessed June 9, 2023, www.nicolacanzano.com.

Recordings:
No commercial recording available

Elliott Carter (1908-2012) — Sonata for Cello & Piano

Date of Composition: 1948
Date of Premiere: February 27, 1950
Premiered by: Bernard Greenhouse, cello with Anthony Makas, piano
Approximate Length: 20 min

I. Moderato (5 min)
II. Vivace, molto leggiero (5 min)
III. Adagio (5 min)
IV. Allegro (5 min)

Background Information:

Aaron Copland referred to Elliott Carter as "one of America's most distinguished creative artists in any field." American composer Carter was a vanguard and at the front of the modern music movement in America. With a catalog of over 150 works, he carved a niche and style of composing that is rarely matched even today. He was awarded the Pulitzer Prize twice, won multiple Grammy Awards, received the United States National Medal of Arts, and was named a Commander of the Legion of Honor by the French government.

A student of Gustav Holst, Walter Piston, and Nadia Boulanger, he studied at Harvard University and in Paris. Later, he would hold teaching positions at schools such as Peabody, Yale and Juilliard. Pre- and post-war Carter were different; before the second world war he favored a more neo-classical approach, while after the war, his music became more experimental, pushing boundaries continuously. While not using full-on serial technique, he favored chromaticism and metric modulation, creating vastly difficult and challenging scores.

His Cello Sonata, written in 1948 contains these elements. Carter speaks of his approach to writing the sonata and embracing the differences in the two instruments. In the first movement, the cello plays long, semi-melodic lines, while the piano is the rhythmic counterpart, all clockwork and angular. The second movement, Vivace, is not far off from jazz in its syncopations and tonal language. The following Adagio, is a world away from the second movement, in that it feels like one long rhapsody for the cello. The final Allegro is a rollicking movement in rondo form, with the cello cascading all over the instrument, the piano interjecting notes and motives in between. It's a fiendishly difficult sonata on multiple fronts, but ultimately is rewarding for the two players and the audience.

Carter writes about the sonata: "...the idea of metrical modulation came to me while writing this piece, and its use becomes more elaborated from the second movement on. The first movement, written last after the concept had been quite thoroughly explored, presents one of the piece's basic ideas: the contrast between psychological time (in the cello) and the chronometric time (in the piano), their combination producing musical or 'virtual' time." (earplay.org)

Carter's Cello Sonata is one of the great American cello sonatas of the twentieth century. It continues to be innovative and has lost none of its brilliance, even after 75 years.

Edition:
Associated Music Publishers

Bibliography:
Official website of the composer, Accessed August 12, 2023, https://www.elliottcarter.com/
Program notes from the composer, Accessed August 12, 2023, http://www.earplay.org/www/notes.php?id=Carter5

Recordings:
There are numerous commercial recordings available of this work.

Pablo Casals (1876-1973) — Song of the Birds (El cant dels ocells) for Cello & Piano

Date of Composition: c. 1939
Date of Premiere: Unknown
Premiered by: Pablo Casals
Approximate Length: 4 min.

Background Information:

Pablo Casals, probably the first international celebrity cellist in history, made a huge impact on the world of music, not to mention the cello. Although he held tightly to his Catalonian heritage, in reality, he belonged to the world, touring extensively and setting up his legendary Casals Festival in Puerto Rico.

The Song of the Birds, a traditional Catalonian melody, became a staple of Casals' live performances, choosing to end his recitals with his arrangement. Later, he used it as a plea for peace, most significantly playing it at the White House for President J. F. Kennedy, and First Lady Jackie Kennedy.

Thematically, The Song of the Birds depicts the Nativity from the viewpoint of the birds, serenading the Christ child with their song. Casals said, "...it is the eagles and the sparrows, the nightingales, and the little wrens that sing a welcome to the infant, singing of Him as a flower that will delight the earth with its sweet scent." (Casals, p. 28)

The meditative piece contains fluttering trills and harmonics, creating an ethereal, meditative landscape. It is just one of many significant contributions this iconic musician left behind.

Edition:
Carl Fischer

Bibliography:
Baldock, Robert. Pablo Casals (Northeastern University Press, Boston, 1992)
Casals, Pablo. Joys and Sorrows (Simon and Schuster, NY, 1970)

Recordings:
There are recordings of this available, namely Casals himself on Regis records.

Andrea Casarrubios (b. 1988) — Seven for Solo Cello

Date of Composition: 2020
Date of Premiere: 2020
Premiered by: Tommy Mesa, cello
Approximate Length: 8 min.

Background Information:

Spanish cellist Andrea Casarrubios has had a major career as a performer and composer. She has performed all over the world and written music for high profile commissions. As a cellist herself, of course, she has composed a fair amount of music for cello, but she has written for chamber and large ensembles as well.

Her piece Seven for solo cello is a moving work of tribute to the loss and heroism that came from the COVID 19 pandemic.

She writes:

Commissioned by Astral Artist Tommy Mesa for his project Songs of Isolation, SEVEN is a tribute to the essential workers during the global COVID-19 pandemic, as well as to those who lost lives and are still suffering from the crisis. Written in Manhattan, the piece ends with seven bell-like sounds, alluding to New York's daily 7 PM tribute during the lockdown, the moment when New Yorkers clapped from their windows, connecting with each other and expressing appreciation for those on the front lines.

Edition:
Available from the composer's website

Bibliography:
Official website of the composer, Accessed July 7, 2023, https://www.andreacasarrubios.com/

Recordings:
Tommy Mesa's recording can be found on his album "Songs of Isolation".

Gaspar Cassadó (1897-1966) — Suite for Solo Cello

Date of Composition: 1926
Date of Premiere: Unknown
Premiered by: most likely by Cassadó himself, but the piece was dedicated to cellist Francesco von Mendelssohn.
Approximate Length: 15 min.

I. Preludio-Fantasia (a Zarabanda) (6 min)
II. Sardana (4 min)
III. Intermezzo e Danza Finale (a Jota) (5 min)

Background Information:

    Gaspar Cassadó was one of the great Spanish cellists of the twentieth century. While not as much of a household name as arguably the greatest Spanish cellist of the twentieth century, Pablo Casals, he still managed to have an international career. Casals essentially discovered him, after hearing him performing a concert when he was nine years old. Cassadó went to study with Casals in Paris, and also studied composition with Maurice Ravel and Manuel de Falla.
His Suite for Solo Cello, written in 1926, is a brilliant work infused with Spanish sounds and rhythms. Due to his connection with Casals, who was such a vocal champion of the Bach Suites, it's not difficult to see them as a background for his solo suite. The use of a Prelude followed by a collection of dances is a page right out of Bach's book.
    The first movement is a broad introduction which introduces us to the character of the piece, before going into a section based on the Sarabande, which was a Baroque dance that originated in Spain.
The second movement is based on the sardana, a folk dance from Catalonia. Harmonics signify a flute, and there is a brilliant section where the melody goes high up in thumb position interspersed with open strings.
In the third movement, based on the jota dance, Cassadó paints such a vivid picture of the dance. You can practically hear the stamping of the feet, the click of the castanets, and the swirl of the colorful dresses. It all ends in a dizzying flurry of triple-stops.

Edition:
Universal

Bibliography:
Internet Cello Society page on Cassado, Accessed on August 14, 2023, http://www.cello.org/cnc/cassado.htm
Program notes from the Vancouver Recital Society, Accessed August 14, 2023, https://vanrecital.com/tag/cellist/

Recordings:
Unfortunately, Cassadó never recorded his own suite (but he did record the Bach Suites). Janos Starker recorded it some time after Cassadó's death, bringing the piece to a whole new audience. There are numerous other recordings made by world-class cellists

Unsuk Chin (b. 1961) — Cello Concerto

Date of Composition: 2009, rev. 2013
Date of Premiere: 2009
Premiered by: Alban Gerhardt, cello; with Ilan Vokov conducting the BBC Scottish Symphony Orchestra/ 2013 version premiered by Alban Gerhardt with Kent Nagano conducting the Bayerisches Staatsorchester
Approximate Length: 28 min.

I. "Aniri" (9'48)
II. (2'57)
III. (8'06)
IV. (7'16)

Background Information:

Unsuk Chin was born in Seoul but was educated in Europe. György Ligeti was one of her main teachers when she studied in Hamburg. She received great acclaim for her Violin Concerto and other works and has forged a collaborative partnership with conductor Kent Nagano who has championed and premiered numerous works of hers.

Cellist Alban Gerhardt met Chin after a concert where he heard her violin concerto. He was immediately struck with how original her compositional language was and hoped that she might write a piece for him someday. His wish came true when she informed him that she was about to embark upon writing a cello concerto for him–the first time she would write a concerto with a specific player in mind. After a considerable time later, she finally finished the score, delivering it to Gerhardt two months before the premiere.

The concerto was incredibly well-received, inspiring a critic from The Guardian to proclaim it as one of the 25 best classical music pieces written in this century. Despite the acclaim, Chin was unsatisfied with the second movement, so she decided to revise it. It was enough of a difference to her that she regarded the revised version as a new premiere, which Gerhardt handled again.

The concerto is broad in scope and covers the entire range of the cello. It is full of lightning-fast, technically demanding passages, not to mention employing numerous extended techniques. There are moments of extreme quiet and terrifyingly loud outbursts. This makes it all the more impressive that Gerhardt learned the piece in less than two months, fully memorized.

Edition:
Boosey & Hawkes

Bibliography:
Alban Gerhardt blog entry on the piece, Accessed August 9, 2023, https://albangerhardt.com/the-unsuk-chin-celloconcerto-preparing-for-a-world-premier/
Publisher page on the piece, Accessed August 9, 2023, https://www.boosey.com/cr/music/Unsuk-Chin-Cello-Concerto/47692

Recordings:
To date, the only commercially available recording is by Alban Gerhardt on Deutsche Grammophone.

Frederic Chopin (1810-1849) — Introduction and Polonaise Brillante, Op. 3 for Cello & Piano

Date of Composition: 1829; Introduction added 1830
Date of Premiere: August 1831
Premiered by: Most likely Józef Kaczyński, cello and Chopin, piano
Approximate Length: 9 mins.

Background Information:

Early in Frederic Chopin's career, he earned the favor of Prince Antoni Radziwiłł, who was an amateur cellist and the dedicatee of Chopin's Piano Trio in G Minor. Chopin taught Radziwiłł's daughter as a piano student and was inspired to compose a piece for the two of them. The result was the Polonaise for Cello and Piano; the introduction would be added later. In a letter to a friend, he self-deprecatingly detailed: "I wrote [...] an alla polacca with cello. Nothing to it but dazzle, for the salon, for the ladies."(Heinemann, p. vi)

Chopin's original design for the work was a rather simplistic and bel canto-style melody line for the cello, with the piano part much more involved and technically demanding, reflecting the level of the modestly-skilled Prince and his much more talented daughter. Chopin later added in the Introduction in 1830 and in the eventual initial publication, dedicated it to the famous cellist Joseph Merk, whom Chopin greatly admired.

Since then, cellists, being rather disappointed with the rather undemanding cello line, have embellished, and in some cases, completely re-written the cello part, making it considerably more difficult and virtuosic than originally intended. Both versions are available, giving cellists an option as to which one they want to do.

Selected Editions:
G. Henle Verlag (Urtext–original Chopin version)
International (revised, embellished edition)

Bibliography:
Heinemann, Ernst Günter, Preface, In. "Polonaise Brillante", München: Henle, 2006.
Polish webpage on Chopin, Accessed July 29, 2023, https://chopin.nifc.pl/en/chopin/kompozycja/16_introduction-and-polonaise-brillante-in-c-major-for-piano-and-cello

Recordings:
Numerous commercial recordings have been released, mostly of the revised versions.

Frederic Chopin (1810-1849)
Sonata for Cello & Piano in G Minor Op. 65

Date of Composition: 1846
Date of Premiere: February 16, 1848 in Paris
Premiered by: Auguste Franchomme, cello, and Frederic Chopin, piano
Approximate Length: 30 min.

> I. Allegro moderato (15 min.)
> II. Scherzo (5 min.)
> III. Largo (4 min.)
> IV. Finale. Allegro (6 min.)

Background Information:

    Frederic Chopin was arguably one of the greatest pianists of the nineteenth century, not only as a performer, but as a composer as well. While he focused almost exclusively on composing for the piano, his one and only sonata for another instrument is his Sonata for Cello and Piano. He had actually written another work for cello and piano earlier, his Polonaise Brillante (see other entry), but this is a much more mature and larger scale work. Feeling somewhat insecure about writing for the cello, he turned to his friend, cellist Auguste Franchomme, for help. Franchomme had helped him extensively in another earlier work for cello and piano, the Grand Duo. Chopin left behind a copious amount of sketches for this sonata, revealing the struggle he went through in conceptualizing the work. He said, "Sometimes I am satisfied with my sonata with violoncello and at other times I am not. I throw it into a corner only to gather it up again later." (Zimmerman, p. iii)

    Casting a shadow over the mood and character of the sonata, it was written during a time which saw the disintegration of his long-standing relationship with George Sand. Indeed a sense of melancholy pervades throughout, and undoubtedly contributed to his lack of confidence in the work.
This would be the last major work that Chopin composed.

Selected Editions:
G. Henle Verlag (Urtext)
International

Bibliography:
Berger, Melvin. Guide to Sonatas (Anchor Books, New York, 1991)
Zimmerman, Ewald, Preface in Chopin, Frederic "Sonata for Cello and Piano", Munich: Henle, 1997.

Recordings:
Most of the major cellists have made commercial recordings of this sonata.

Rebecca Clarke (1886-1979) — Sonata for Cello & Piano

Date of Composition: 1919
Date of Premiere: September 1920
Premiered by: May Mukle, cello
Approximate Length: 23 min.

I. Impetuoso (8 min)
II. Vivace (4 min)
III. Adagio - Allegro (11 min)

Background Information:

Rebecca Clarke has the distinction of being one of the first professional female orchestra players as a violist. She also performed in one of the first all-female professional string quartets. But it was her Viola Sonata which brought her to quick fame. Entering it into a competition sponsored by Elizabeth Sprague Coolidge, it tied for first place, with the top prize ultimately going to Ernest Bloch. The feedback and reviews were ecstatic and overwhelmingly positive, although many (including Coolidge herself) couldn't believe it hadn't been written by a man.

A year after the premiere, she made a transcription of the sonata for cello for her friend and quartet-mate, cellist May Mukle. The cello version appeared as a supplement in the 1921 publication of the viola sonata; the piano part being identical.

Clarke included an inscription at the very beginning of the piece, which is a quote from French poet Alfred Musset: "Poet, take up your lute; the wine of youth this night is fermenting in the veins of God." Clarke didn't make much of the quote, simply including it as somewhat of an inspirational point, not something to be taken overly literally.

However, from the opening notes of the piece, it's difficult not to hear those poetic words and connect them with the music. The piece starts with a striking declaration from the cello, not unlike a trumpet call, and rarely lets up. The second movement skitters with nervous, yet humorous energy with the cellist employing an extensive use of harmonics and pizzicato. The last movement brings the whole work full circle–literally, as the opening material returns at the end.

The sonata is certainly full of vigor and passion and shows off the two instruments incredibly well. It's an epic work that is rightly taking its place firmly in the repertoire of many players.

Edition:
Masters Music Publications

Bibliography:
Hodges, Betsi. W.W. Cobbett's Phantasy: A Legacy of Chamber Music in the British Musical Renaissance (VDM Verlag Dr. Müller, 2009)
Official website for the composer, Accessed August 9, 2023, https://www.rebeccaclarke.org/
Curtis, Liane, Liner notes for Clarke, Rebecca "Sonata for Cello and Piano", Pamela Frame, cello, Barry Snyder, piano, Koch Classics, 1994.

Recordings:
A number of commercial recordings are available, notably the first recording of the sonata on cello by cellist Pamela Frame on Koch Classics.

Anna Clyne (b. 1980) — Dance for Cello & Orchestra

Date of Composition: 2019
Date of Premiere: August 3, 2019
Premiered by: Inbal Segev, cello; Cristian Macelaru conductor at the Cabrillo Festival of Contemporary Music
Approximate Length: 25 min.

> I. when you're broken open (5 min)
> II. if you've torn the bandage off (4 min)
> III. in the middle of the fighting (4 min)
> IV. in your blood (6 min)
> V. when you're perfectly free (6 min)

Background Information:

Dance for Cello and Orchestra was born out of a meeting between cellist Inbal Segev and composer Anna Clyne set up by conductor Marin Alsop. The connection was instant and this multi-movement work was created. British composer Clyne, one of the most prolific composers working today, was inspired by a poem by Rumi, which gives each of the movements its titles.

She says, "I knew that I wanted to write a multi-movement work in which each movement had its own personality, its own character. I've known this Rumi poem for a while and always thought it would be a good source of inspiration—it's short, has repetition, a clear form of five lines, and a strong physicality (for example, "broken open," "in your blood"). It also has a sense of urgency that I found compelling for this piece. It was a great way to structure the piece—to break it up into the five movements according to the five lines of the poem." (www.boosey.com)

The finished concerto was dedicated to Clyne's father, Leslie. It was premiered and subsequently recorded by Inbal Segev.

Edition:
Boosey & Hawkes

Bibliography:
Official website of the composer, Accessed August 1, 2023, http://www.annaclyne.com
Publisher page on the piece, Accessed August 1, 2023, https://www.boosey.com/cr/news/Anna-Clyne-discusses-poetic-inspiration-for-her-new-cello-concerto/101385&LangID=1

Recordings:
Inbal Segev made a recording with Marin Alsop conducting the London Philharmonic Orchestra for Avie Records.

Samuel Coleridge-Taylor (1875-1912) — Variations in B Minor for Cello & Piano

Date of Composition: 1905
Date of Premiere: 1907
Premiered by: C.A. Crabbe, cello
Approximate Length: 13 min.

Background Information:

Samuel Coleridge-Taylor was an English-born composer who, in his lifetime, found fame in the UK and in the United States. At a young age, he showed advanced musical aptitude, which his mother helped to foster. He caught the attention of Edward Elgar and Charles Villiers Stanford who took him on as a student, becoming a mentor to him. Under Stanford's influence, his earliest mature pieces, while still a student, were mostly in the realm of chamber music. Coleridge-Taylor also had a penchant for vocal and theatrical works; his early set of three cantatas based on Longfellow's poem "The Song of Hiawatha" got him instant fame, and cemented his career as a professional composer.

Due to the success of Hiawatha, many African-Americans were enthralled with him and his music, and in 1902 formed the Samuel Coleridge-Taylor Society to bring his music to a wider audience. This brought him the opportunity to tour the United States, even getting an invitation from the White House. It was on these visits to America that he became increasingly more interested in his African heritage, and he sought to incorporate African folk songs and spirituals into his music from then on.

Throughout his career, he moved between larger scale works for orchestra and the stage, and smaller works, such as chamber music. The Variations in B Minor for Cello and Piano was written on an original theme of his own. The theme is a lovely, lilting melody, and gives Coleridge-Taylor plenty of material in which to base his variations on. It's a beautiful work that showcases both instruments equally in an elegant and charming set of variations.
After it premiered, the piece was thought lost. Fortunately, it was found later, after Coleridge-Taylor's death, finally getting published in 1918.

Editions:
Silvertrust Edition Performer's Edition
Stainer & Bell

Bibliography:
Carr, Catherine The Music of Samuel Coleridge-Taylor (1875-1912) dissertation from Durham University, 2005.
Website for the Samuel Coleridge-Taylor Foundation, Accessed August 12, 2023, https://sctf.org.uk/

Recordings:
A couple of commercial recordings have been made, as well as a number of performances on youtube.

John Corigliano (b. 1938) — Fancy on an Air by Bach for Solo Cello

Date of Composition: 1996
Date of Premiere: August 24, 1997
Premiered by: Yo-Yo Ma, cello
Approximate Length: 5 min.

Background Information:

John Corigliano is one of the most well-known contemporary composers of the late twentieth and early twenty-first centuries. He shot to international fame with his score for the film The Red Violin, which earned him the Academy Award for Best Score. He followed that up with a Pulitzer Prize for his Symphony No. 2. He serves on the faculty at Juilliard and has taught many of the rising up-and-coming composers of this time.

Fancy on an Air by Bach grew out of a request to write a piece for a friends' wedding anniversary. Corigliano thought it would be better to have a group of composers write variations on the Goldberg theme by Bach for the occasion (the friends' last name was Goldberg). He enlisted his friends Yo-Yo Ma and Emmanuel Ax to perform the finished work.

Unfortunately, the husband passed away, and the piece was then performed at his funeral rather than their anniversary celebration. Corigliano has since published his variation alone for unaccompanied cello. He writes, "My 'Goldberg Variation' Fancy on a Bach Air...Its dual inspiration was the love of two extraordinary people and the solo cello suites of a great composer–both of them strong, long-lined, passionate, eternal, and for me, definitive of all this is beautiful in life."(www.johncorigliano.com)

Edition:
G. Schirmer

Bibliography:
Official website of the composer, Accessed August 10, 2023, https://www.johncorigliano.com/
Page from the composer's website on the piece, Accessed August 10, 2023, https://www.johncorigliano.com/works/fancy-on-a-bach-air-1996

Recordings:
Yo-Yo Ma has recorded it on the Sony Classical label.

George Crumb (b. 1929-2022)   Sonata for Solo Cello

Date of Composition: 1955
Date of Premiere: March, 1957
Premiered by: Camilla Doppmann, cello

Approximate Length: 11 min.

> I. Fantasia (4 min)
> II. Tema Pastorale con variazioni (4 min)
> III. Toccato (3 min)

Background Information:

George Crumb was an innovative and progressive voice among American composers throughout the twentieth century. Originally from West Virginia, he studied at the University of Illinois and the University of Michigan; in between, he received a Fulbright Scholarship to study in Berlin. He spent most of his career teaching at the University of Pennsylvania, while continuing his composition career, earning a Pulitzer in 1968.

Crumb's music sits in a space between more traditional, neoclassical methods, and more modern contemporary techniques. Pushing the boundaries of sound and timbre in his music, he even was creative in the notation of his scores. Many of his scores are massively oversized and employ a system of graphic notation, often done in designs and patterns, such as a spiral, on the page. His seminal work, Black Angels, is a groundbreaking work for amplified string quartet, which calls for the string players to play a variety of percussion instruments, water goblets, whistle, hum and shout.

His Sonata for Solo Cello is an early work, composed when he was studying in Berlin, and is the first one that he published. It was inspired by and dedicated to his mother, who was a cellist. Despite it being an early work, many elements typical of Crumb are present. Using standard forms such as a Baroque Suite as a framework, he layers the piece in an expanding tonal language.

The opening Fantasia alternates between strumming pizzicato chords, which get more and more insistent, and a plaintive arco line. The movement builds to a climax high up in the register in thumb position double-stops before wearily winding down to nothing. A theme and variations gives the second movement its structure, opening with a swinging melody, involving harmonics and double-stops. The variations following expand the theme in acrobatic string crossing and rapid pizzicatos. The main theme returns at the end to close the movement off neatly. The third movement is a swirling, driving series of arpeggios, broken up by a jazzy, swung groove, and ending the movement and the entire piece with a melodramatic cadence.

The Sonata is a concise and charged work, showing Crumb's wonderful combination of traditional forms and structure with an ever-broadening sense of tonality and possibility for expression.

Edition:
Peters

Bibliography:
Official website of the composers, Accessed August 13, 2023, https://www.georgecrumb.net/
Program notes, Accessed August 13, 2023, http://www.earplay.org/www/notes.php?id=Crumb4

Recordings:
Many cellists have released commercial recordings of this work.

Giuseppe Dall'Abaco (1710-1805) — 11 Capricii for Solo Cello

Date of Composition: 1766 (as indicated on the title page of the manuscript copy)
Date of Premiere: Unknown
Premiered by: Unknown, but most likely Dall'Abaco
Approximate Length: 62 min.

Caprice No. 1 in c minor (4 min.)
Caprice No. 2 in g minor (3 min.)
Caprice No. 3 in Eb Major (7 min.)
Caprice No. 4 in d minor (7 min.)
Caprice No. 5 in Bb Major (2 min.)
Caprice No. 6 in e minor (6 min.)
Caprice No. 7 in Bb Major (9 min.)
Caprice No. 8 in G Major (4 min.)
Caprice No. 9 in C Major (3 min.)
Caprice No. 10 in A Major (4 min.)
Caprice No. 11 in F Major (7 min.)

Background Information:

Giuseppe Maria Evaristo Clemente Dall'Abaco was the son of composer, violinist and cellist, Evaristo Felice Dall'Abaco. He spent some time at the court in Bonn, Germany, before settling in Verona, where he became a member of the Accademia Filarmonica.

Despite living to the age of 95 (an anomaly at that time), he wrote all of his major extant works early in his life in a very short amount of time. His entire output consists of 35 sonatas for cello and continuo, several cello trios (the number dubious) and his most well-known works, the 11 solo capricci. There is only one handwritten manuscript for these capricci dating from the 19th century, which is a copy of his original manuscript.

A curious quirk occurs in the manuscript in the 11th capriccio, where the music abruptly stops, leaving it in an unfinished state. Many theories have been posed as to why, but cellists are left to create their own ending (which likely also would have included a 12th caprice originally as well).

Each caprice occupies a particular key and affekt with little to nothing in the way of tempo or expressive markings. There are a few possibilities as to why these were written, perhaps for instructional, performing purposes, or both. Nonetheless, these capricci offer the performer a wide landscape in which to embellish, ornament and express themselves that stand as worthy counterparts to Bach's monumental Six Suites for Solo Cello. Other than the Gabrielli Ricercare, they represent the only other major unaccompanied collection of works for cello in the Baroque era.

Selected Edition:
Musedita

Bibliography:
Frey, Elinor, Liner notes, Dall'Abaco, Giuseppi Clemente "Cello Sonatas" Elinor Frey, cello, Passacaille Records, 2020
Galliglioni, Francesco, Liner notes, Dall'Abaco, Giuseppi "Capricci a violoncello solo", Francesco Galliglioni, cello, Brilliant Classics, 2018. Accessed June 9, 2023, https://issuu.com/klassiek.nl/docs/digital_booklet_dall_abaco_capricci

Recordings:
A couple of commercial recordings exist on both period and modern instruments.

Michael Daugherty (b. 1954) — Tales of Hemingway for Cello & Orchestra

Date of Composition: 2015
Date of Premiere: April 17, 2015
Premiered by: Zuill Bailey, cello; Giancarlo Guerrero, conductor; Nashville Symphony Orchestra
Approximate Complete Length: 28 min.

I. Big Two-Hearted River (5 min)
II. For Whom the Bell Tolls (7 min)
III. The Old Man and the Sea (7 min)
IV. The Sun Also Rises (9 min)

Background Information:

Michael Daugherty is a product of the variety of composers and mentors he studied with in his formative years, including Györgi Ligeti, Conlon Nancarrow, and Leonard Bernstein. Daugherty is currently on faculty at the University of Michigan and has won numerous awards and honors for his compositions.

His program notes on Tales of Hemingway:

Tales of Hemingway evokes the turbulent life, adventures, and literature of American author and journalist Ernest Hemingway (1899-1961). His terse, direct, accessible writing style, combined with a mastery of dialogue and brilliant use of omission and repetition, made him one of the most influential and original writers of the 20th century. Hemingway's distinctive body of work was also informed by his larger-than-life experiences…Twenty-five minutes in duration, my cello concerto is divided into four movements, which are inspired by one of Hemingway's short stories or novels.

The recording with the premiere artists won three Grammy awards in 2017.

Edition:
Michael Daugherty publishing; Score is available for purchase/parts are available to rent

Bibliography:
Official website of the composer, Accessed November 17, 2020, www.michaeldaugherty.net
Page on the composer's official website of the piece, Accessed November 17, 2020, https://michaeldaugherty.net/works/concerti-with-orchestra/tales-of-hemingway/

Recordings:
To date, there has only been one commercial recording made by Zuill Bailey on Naxos in 2016.

Kevin Day (b. 1996) Sonata for Cello and Piano (2016)

Date of Composition: 2016
Date of Premiere: Spring 2017
Premiered by: Emmanuel Kwok, cello and Daria Kiseleva, piano
Approximate Length: 15 min.

> I. Allegro agitato (5 min)
> II. Lento (for Naomi) (5 min)
> III. Giocoso (5 min)

Background Information:

Kevin Day, originally from Arlington, Texas, studied at Texas Christian University and The University of Georgia. He was one of the winners of the BMI Student Composers Award and in the 2019-2021 season, he was the composer-in-residence with the Mesquite Symphony. He was a finalist for the Pulitzer Prize in 2022. He has composed for band, orchestra, chamber music, choral music, and for film.

From the program notes for his sonata:

I had the idea for my first cello sonata when I was playing in the Disneyland All-American College Band in Los Angeles in Summer 2016. I've always loved the cello and how musical and expressive it can be and wanted to push myself to write a piece that would expand my compositional skills and write for an instrument I've never composed for as a soloist. This piece was also inspired by composer Frank Ticheli, whom I had a composition lesson with while I was in Los Angeles. He encouraged me to expand my tonal and harmonic language and believes that "tonality and atonality should go hand in hand with each other." This is what I was hoping to accomplish in this piece. (soundcloud.com/kevindaymusic)

Edition:
Score and parts available via www.kevindaymusic.com

Bibliography:
Official website for the composer, Accessed August 20, 2020, https://kevindaymusic.com/
Program notes from Day's SoundCloud page, Accessed August 20, 2020, : https://soundcloud.com/kevindaymusic/cello-sonata-2016 (audio examples are present, however program notes are no longer available)

Recordings:
No commercial recording is available as of yet. Live recordings can be found on his youtube page.

Claude Debussy (1862-1918)   Sonata for Cello & Piano

Date of Composition: 1915
Date of Premiere: 1915
Premiered by: Joseph Salmon, cello, Claude Debussy, piano
Approximate Length: 12 min.

> I. Prologue: Lent, sostenuto e molto risoluto (5 min)
> II. Sérénade: Modérément animé (3 min)
> III. Finale: Animé, léger et nerveux (4 min)
> (the 2nd and 3rd movements are played without pause)

Background Information:

Claude Debussy was one of the pivotal figures transitioning into the new sound world at the dawn of the twentieth century. While respecting German-style Romantic music, he also made great strides in moving away from that style, preferring a more concise music that focused more on moods and feelings rather than specific themes.

Towards the end of his life, after the outbreak of World War I and a devastating cancer diagnosis, he stayed away from composing for several years. He finally came back to composing with a plan to write Six Sonates pour Divers Instruments, of which he was only able to complete three, the cello sonata being one of them.

The Cello Sonata is the definition of brevity as the entire work is no longer than around 12 minutes. Debussy described the work saying, "The proportions and the form of the Sonata were almost classical in the true sense of the word."(Back, xiii) He must not have been referring to the actual form, as it doesn't follow a traditional Sonata-Allegro form, a standard for Classical sonatas, but possibly more the treatment of melodic ideas.

As his career progressed, he moved farther and farther away from programmatic titles, something that was all the rage in the previous century, instead crafting titles that were more suggestions rather than spelling out anything specific. The cello sonata, at one point, had a title, Pierrot fâché avec la lune (Pierrot is angry with the moon), referencing the Harlequin stock character of the sad-clown Pierrot. He ultimately removed it, keeping it to the simple and straightforward Sonata for Cello and Piano. However, the music still bears quite a few traces of the more descriptive title, particularly in the second movement which seems to evoke Pierrot strumming his guitar and playing the flute to serenade and woo the object of his affection.

The Sonata is a tour de force for both instruments allowing for virtuosity with plenty of room for a variety of moods and colors. This is highly expressive music full of character and energy, which, incidentally, makes for a successful recital opener.

Selected Editions:
Barenreiter (Urtext)
Durand
G. Henle Verlag (Urtext)

Bibliography:
Back, Regina, Preface, Debussy, Claude "Sonata for Cello and Piano", Kassel: Barenreiter, 2008.
Berger, Melvin. Guide to Sonatas (Anchor Books, New York, 1991)

Recordings:
Most of the major cellists have released commercial recordings.

Bryce Dessner (b. 1976) — Tuusula for Solo Cello

Date of Composition: 2015
Date of Premiere: 2015
Premiered by: Nicolas Altstaedt, cello
Approximate Length: 10 min.

Background Information:

Bryce Dessner wears many hats, including composer of classical music, film scores, and guitarist of the rock band, The National. He has won many awards and has collaborated with a wide variety of musicians in all genres. His most well-known film score is for the film The Revenant for director Alejandro Gonzàlez Iñàrritu.

His own program notes for Tuusula:

I composed this solo work for cellist Nicolas Altstaedt two summers ago when I was composer in residence at Pekka Kuusisto's beautiful chamber music festival, Meidän Festivaali, in Sibelius's hometown of Tuusula. Tuusula is a small lake town about 40 minutes from Helsinki, and was a haven for composers and painters in the 19th and early 20th centuries…The place itself, the woods and water and light, inspired me to write this cello solo for Nicolas, which was not planned as part of the festival. I would write a bit of the piece every day, which accounts for its improvisatory feeling, and at the end of the week Nicolas premiered it in a chapel on the edge of the lake where Sibelius was baptized.

Edition:
Chester Music

Bibliography:
Official website of the composer, Accessed November 17, 2020, www.brycedessner.com
Publisher page on the piece, Accessed November 17, 2020, https://www.wisemusicclassical.com/work/56281/Tuusula--Bryce-Dessner/

Recordings:
There is a commercial recording available made by cellist Lavena on the Bright Shiny Things label, 2021.

Tan Dun (b. 1957)   Crouching Tiger Concerto for Cello & Orchestra

Date of Composition: 2000
Date of Premiere: September 28, 2000
Premiered by: Yo-Yo Ma, cello; Tan Dun conducting the London Sinfonietta
Approximate Length: 32 min.

I. Crouching Tiger, Hidden Dragon (8 min)
II. Through the Bamboo Forest (5 min)
III. Silk Road: Encounters (5 min)
IV. Eternal Vow (7 min)
V. To the South (3 min)
VI. Farewell (4 min)

Background Information:
Tan Dun shot to international fame thanks to his score for the film Crouching Tiger, Hidden Dragon. The score heavily features cello solos by Yo-Yo Ma and won an Academy Award for Best Original Score. Already having a substantial career up to that point, Chinese-American composer Tan Dun was well known for blending Western and Eastern music styles. He has written solo, chamber, symphonic, vocal and operatic works, often incorporating video and multimedia into the live performances. He wrote music for the 2008 Olympic Games in Beijing, conducted at the opening of Disneyland Shanghai, and is a UNESCO Goodwill Ambassador.

Due to the success of the Crouching Tiger, Hidden Dragon score, Dun transformed it into a concerto for cello and orchestra using themes from the original score. Like the film score, the music features a robust percussion section, which offers pouding, driving rhythms throughout, with the cello soaring above. Yo-Yo Ma gave the world premiere in London at the Barbican Festival in 2000. It has also been arranged as a sonata for cello and piano, triple concerto for violin, cello and piano, and a concerto for erhu and orchestra.

Dun has written quite a number of other cello works (the majority of which, sadly, are not available for performance) including a couple of unaccompanied works for cello, such as Intercourse of Fire and Water.

Edition:
G. Schirmer-unfortunately, at this time, it is only available to rent

Bibliography:
Publisher's page on the composer, Accessed August 11, 2023, https://www.wisemusicclassical.com/composer/1561/Tan-Dun/
Publisher's page on the piece, Accessed August 11, 2023, https://www.wisemusicclassical.com/work/33553/

Recordings:
Strangely, there is no commercial recording of this concerto that has been released. The original score to the film is available on the Sony Classics label. There are, however, a number of performances of the concerto available on youtube.

Melissa Dunphy (b. 1980) — Baroque Variations on The Frail for Cello & Piano

Date of Composition: 2007
Date of Premiere: 2007
Premiered by: Ioana Velicu, cello, and Melissa Dunphy, piano
Approximate Length: 5 min.

Background Information:

Originally from Australia, composer Melissa Dunphy has written for a variety of mediums. She shot to fame when her work the Gonzalez Cantata was featured on the Rachel Maddow Show in 2009. Not just confined to concert hall works, she has also been actively involved with works for the theater where she has been nominated for a Barrymore Theatre award and been music director of the O'Neill National Puppetry Conference. She and her husband own the Hannah Callowhill Stage, an intimate multi-disciplinary performing arts venue in Philadelphia.

While the majority of her works tend to be vocal in nature, she has written a fair amount of instrumental works, including this set of variations for cello and piano. The theme for the set of variations is based on a song called "The Frail" by Nine Inch Nails' lead singer and songwriter, Trent Reznor. It is written in a neo-Baroque style, which at first, wouldn't seem to fit the dark tenor of Nine Inch Nails' music, but is incredibly clever, a highlight being the polyphonic variation.

Dunphy has a new piece of cello and piano forthcoming entitled, Brisbane: Spring of 1987.

Edition:
Available from www.melissadunphy.com

Bibliography:
Official website of the composer, Accessed July 7, 2023, https://melissadunphy.com/compositions.php

Recordings:
No commercial recording is available. A video of the composer performing the piece is on her website.

Henri Dutilleux (1916-2013)

Tout un monde lointain... for Cello & Orchestra

Date of Composition: 1970
Date of Premiere: July 25, 1970
Premiered by: Mstislav Rostropovich, cello, with Serge Baudo conducting the Orchestre de Paris.
Approximate Length: 27 min.

> I. Énigme (7 min.)
> II. Regard (6 min.)
> III. Houles (4 min.)
> IV. Miroirs (6 min.)
> V. Hymne (4 min.)
> [played without pause]

Background Information:

French composer Henri Dutilleux's music was a combination of his French musical heritage, that of the music of Debussy and Ravel, and more contemporary modern writing. Studying at the Paris conservatory, his big break came from winning the Grand Prix de Rome in 1938. Refusing to be pinned down to any one style, his music is a kaleidoscope of influences and techniques.

Tout un monde lointain… for Cello and Orchestra (A whole, distant world…) was written for Mstislav Rostropovich and is based on poetry by Charles Baudelaire. The title comes from a line of his poem La Chevelure : "Tout un monde lointain, absent, presque défunt…"("A whole, distant, absent, almost defunct world…"). Each movement has another poetry quote, which acts as more of a spiritual guide to the music rather than the music being a literal interpretation of it.

The music across all five movements (which are played without pause) covers a wide spectrum of timbres, colors, and textures, the cello acting as the guide. At times the music is spacious, expansive, other times it is insistent and aggressive. It covers the full spectrum of dynamic range from its opening whispery shimmers in the percussion section to jagged outbursts at top volume. The quotation before the last movement Hymne "Keep your dreams: wise men do not have as beautiful ones as fools!", could be seen as a summation of the entire work. At times, the concerto does seem like we've entered into a dreamscape, concrete and surreal images and sounds swirling around us. It's a challenging work, but one that gets more lucid with repeated listens.

Edition:
Leduc; Heugel & Cie

Bibliography:
Program notes on the works, Accessed August 15, 2023, https://www.laphil.com/musicdb/pieces/4327/tout-un-monde-lointain
Publisher's page on the composer, Accessed August 15, 2023, https://www.wisemusicclassical.com/composer/4424/Henri-Dutilleux/

Recordings:
Many cellists have recorded this work, with Rostropovich making the premiere recording in 1974

Antonín Dvořák (1841-1904) — Cello Concerto in B Minor, Op. 104

Date of Composition: 1895
Date of Premiere: March 19, 1896
Premiered by: Leo Stern, cello; Antonín Dvořák, conductor; London Philharmonic Society
Approximate Complete Length: 42 min.

> I. Allegro (16 min)
> II. Adagio ma non troppo (12 min)
> III. Finale: Allegro moderato (14 min)

Background Information:

If you were to ask anyone to name a piece written for cello just off of the top of their head, chances are, Dvořák's Cello Concerto would be the first that they name. Easily one of the most famous pieces for cello, and aside from the American String Quartet and the New World Symphony, one of the most well-known pieces he wrote, Dvořák's work remains one of the standout works for cello in the 19th century, demanding comparison from every piece to come after. Johannes Brahms was to grouse that if he had known a piece like this was possible for the cello, he would've written one himself. A touch of ego aside, this was a huge compliment to Dvořák, and shows what level of esteem he had reached at this point in his career.

Dvořák lived in New York City for a couple of years, where he had answered an invitation to become the director of the National Conservatory of Music. At one point, he attended a performance of the New York Philharmonic, which was performing the premiere of principal cellist Victor Herbert's second cello concerto (see entry in this book). Despite having been asked to write a cello concerto previously, Dvořák was supposedly suspicious of the cello's abilities as a concerto soloist, particularly in the higher registers. He became convinced, however, after hearing Herbert's masterful playing and soon began work on his own concerto.

During composition, Dvořák sought the advice of his friend and cellist of the Czech String Quartet, Hanuš Wihan, who was more than eager to give his thoughts and suggestions for changes. Dvořák was not overly impressed with Wihan's improvements, but the first edition published by Simrock does contain a few alternate passages. Wihan, being the dedicatee, was supposed to give the premiere, but due to a miscommunication with the date, it ended up being premiered by Leo Stern, with Wihan giving his performances soon after.

The concerto is grand, and makes great use of the cello solo and instruments across the orchestra, with standout moments for the horn and clarinet. It begins foreboding and dark, but soon opens up, building to the cello's emphatic first entrance, asserting its presence from the first note. Virtuosic passages contrasting with heart-melting melodies abound, with Dvořák making full use of the cello's prodigious range.

Perhaps one of the most poignant moments comes in the second movement. During the time he was working on the piece, his sister-in-law, Josefina Kaunitzová, whom Dvořák had had romantic feelings for earlier in his life, passed away. Deeply charged with grief, he inserted a quote from a song of his, Lasst mich allein, Josefina's favorite. He also crafted a coda at the end of the concerto, a reflective memorial to her, which he made sure his publisher left intact and untouched.

Johannes Brahms, in addition to his famous quote about the concerto, actually did some editing of the first publication for his and Dvořák's mutual publisher, Simrock. In a letter to them, he wrote that "cellists can be grateful to your Dvořák for bestowing on them such a great and skilled work." (Steinberg)
Cellists, and audiences alike, are indeed grateful.

Antonín Dvořák (1841-1904) — Cello Concerto in B Minor, Op. 104

Selected Editions:
Barenreiter (Urtext)
Breitkopf und Härtel
International

Bibliography:
Sadie, Stanley, ed. The New Grove: Late Romantic Masters (W. W. Norton & Company, New York, 1985)
Steinberg, Michael. The Concerto: A Listener's Guide (Oxford University Press, New York, 1998)

Recordings:
Virtually every major cellist has recorded this work.

Antonín Dvořák (1841-1904) — Silent Woods for Cello & Orchestra

Date of Composition: 1891, cello and piano version; 1892 cello and orchestra version
Date of Premiere: 1891 cello and piano version
Premiered by: Hanuš Wihan, cello with Antonín Dvořák, piano
Approximate Length: 6 min.

Background Information:

Dvořák's contribution to the cello world is without dispute given the status of his Cello Concerto (see other entry), which many consider to be the greatest cello concerto ever written. He did, in fact, compose a couple of other pieces for cello, the Rondo for Cello and Orchestra, Op. 94, and Silent Woods for Cello and Orchestra, which, understandably tend to get overshadowed by the magnitude of the concerto. The two smaller pieces were written before the concerto; perhaps as a way for Dvořák to warm up to the much more substantial concerto.

Silent Woods is an arrangement from a keyboard work called Waldesruhe. It proved to be very popular, motivating Simrock, Dvořák's publisher, to request arrangements for other instruments, a popular thing to do in that era. A violin and piano arrangement was made first before the cello and piano. Shortly after, he arranged it for cello and orchestra.

It is a gorgeous work that showcases Dvořák's gift for melody. Aside from a slightly faster, more urgent middle section, the rest of the piece is more tranquil, luxuriating in its beautiful melodies and harmonies. It ends in quiet serenity.

Selected Edition:
G. Henle Verlag (Urtext)

Bibliography:
Pospíšil, Milan, Preface, Dvorak, Antonin "Silent Woods", Munich: G. Henle Verlag, 1999.
Sadie, Stanley, ed. The New Grove: Late Romantic Masters (W. W. Norton & Company, New York, 1985)

Recordings:
Many cellists have made recordings of this work.

Edward Elgar (1857-1934) — Cello Concerto in E Minor, Op. 85

Date of Composition: 1919
Date of Premiere: October 27, 1919
Premiered by: Felix Salmond, cello; Albert Coates, conductor; London Symphony Orchestra
Approximate Complete Length: 30 min.

> I. Adagio--Moderato (8 min)
> II. Lento--Allegro molto (4:30 min)
> III. Adagio (5 min)
> IV. Allegro--Moderato--Allegro, ma non troppo--Poco più lento--Adagio (13 min)

Background Information:

One of Elgar's most famous and enduring works, his Cello Concerto in E Minor encapsulates a world of emotions and experience, with Elgar describing it as "a man's attitude to life". Written on the other side of World War I from his Violin Concerto, the Cello Concerto is dark, brooding and melancholy, and yet, contains a jubilance and impish sense of humor, mostly to be found in the breezy second movement.

In early 1918, Elgar entered the hospital, being in great pain, and reportedly, while lying in recovery, he came up with the opening theme. Immediately, upon arrival home after the hospital, he sketched out the theme, which he described as "Very full, sweet and sonorous". He continued to work on the concerto over the better part of the year, trying to shake off the effects of his illness and the dark shadow the war had cast over him. Before completing it, he reached out to cellist Felix Salmond not only asking him to premiere the work, but to offer feedback on the solo part as well. He delivered the finished work to his publisher, Novello, on August 8, 1919.

The first performance of the concerto was by Salmond and the London Symphony Orchestra under the baton of Albert Coates. While Coates was more interested in attending to the other works on the program, there was barely enough time to rehearse the cello concerto. The rehearsals and the resultant premiere were a reported disaster, coloring critical and audience reception of the work for many years following.

The concerto languished with relative indifference until the young Jacqueline du Pré began to champion the work, culminating in her landmark recording of it in 1965 with Sir John Barbirolli and the London Symphony Orchestra. The concerto had been recorded previously by Beatrice Harrison and Pablo Casals, but it was du Pré's close association with the piece and her breathtaking interpretation of it that finally gave the piece its due, cementing its place as one of the greatest written for the instrument.

Selected Editions:
Bärenreiter (Urtext)
Masters Music
Novello Publishing

Bibliography:
Kennedy, Michael. Portrait of Elgar (Oxford University Press, New York, 1992).
Steinberg, Michael. The Concerto: A Listener's Guide (Oxford University Press, New York, 1998).
Wilson, Elizabeth. Jacqueline du Pré: Her Life, Her Music, Her Legend (Arcade Publishing Inc, New York, 1998).

Recordings:
Most of the major cellists have recorded this work.

Reena Esmail (b. 1983) — Perhaps for Solo Cello

Date of Composition: 2015
Date of Premier: April 15, 2015/April 20, 2015
Premiered by: Matt Zalkind, cello at the Juilliard School/Colin Stokes, cello at the National Sawdust Festival
Approximate Length: 5 min/10 min

Background Information:

Indian-American composer Reena Esmail studied at Juilliard and Yale, and studied the Hindustani music style extensively in India thanks to a Fulbright grant. She combines characteristics of both Western and Indian music into her works.

Her piece Perhaps for Solo Cello, which exists in two versions, came out of a collaboration with filmmaker and dancer Heather McCalden.

McCalden writes about the piece:

The title of Reena's music is derived from an essay by Jacques Derrida called, "The Loving in Friendship: Perhaps: – the Adverb, and the Noun". The noun version of perhaps is one that has gone into this work, for I find it to be something quite wonderful, yet naturally, impossible to summarize. In extremely reduced form, the perhaps is an "opening" which allows room for uncertainty, and room for something Derrida calls the "impossible possibles" — which are the only real possibles for, "a possible surely and certainly possible…would be a poor possible." Perhaps as both a noun and an adverb is a suspension that creates space to allow anything to happen; in this sense, the concept for me is something that allows room for hope — something very rare these days.

Esmail explains that the work can be performed with or without the film.

Edition:
From the composer herself: reenaesmail.com

Bibliography:
Official website of the composer, Accessed November 18, 2020, www.reenaesmail.com
Program notes on the piece by the composer, Accessed November 18, 2020, https://www.reenaesmail.com/catalog-item/perhaps/#programnotes

Recordings:
No recording available as of yet.

Elisenda Fábregas (b. 1955) — Colores Andaluces for Cello & Piano

Date of Composition: 2006
Date of Premiere: October 13, 2006
Premiered by: Françoise Groben, cello
Approximate Length: 10 min.

I. Tres morillas (2 min)
II. Duende (2 min)
III. Nana (2 min)
IV. El Jinete (1:30 min)
V. Zapateado (2 min)

Background Information:

Spanish/American composer Elisenda Fábregas has had a broad international career. She has performed all over the world as a pianist, and her compositions have reached international acclaim. Now residing in Spain, she has written many works for cello, mostly stemming from her work with cellist Roger Morelló Ros.

Colores Andaluces (Andalusian Colors) is a set of five short pieces exploring different aspects of Spanish music styles.

On the work, Fábregas writes:

Colores Andaluces was written at the request of cellist Françoise Groben. I had the chance to experience the artistry and charisma of Françoise at several extraordinary performances of Voces de mi tierra, a work written for the Meininger-Trio, where Françoise enjoyed an extended cadenza…The result was this collection of short pieces in the Spanish style. Françoise Groben premiered this work at Celloherbst in Germany on October 13, 2006.

Edition:
Friedrich Hofmeister Musikverlag

Bibliography:
Official website of the composer, Accessed July 31, 2023, https://elisendafabregas.com/

Recordings:
The premiere cellist Françoise Groben released a commercial recording of this work.

Louise Farrenc (1804-1875)   Sonata in B-flat Major, Op. 46 for Cello & Piano

Date of Composition: 1857
Date of Premiere: unknown
Premiered by: unknown
Approximate Length: 25 min.

> I. Allegro moderato (11 min)
> II. Andante sostenuto (6 min)
> III. Finale. Allegro (8 min)

Background Information:

    Louise Farrenc was one of the great piano talents and composers of the nineteenth century. She studied piano at the Paris Conservatory, and wanted to study composition with Anton Reicha there as well, but, as a female, wasn't allowed in his composition classes. Instead, she studied privately with him. Later, she became the second female professor at the conservatory in its history, but wasn't allowed to teach composition, despite her growing status as a composer in Paris.

    She not only wrote music for solo piano, but a wide array of chamber music– including several trios with piano, two piano quintets, and a nonet, choral works and three symphonies. For years, many of her works were lost, which contributed greatly to the decline in awareness of her and her music after her death. Thankfully, many of those works have been rediscovered, and her music is entering into the performance halls more often where it belongs.

    Her Sonata in B-flat Major for Cello and Piano was written in 1857 and published in 1861. It then went out of print and was largely forgotten until it was rediscovered and brought back into print. It is a lovely sonata, filled to the brim with exquisite melodies, clever conversational writing between the cello and piano, and virtuosic passages. Like sonatas of Mendelssohn and Schubert, the sonata has echoes of the Classical style with some of the darker, lusher sonorities of the Romantic era as well.

    The first movement begins with a tender, undulating piano line underneath a highly lyrical cello melody. The rest of the movement ebbs and flows through highly vocal melodic lines, weaving their way around the active piano part. More gorgeous melodic material appears in the charming second movement. It gently lilts along in a sicilienne-like rhythm. This could very easily be a tear-jerking art song or opera aria. The last movement is in a grand and upbeat, not to mention virtuosic, mood. Just when you think she is going to end it rather demurely and sweetly, the final triumphant cadential chords cap off this gem of a sonata.

Edition:
Edition Silvertrust
Hildegard Publishing

Bibliography:
Biography on Farrenc, Accessed August 13, 2023, https://www.musicbywomen.org/composer/louise-farrenc/
Publisher page on the piece, Accessed August 13, 2023, https://www.editionsilvertrust.com/farrenc-cello-sonata.htm

Recordings:
There have been a few commercial recordings made of this work.

Gabriel Faure (1845-1924) — Élégie, Op. 24 for Cello & Piano

Date of Composition: 1880
Date of Premiere: 1883
Premiered by: Jules Loeb, cello; Gabriel Faure, piano [Premiere of version for cello and orchestra in 1901 with Pablo Casals, cellist, and Faure conducting.]
Approximate Length: 7 min.

Background Information:

During his career, Gabriel Fauré wrote in most of the major genres (symphonic, vocal, chamber, etc.), and turned to solo works for cello frequently. He composed a handful of shorter works for cello and piano (the Sicilienne being the most well-known), and two sonatas for cello and piano late in his life.

Fauré began composing a slow movement for cello and piano in 1880, which originally was to be part of a standard sonata for cello and piano; this was a typical routine for Fauré, beginning the work on a piece with the slow middle movement. Eventually, he abandoned the plan for the whole sonata, deciding to leave the movement alone, titling it Élégie.

It's not known if the piece was actually inspired by the death of someone, or if it was just an abstract concept in his mind, but the piece certainly feels like an ode to someone who has passed. The piece starts with repeated dirge-like chords, while the cello comes in with a suitably, mournful melody. The middle section concludes with a fiery, acrobatic triplet section with the cello whizzing up and down in scalar motion, before returning to the opening theme high up in its register. It eventually winds its way down, culminating on the low, open C string. It's as if the piece moves through all the stages of grief: from sorrow to anger to acceptance with the cello as the tour guide.

The piece proved to be so successful that Fauré was asked to arrange it for cello and orchestra, which was premiered by Pablo Casals.

Selected Editions:
G. Henle Verlag (Urtext)
International
Universal

Bibliography:
Nectoux, Jean-Michel The New Grove: Twentieth-Century French Masters (Norton, New York, 1986)

Recordings:
Many commercial recordings have been released of both the piano and orchestral versions.

Gabriel Fauré (1845-1924) — Sonata No. 2 in G Minor, Op. 117 for Cello & Piano

Date of Composition: 1921
Date of Premiere: 1922
Premiered by: Gérard Hekking, cello; Alfred Cortot, piano
Approximate Length: 20 min.

> I. Allegro (6 min)
> II. Andante (8 min)
> III. Finale - Allegro vivo (5 min)

Background Information:

Gabriel Fauré, one of the most well-known late Romantic French composers, wrote a sizable amount of solo works for cello. Late in his life, he composed two sonatas for cello and piano three years apart. The second sonata of the two grew out of a commission from the French government to write a slow movement commemorating the anniversary of the death of Napoleon. Upon finishing the slow, dirge-like movement–which bears a striking resemblance to his earlier Elegie for cello (see other entry)--he was inspired to turn it into a full sonata.

The work is divided into three movements in the exact layout as the first sonata: Allegro, Andante, Allegro. The first movement moves along in a rather affable, yet brisk, continuous motion, barely coming up for air. The final movement charges along even faster, with the piano churning dizzily underneath the long cello lines. Fauré does allow the music to relax and quiet down, before resuming its energetic pace again.

The real standout is the second movement. It's a luxurious, gorgeous, melancholy movement–the longest of the sonata– that ends in a prayer-like whisper, weary from the big displays of emotion throughout.

Selected Editions:
Edition Kunzelmann
G. Henle Verlag (Urtext)

Bibliography:
Berger, Melvin. Guide to Sonatas (Anchor Books, New York, 1991).

Recordings:
Numerous commercial recordings are available.

Vivian Fine (1913-2000) — Sonata for Cello and Piano

Date of Composition: 1986
Date of Premiere: March 13, 1988
Premiered by: Maxine Neuman, cello with Joan Stein, piano
Approximate Length: 13 min.

> I. Poco lento–tempo giusto (4 min)
> II. Elegia (4 min)
> III. Allegro–Con piena voce (5 min)

Background Information:

Vivian Fine was a prolific composer with a catalog of over 140 works, including many art songs, choral, symphonic and chamber works. Her main composition teachers were Ruth Crawford and Roger Sessions, and her style evolved from atonal to tonal to a mixture of the two. She was a member of Aaron Copland's Young Composers Group and was a founding member of the American Composers Alliance. She taught for many years at Bennington College, as well as New York University and Juilliard. In addition to being a successful composer, she was also a concert pianist, premiering the works of such famous composers as Charles Ives and Copland.

Her Sonata for Cello and Piano was written in 1986 and is subtitled "in homage to Claude Debussy". In a note on the score, she says, "[The piece] was directly inspired by a recorded performance of the Debussy Sonata by Benjamin Britten and Mstislav Rostropovich, which I felt penetrated the music in new and wonderful ways. My musical language is very different from Debussy's, but I sought to capture some of the textures and momentum of his sonata. The careful listener will find a brief quotation in the first movement."

Edition:
Vivian Fine Estate publishing–available for free on imslp.org

Bibliography:
Fuller, Sophie, The Pandora Guide to Women Composers (Pandora Publishing, London, 1994).
Official website of the composer, Accessed August 8, 2023, https://www.vivianfine.org/main/biography.htm

Recordings:
A professional recording is available from the composer's website under the title Demo CD, however, the performers are not listed.

Gerald Finzi (1901-1956) — Cello Concerto in A Minor, Op. 40

Date of Composition: 1955
Date of Premiere: 1955
Premiered by: Christopher Bunting, cello with John Barbirolli, conducting the Hallé Orchestra
Approximate Length: 41 min.

> I. Allegro moderato (16 min)
> II. Andante quieto (15 min)
> III. Rondo: Adagio - Allegro giocoso (10 min)

Background Information:

Twentieth century English composer Gerald Finzi might not be a household name on the level of Edward Elgar or Gustav Holst, but he did enjoy a successful career in his lifetime. His life and career were interrupted by both world wars, not to mention the devastating diagnosis of Hodgkin's disease, to which he succumbed five years later.

His cello concerto was one of the last pieces he ever wrote. Sir John Barbirolli had asked for a work from Finzi for the Cheltenham Festival. He had been working on a cello concerto for several years, and the request from Barbirolli provided the impetus he needed. The cellist Christopher Bunting supposedly gave suggestions to Finzi on the writing of the cello part.

It's quite possible that the diagnosis of Finzi's illness cast a shadow over the concerto. The mood is highly charged and emotional. The first movement is anguished and ends with the cello in a pained high note. The second movement is gentler, with the cello rolling out waves of heartfelt phrases. After a quirky, slow, pizzicato introduction, the last movement picks up the mood and tempo. It's a rousing finishing to an otherwise largely melancholic work.

Finzi's health was failing rapidly shortly after finishing the concerto. He was admitted to the hospital just prior to the radio broadcast premiere. He was able to hear the broadcast from his hospital bed, and died the very next day. It was to be the last music he heard before he passed.

Edition:
Boosey & Hawkes

Bibliography:
Burn, Andrew, Liner notes, Finzi, Gerald "Cello Concerto", Tim Hugh, cello, Northern Sinfonia, Howard Griffiths, cond., Naxos, 2001.
Official website of the composer, Accessed August 15, 20203, https://www.geraldfinzi.org/

Recordings:
There are a couple of commercial available recordings of this work.

Lukas Foss (1922-2009) — Capriccio for Cello & Piano

Date of Composition: 1946
Date of Premiere: 1947
Premiered by: Gregor Piatigorsky, cello and Lukas Foss, piano at Tanglewood
Approximate Length: 6 min.

Background Information:

Lukas Foss was born in Germany in 1922. He studied in Berlin and Paris before immigrating to the United States as the war was heating up. He went on to study at the Curtis Institute, and began conducting lessons with famed conductor Serge Koussevitsky, and a side sojourn studying composition with Paul Hindemith at Yale. He was composer-in-residence at Tanglewood and the Manhattan School of Music, taught in a number of institutions, and was conductor of the Buffalo Philharmonic and the Milwaukee Symphony.

The Koussevitzky Foundation commissioned him for a cello piece, which he wrote specifically for Gregor Piatigorsky. Piatigorsky and Foss premiered the resultant Capriccio for Cello and Piano at Tanglewood the following year.

The Capriccio is glowing with Americana. It's a vibrant and exultant short work, that starts off with a fanfare from the cello that could be straight out of the score to a Western film. It evokes images of old pioneer towns and wide open landscapes. The cello part is considerable, with acrobatic leaps across the strings. It's a joyous six minutes that is one of Foss' most performed works in his oeuvre.

Edition:
Carl Fischer

Bibliography:
Publisher's page on the composer, Accessed 15, 2023, https://www.keisersouthernmusic.com/composers/lukas-foss

Recordings:
There are a number of commercial recordings available, notably the recording made by Piatagorsky and Foss on Sony Classics label.

César Franck (1822-1890) — Sonata in A Major for Cello & Piano

Date of Composition: 1888
Date of Premiere: 1888
Premiered by: Jules Delsart, cello
Approximate Length: 30 min.

> I. Allegretto ben moderato (7 min)
> II. Allegro (8 min)
> III. Recitativo - Fantasia: Ben moderato - Molto lento (8 min)
> IV. Allegretto poco mosso (7 min)

Background Information:

César Franck was a beloved and well-known French Romantic composer, whose Violin Sonata in A Major is probably his most famous work. It was a big hit as soon as it premiered in 1886, and shortly after, cellist Jules Delsart embarked on adapting it for cello.*

After hearing a performance of the violin sonata, Delsart was so taken with the piece, that he asked Franck's permission to make a version for cello. Franck obliged and gave his blessing. Delsart adapted only the violin version, leaving the piano part untouched; most of the cello version is identical to the violin part save the octave.

It is a towering work (perhaps Franck's answer to Saint Säens's Violin Sonata in D Minor), the true epitome of a Romantic-era sonata, that appears to get all of its themes for the entire sonata from the opening bars. It has been described as a cyclic work and evidence of Franck's commanding skills as a composer.

It remains hugely popular for both violinists, cellists, and many other instruments have their own transcriptions.

*There are some reports that the cello was actually the instrument the sonata was originally intended for, but this has never been verified.

Selected Editions:
Barenreiter (Urtext)
G. Henle Verlag (Urtext)
International

Bibliography:
Jost, Peter, Preface to Frank, Cesar "Sonata for Cello and Piano", Munich: G. Henle Verlag

Recordings:
Many of the major cellists have released commercial recordings of this sonata.

Gabriela Lena Frank (b. 1972) & David Fetherolf (b. 1956)

Serenata for Solo Cello

Date of Composition: 2018
Date of Premiere: March 16, 2018
Premiered by: Kate Dillingham, cello
Approximate Length: 14 min.

Background Information:
    Hailed by the Washington Post as one of the most significant composers in history, Gabriela Lena Frank has led a very distinguished career. Inspired by her heritage–she is of Chinese/Peruvian and Lithuanian/Jewish descent–she has studied South American culture specifically, guiding her in her creative endeavors. She is the composer-in-residence for the Philadelphia Orchestra and has written works for the Detroit Symphony, the Chicago Symphony, Boston Symphony, Atlanta Symphony, San Francisco Symphony, the San Diego Opera and San Francisco Opera. She has even had a PBS documentary made about her life and place in the current classical music world.
    Her work Serenata is actually a collaboration with fellow composer David Fetherolf. Fetherolf and Frank had discussed the possibility of composing a work for unaccompanied cello in a collaborative effort, but their schedules had yet to align. Some time later, cellist Kate Dillingham approached Fetherolf about writing a new piece and he thought of involving Frank. They were able to make it work and Serenata was born out of this duo project.
    Frank says, "In a new and, for me, daring endeavor, I've taken musical ideas from the American composer David Fetherolf, longtime friend and mentor, and spun them into new shapes. He, in return, has reworked these according to his own whims. Our dance has not been unlike my dance with past ghosts, but it is more beautiful and personal for me, animated by real affection."

Edition:
Schirmer

Bibliography:
Official website of the composer, Accessed August 8, 2023, https://www.glfcam.com/people/gabriela
Publisher's page for the piece, Accessed August 8, 2023, https://www.wisemusicclassical.com/work/57928/Serenata--Gabriela-Lena-Frank--David-Fetherolf/

Recordings:
At press time, no commercial recording has been released.

Domenico Gabrielli (c. 1659-1690) — 7 Ricercari per violoncello solo

Date of Composition: between 1687 and 1691
Date of Premiere: Unknown
Premiered by: presumably Gabrielli himself
Approximate Length: 5 min. average

Background Information:

The cello began its journey primarily as an accompanying instrument. Eventually, it began to break free of its supporting role, and be considered as an instrument with more soloistic properties. A fair amount of mystery clouds a lot of concrete information about where, when and how the cello was used in these early days (not to mention which specific bass string instrument they were referring to; nomenclature was far from being standard across Europe). We can, however, point to a few epicenters of cello activity and player/composers that started forging a substantive catalog of repertoire for the instrument.

Bologna and Modena were two cities that saw an early flurry of cello activity. Giovanni Battista Degli Antonii and Domenico Galli, two early cellists, were members of the Accademia Filarmonica of Bologna, one of the most important organizations for musicians in Bologna. It counted among its other members: Arcangelo Corelli, Carlo Farinelli, and Domenico Gabrielli.

Gabrielli was one of the first virtuosic cellists, earning him the nickname of Minghén dal viulunzèl (literally Dominic of the violoncello), which was a very flattering term. His 7 Ricercari are considered the first music published for solo, unaccompanied cello. Naturally, when comparing them against later unaccompanied works, such as the Bach Suites, they seem antiquated and sparse. Of course, this is hardly fair, as the cello as a soloistic instrument was still in its infancy, and far more established by the 1720s when Bach likely wrote his six suites.

Some scholars and cellists have suggested that these are mere study pieces, or works that require a bass line to be added. But it is entirely possible that the works appear as Gabrielli intended. They are for the most part free and rhapsodic with plenty of space for ornamentation and embellishment. Whatever scenario Gabrielli envisioned for these lovely early gems of music for solo cello, they give us a fascinating insight into the early world of our beloved instrument .

Selected Edition:
Barenreiter (Urtext)

Bibliography:
Article by Brian Carter about Gabrielli for the Internet Cello Society, Accessed August 14, 2023, https://www.cello.org/Newsletter/Articles/gabrielli/gabrielli.htm
Bylsma, Anner, Liner notes "The Violoncello in the 17th Century", Anner Bylsma, cello, Deutsche Harmonia Mundi, 1989
Hoffman, Bettina, Preface to Gabrielli, Domenico "The Complete Works for Violoncello", Kassel: Barenreiter, 2001.

Recordings:
A handful of commercial recordings, mostly on period instruments, are available.

Albert Ginastera (1916-1983) — Pampeana No. 2 Rhapsody for Cello & Piano, Op. 21

Date of Composition: 1950
Date of Premiere: Unknown
Premiered by: Unknown, but written for his future wife, Aurora Natola, cello
Approximate Length: 9 min.

Background Information:

Albert Ginastera was the most important Argentine composer of the twentieth century. He incorporated Argentine folk songs and melodies into his music, much the same way Bèla Bartòk did with Hungarian folk songs. He studied at the National Conservatory in Buenos Aires, before coming to the States and studied with Aaron Copland. He held a number of teaching positions throughout his life–Astor Piazzolla was a student of his–all the while continuing to compose.

His works are separated into three periods. The first was characterized by the predominant use of folk songs; the second was where the use of folk songs was less overt, yet still there in the background; the third is where he moved further into more modern techniques, including the use of the twelve-tone system.

Over the course of seven years, he wrote three Pampeanas: No. 1 for violin and piano, No. 2 for cello and piano and No. 3 for orchestra. The works reflect the region of Pampas. Ginastera wrote, "Whenever I have crossed the pampas, my spirit felt itself inundated by changing impressions, now joyful, now melancholy, produced by its limitless immensity and by the transformation that the countryside undergoes in the course of the day . . . from my first contact, I desired to write a work reflecting these states of my spirit." (Kosower)

Pampeana No. 2 contains a series of cello cadenzas interspersed by wild and brilliant dances.

This work, as well as his other cello pieces, was written for his second wife, cellist, Aurora Natola.

Edition:
Boosey & Hawkes

Bibliography:
Publisher page on the composer, Accessed August 14, 2023, https://www.boosey.com/pages/cr/composer/composer_main?composerid=2699&ttype=BIOGRAPHY
Kosower, Mark, Liner notes from Ginastera, Albert "Ginastera Works for Cello and Piano", Mark Kosower, cello, Jee-Won Oh, piano, Naxos, 2008.

Recordings:
A number of commercially made recordings are available.

Philip Glass (b. 1937) — Orbit for Solo Cello

Date of Composition: 2013
Date of Premiere: April 2, 2013
Premiered by: Yo-Yo Ma, cello
Approximate Length: 7 min.

Background Information:

    Philip Glass has written a fair amount of music for solo cello, although, sadly, not much of it is readily available, aside from his Partita for Solo Cello (Songs and Poems) (see other entry) and Orbit for Solo Cello.

    Orbit was commissioned by choreographer Damian Woetzel and was premiered by Yo-Yo Ma with dancer Lil' Buck. The music, fairly removed from Glass' normal style and motives, spins and twirls, taking slight detours and pauses, but almost continuously moving. It has a slightly solemn tone, but resonates with a stark beauty. While smaller in scope to his Partita for Solo Cello, it is nonetheless a lovely little kaleidoscope of a piece.

Edition:
Chester Music

Bibliography:
Official website page on the piece, Accessed August 23, 2023, https://philipglass.com/compositions/orbit/

Recordings:
Only two commercial recordings are available, the premiere recording made by Jeffery Ziegler, and Matt Haimovitz. [N.B.: there is a video on youtube recreating the premiere performance containing the original choreography.]

Philip Glass (b. 1937) — Partita No. 1 for Solo Cello (Songs & Poems)

Date of Composition: 2007
Date of Premiere: February 13, 2007
Premiered by: Wendy Sutter, cello
Approximate Length: 30 min.

I. Song I (4 min)
II. Song II (6 min)
III. Song III (2 min)
IV. Song IV (3 min)
V. Song V (6 min)
VI. Song VI (4 min)
VII. Song VII (5 min)

Background Information:

Philip Glass is arguably one of the most recognizable names in contemporary Classical music. Coming to notoriety in the late-1960's and '70's, particularly with his quasi-opera Einstein on the Beach, he has continued to compose well into his eighties. He is part of the minimalist movement, however he rejects that term to describe himself, clarifying that he writes "music with repetitive structures." His music is instantly recognizable with his almost omnipresent, ever-repeating triplets, and he is currently one of the most performed living composers. He has written for instrumental solos, chamber music, orchestra, operas and film.

Partita No. 1 for Solo Cello (Songs and Poems) (originally titled "Seven Songs and Poems for Solo Cello") was written in 2007 for cellist Wendy Sutter. The two had met when she was a member of the contemporary ensemble Bang on a Can. Glass was inspired by her playing, and with her input, crafted this work for solo cello. Portions of the music are based on his score to the film "Chaotic Harmony".

In some ways, the music in these seven movements is not wholly identifiable as Philip Glass. There are repetitions and triplets all throughout, but his prevalent characteristics are muted somewhat. Glass has repeatedly stated that he is most inspired by the music of J.S. Bach, and one certainly hears echoes of Bach's famous Six Suites for Solo Cello. Using the suites as a framework, he weaves in and out of different moods and motives, utilizing the low strings a considerable amount. At times, the music is full-throated and declamatory with lots of double stops, at other times, it is linear and unsettled, relentlessly moving. Full of breadth and poignancy, this is a grand work, a great addition to the solo cello repertoire from one of the giants of contemporary music.

[NB. Glass has written a follow-up, a second partita for solo cello, which was premiered by Matt Haimovitz in 2017, however the music is unfortunately not available at press time.]

Edition:
Chester Music

Bibliography:
Glass, Philip. Words Without Music: A Memoir (Liveright Publishing, New York, 2015)
Guerin, Richard, Liner notes for Glass, Philip "Songs and Poems for Solo Cello", Wendy Sutter, cello, Orange Mountain Music, 2007.
Official website of the piece, Accessed August 23, 2023, https://philipglass.com/compositions/songspoemssolocello/

Recordings:
Thus far, there is only one commercial recording that has been released, the phenomenal, iconic premiere recording by Wendy Sutter.

Osvaldo Golijov (b. 1960) — Azul for Cello and Orchestra

Date of Composition: 2006
Date of Premiere: August 4, 2006
Premiered by: Yo-Yo Ma, cello; Donald Runnicles conductor with the Boston Symphony Orchestra at the Tanglewood Festival
Approximate Length: 27 min.

Background Information:

Argentinian composer Osvaldo Golijov has written in a variety of mediums, including chamber, orchestral, choral and for film. He has had high profile collaborations with the Kronos Quartet and soprano Dawn Upshaw.

In addition to a solo cello piece called Omaramor (1991), he composed this towering cello concerto entitled Azul in 2006 for Yo-Yo Ma.

Azul, meaning 'blue', weaves a multitude of influences together into a poetic whole. Inspired by the writings of Pablo Neruda, landscapes and Baroque music, Golijov's score, in addition to the solo cello and orchestral accompaniment, includes an instrument called a "hyper accordion", and an enlarged percussion section.

After Ma premiered the work at Tanglewood, Golijov made revisions to the work, filling it out into four interlocked sections. The revised version was premiered by Alisa Weilerstein in 2007.

Edition:
Boosey & Hawkes

Bibliography:
Official composer's website of the piece, Accessed July 31, 2023, https://osvaldogolijov.com/arc/azul
Program notes from the Los Angeles Philharmonic, Accessed July 31, 2023, https://www.laphil.com/musicdb/pieces/213/azul

Recordings:
Yo-Yo Ma released a recording of the concerto on Warner Classics in 2017.

Georg Goltermann (1824-1898) Cello Concerto No. 4 in G Major, Op. 65

Date of Composition: Between 1853-1898
Date of Premiere: Unknown
Premiered by: Unknown
Approximate Length: 16 min.

I. Allegro (5 min)
II. Andantino (3 min)
III. Allegro Molto (8 min)

Background Information:

    Georg Goltermann was one of the leading German virtuoso cellists of the nineteenth century. For many years he toured extensively around Europe before retiring from public performing to focus on conducting and composing. Composing well over 100 works, the majority of his pieces naturally centered on the cello, with eight concerti and a number of other incidental works for cello. The Cello Concerto No. 4 in G Major is probably his best known of the concerti.

    His 4th concerto is considered to be of a milder difficulty, which makes it popular for students to learn. The piece involves a number of techniques, such as fast sixteenth or triplet passages, some early thumb position, very emotive lyrical passages, and a syncopated bowing pattern in the final movement theme that tends to challenge students. The third movement Rondo is included in Book 5 of the Suzuki Cello School, ensuring its legacy will continue.

    His other concerti tend to be of a higher difficulty level.

Selected Edition:
International

Bibliography:
Campbell, Margaret The Great Cellists (Trafalgar Square Publishing, Vermont, 1988)
Geeseman, Katherine Ann. The Rise and Fall of the Cellist-Composer of the Nineteenth Century: A Comprehensive Study of the Life and Works of Georg Goltermann Including a Complete Catalog of his Compositions dissertation for Florida State University, 2011.

Recordings:
Sadly, it is rare to find any of Goltermann's solo works committed to recording, other than the Suzuki recordings that accompany the books.

Edvard Grieg (1843-1907)   Sonata in A Minor for Cello & Piano, Op. 36

Date of Composition: 1883
Date of Premiere: October 22, 1883
Premiered by: Friedrich Grützmacher, cello; Edvard Grieg, piano
Approximate Length: 27 min.

> I. Allegro agitato (9 min)
> II. Andante molto tranquillo (6 min)
> III. Allegro molto e marcato (12 min)

Background Information:

Famed Norwegian composer Edvard Grieg ventured into instrumental chamber music here and there over the course of his life, composing three violin sonatas, a string quartet, and his Cello Sonata in A minor.

The cello sonata was written after a gap in his compositional output due to his conducting responsibilities and an illness. It was not an easy process writing the work apparently. Grieg wrote in a letter, "To all appearances, I am living a more peaceful life than ever before, but in reality it is a life full of inward struggle. I am both spiritually and bodily unwell and decide every other day not to compose another note, because I satisfy myself less and less." (Berger, p. 102)

He soldiered on and completed the work the following year. Despite his misgivings and insecurity, the sonata is incredibly successful and reflects little of what he was feeling while writing it. The first movement is full of bluster and intensity, contrasting with a tender second theme. The highly lyrical second movement is roughly based on a theme from his "Triumphal March" from incidental music to Sigurd Jorsalfar, and the third movement–after a mournful cello soliloquy–resembles a 'halling', an energetic Norwegian dance.

The sonata is dedicated to Grieg's older brother John, who was an amateur cellist. Grieg seemed to be quite fond of this sonata, performing it numerous times in the years following, with noted cellists Friedrich Grützmacher, Julius Klengel, and a young Pablo Casals.

Selected Editions:
G. Henle Verlag (Urtext)
Peters
International

Bibliography:
Berger, Melvin A Guide to Sonatas (Anchor Books, New York, 1991)
Heinemann, Ernst-Günter, Preface to Grieg, Edvard "Sonata for Cello and Piano", Munich: W. Henle Verlag, 2005.

Recordings:
Many famed cellists have released commercial recordings of this sonata.

Sofia Gubaidulina (b. 1931) — 10 Preludes for Solo Cello

Date of Composition: 1974
Date of Premiere: 1977
Premiered by: Vladimir Tonkha, cello
Approximate Length: 26 min.

> I. Staccato, legato (1 min)
> II. Legato, staccato (3 min)
> III. Con sordino, senza sordino (3 min)
> IV. Ricochet (2 min)
> V. Sul ponticello, ordinario, sul tasto (4 min)
> VI. Flagioletti (4 min)
> VII. Al Taco, da punta d'arco (1 min)
> VIII. Arco, pizzicato (2 mi)
> IX. Pizzicato, arco (3 min)
> X. Senza arco, senza pizzicato (3 min)

Background Information:

Sofia Gubaidalina is one of the major Russian composers of the late twentieth and early-twenty-first centuries. She incorporates spirituality and religion in her works, as well as the Fibonacci sequence and elements of improvisation. In the late 70's, a professor at the Novosibirsk Conservatory in Russia reached out to Gubaidulina, commissioning a set of varied and pedagogical works for students. In Gubaidulina's words, "...he wanted the etudes for cello to be for specifically pedagogical purposes. But for this purpose, the etudes don't work. They are my fantasy rather than etudes examining a pedagogical aspect." (Biber) Indeed Gubaidulina, through these etudes, explores all kinds of textures and sounds across the cello, many incorporating extended techniques. The professor was apparently not very taken with them and did nothing with them.

A few years later, she reached out to cellist Vladimir Tonkha in the hopes he would agree to perform them. He agreed and championed them, earning Gubaidulina's respect and praise. She would go on to compose further cello works, dedicating a number of them to Tonkha.

Tonkha was the one who suggested she change the name from "Ten Etudes" to "Ten Preludes". Despite preferring the original title, Gubaidulina reluctantly agreed and "Ten Preludes" is how it is known today.

Editions:
Sikorski
Boosey & Hawkes

Bibliography:
Biber, Julia A. "Ten Etudes by Sofia Gubaidulina: A Dissertation" CUNY Academic Works, 2016
Publisher page on the composer, Accessed July 31, 2023, https://www.boosey.com/composer/Sofia+Gubaidulina

Recordings:
A few commercial recordings have been released.

Adolphus Hailstork (b. 1941) — Theme and Variations on Draw the Sacred Circle Closer for Solo Cello

Date of Composition: 2009
Date of Premiere: 2010
Premiered by: Timothy Holley, cello
Approximate Length: 11 min.

Background Information:

Adolphus Hailstork, born in Rochester, NY, studied at Howard University, Michigan State University, Manhattan School of Music and the American Conservatory at Fontainebleau with the famed composer and teacher Nadia Boulanger. He has written across multiple genres and has had works premiered by the Detroit Symphony, Los Angeles Philharmonic, the Norfolk Chamber Ensemble, Cincinnati Opera Company and the Opera Theater of St. Louis.

"Theme and Variations on Draw The Sacred Circle Closer" for solo cello was written for cellist Timothy Holley. It is based on the Shaker hymn "Draw the Sacred Circle Closer", which Hailstork used for his choral work "Earthrise" in 2005.

Hailstork has also written a Sonata for Solo Cello (2012) for Timothy Holley as well.

Edition:
Theodore Presser Company

Bibliography:
Official website on the piece, Accessed July 31, 2023, https://www.presser.com/114-41579-theme-and-variations-on-22draw-the-sacred-circle-closer-22.html

Recordings:
No commercial recording is available, although video performances made by Timothy Holley are available on youtube.

Franz Joseph Haydn (1732-1809)   Cello Concerto No. 1 in C Major, Hob. VIIb:1

Date of Composition: 1765
Date of Premiere: Unknown
Premiered by: Joseph Franz Weigl, cello
Approximate Length: 26 min.

         I. Moderato (10 min)
         II. Adagio (9 min)
        III. Allegro molto (7 min)

Background Information:

  Franz Joseph Haydn was one of the leading composers of the Classical Period. His music was hugely influential, and his generous and magnanimous spirit made a big impact on the musical community of Europe. Known mainly for his symphonies (104 of them total) and his chamber music (88 string quartets namely), his concerti aren't usually the pieces people immediately think of (his violin concerti, for instance, get passed over for Mozart's five concerti all the time), yet, his two cello concerti are at the forefront of cellists' repertoire.

  Written roughly twenty years before the Cello Concerto in D Major (see other entry), the Concerto in C Major's origin is a bit murky. It was composed in the early days of Haydn's tenure at the Esterházy court, most likely written and premiered by the principal cellist at the court, Joseph Weigl, although that is still a bit in question.

  Even though it appeared in his catalog of works, the manuscript was lost for a couple of centuries before it was rediscovered by a musicologist in 1961. It quickly made its way into publication and onto the music stands of most cellists. It sits today, with its sibling concerto in D Major, as one of the most beloved cello concerti of all time.

Selected Editions:
Barenreiter (Urtext)
G. Henle Verlag (Urtext)
International

Bibliography:
Gerlach, Sonja, Preface to Haydn, Franz Joseph "Cello Concerto in C Major", Munich: G. Henle Verlag, 1989.
Stevens, Denis, Liner notes to Haydn, Franz Joseph "Haydn and Kraft Cello Concertos", Anner Bylsma, cello, Tafelmusik, Jean Lamon, cond., Deutsche Harmonia Mundi, 1990.

Recordings:
Innumerable recordings exist of this concerto (and the D Major) both on period and modern instruments.

Franz Joseph Haydn (1732-1809) Cello Concerto No. 2 in D Major, Hob. VIIb:2

Date of Composition: 1783
Date of Premiere: Unknown
Premiered by: James Cervetto, cello
Approximate Length: 26 min.

I. Allegro moderato (15 min)
II. Adago (6 min)
III. Rondo: Allegro (5 min)

Background Information:

It's hard to overstate just how impactful the music and career of Franz Joseph Haydn was on the music world in the eighteenth century. Ensconced at the court of Prince Nikolaus Esterházy, he was in one of the most prominent musical positions in one of the most powerful monarchies in the western world. He is widely considered the "father" of the symphony and the string quartet. While this is a bit inaccurate since he was not the first to write either of those genres of pieces, it is a testament to how persuasive and commanding his writing was in those pieces that inspired an entire generation of composers.

The journey of the Concerto in D Major, with its dubious history, to its eventual place among the most favored and performed cello concertos in the world is fascinating. For many years it was misattributed to Anton Kraft, the famed cellist at the Esterházy court, and a composer in his own right (see other entry), until the true authorship of Haydn came into certainty.

Recent scholarship has cleared the air of where and when it was written. The concerto was written for a series of concerts in London and the premiere cellist was James Cervetto. Cervetto was known for his prodigious use of thumb positions in "violin range", which goes a long way to understanding the way Haydn wrote the solo part, with its lengthy passage up in high thumb position.

The concerto languished in heavily edited and altered editions in the latter half of the nineteenth century, before scholarship set everything in its right place. The manuscript was rediscovered in 1951 and urtext editions were published finally allowing Haydn's original to be heard. Thanks to the copious amounts of recordings that were eventually made, the concerto cemented its place in the pantheon of the great cello concerti in history.

Selected Editions:
G. Henle Verlag (Urtext)
Schott (Urtext)
International

Bibliography:
Article on cellobello.org on the Haydn D Major Cello Concerto, Accessed August 15, 2023, https://www.cellobello.org/cello-blog/artistic-vision/the-origins-of-haydns-cello-concerto-no-2-in-d-major-part-1-of-2/
Gerlach, Sonja, Preface to Haydn, Franz Joseph "Cello Concerto in C Major", Munich: G. Henle Verlag, 1989.
Stevens, Denis, Liner notes to Haydn, Franz Joseph "Haydn and Kraft Cello Concertos", Anner Bylsma, cello, Tafelmusik, Jean Lamon, cond., Deutsche Harmonia Mundi, 1990.

Recordings:
Innumerable recordings exist of this concerto (and the C Major) both on period and modern instruments.

Victor Herbert (1859-1924)   Cello Concerto No. 2 in E Minor, Op. 30

Date of Composition: 1894
Date of Premiere: March 9, 1894
Premiered by: Victor Herbert, cello; New York Philharmonic, Anton Seidl, conductor
Approximate Length: 23 min.

> I. Allegro impetuoso (8 min)
> II. Lento - Andante tranquillo (8 min)
> III. Allegro (7 min)

Background Information:

Victor Herbert was an Irish-born composer and cellist, who is today mostly known for his works for the stage. Having a successful career as a teacher and cellist in the Stuttgart Court Orchestra, he composed works on the side. He eventually moved to New York and began composing operettas and other orchestral works.

Herbert's Cello Concerto No. 2 was written and premiered in 1894. Serendipitously, in attendance, was Antonin Dvořák, who was impressed and very complimentary of the work. Dvořák had ideas of writing a cello concerto, but feared that the balance would prohibit the cello from being heard. After hearing Herbert's concerto and the deft way he scored it, matched against the prominent brass, he was convinced that it could work. Shortly thereafter, Dvořák wrote his iconic Cello Concerto in B Minor.

The Concerto in E Minor is written in three sections, but they are generally played seamlessly without pause. The concerto is highly dramatic, but a beautiful melody and tune never seem to be far away at any moment, no doubt thanks to Herbert's experience writing vocal works for the stage. It is virtuosic, without being overly flashy, instead relying more on expression.

Of course, once Dvořák's concerto came on the scene, it very quickly all but eclipsed all of the other cello concerti, particularly of a late Romantic style. Herbert's concerto laid in the shadow of Dvořák's concerto for some time, but has been getting its due more recently.

Edition:
International

Bibliography:
Campbell, Margaret. The Great Cellists (Trafalgar Square Books, Vermont, 1989).
Pegis, Jason. Lighting the Shadows of the Canon: A Modern and Contextual Reexamination of Victor Herbert's Cello Concerto No. 2 Op. 30 dissertation for UCLA, 2021.

Recordings:
There are a number of commercial recordings available.

Jennifer Higdon (b. 1962) — Nocturne for Cello & Piano

Date of Composition: 2006 violin version/ 2016 cello version
Date of Premiere: 2006/ cello version unknown
Premiered by: Violin version by Jennifer Koh, violin/ cello version unknown
Approximate Length: 5 min.

Background Information:

Jennifer Higdon is one of the most well-known contemporary composers of our time. A Pulitzer prize and multiple Grammy award winner, her works from orchestral to chamber to operatic are well known within and without the Classical music world. Having received commissions from some of the world's best known orchestras, string quartets, opera companies, and performers, her name and music is one of the most respected and performed in the field.
In 2006, she was commissioned by violinist Jennifer Koh to write a work for violin and piano that reflected Koh's love of poetry. Higdon obliged and composed "String Poetics", a five-movement work ("Jagged Climb", "Nocturne", "Blue Hills of Mist", "Maze Mechanical", and "Climb Jagged") that emulates poetry in the different movements and textures of the music.

Over the years since, the second movement "Nocturne" has been played outside of the full piece. With its subtitle of "gentle, serene, and lyrical", the work stands on its own as a beautiful and tender work. Its popularity inspired Higdon to publish the movement separately, and in 2016 created a version for cello and piano.

Edition:
Available from the composer's website.

Bibliography:
Official website of the composer, Accessed, August 10, 2023, http://jenniferhigdon.com/index.html
Program notes on the piece, Accessed August 10, 2023, http://www.jenniferhigdon.com/pdf/program-notes/String-Poetic.pdf

Recordings:
At the time of writing, no commercial recording is available of the cello and piano version, however there are a couple of performances on youtube. The premiere recording of the original version by Jennifer Koh is available on Cedille Records.

Paul Hindemith (1895-1963) — Sonata for Solo Cello

Date of Composition: 1922
Date of Premiere: May 1923
Premiered by: Maurits Frank, cello
Approximate Length: 11 min.

I. Lively, very marked (2 min)
II. Moderately fast, comfortable (2 min)
III. Slow (4 min)
IV. Lively, at the quarter note (1 min)
V. Moderately fast (2 min)

Background Information:

Paul Hindemith was a violist and composer who pushed boundaries in his music. He wrote both Romantic music, Gebrauchsmusik (functional) music for amateurs, and progressive music that was neither tonal or atonal. He often eschewed using a key signature, and the music exists in a space between being rooted in a tonic and the twelve-tone system.

The Sonata for Solo Cello was written in 1922 while Hindemith was at the Donaueschingen Chamber Music Festival, a contemporary music festival held in the Black Forest. There was a tradition of competing to write a piece in one evening–Hindemith wrote the first four movements of the Sonata in one evening at the festival, adding the fifth movement later. His quartet-mate, cellist Maurits Frank received the dedication and premiered the work.

The Sonata is included in his Op. 25 works, most of which are other sonatas for solo instruments. It is one of a number of pieces for solo cello that he wrote, including several works for cello and piano, and two cello concerti.

Edition:
Schott

Bibliography:
Official website of the composer, Accessed August 15, 2023, https://www.hindemith.info/en/home/
Official website page on the piece, Accessed August 15, 2023, https://www.hindemith.info/en/institute/news/lightbox/paul-hindemith-sonata-for-solo-cello-op-25-nr-3/

Recordings:
Many cellists have recorded this and Hindemith's other works for cello.

Lee Hoiby (1926-2011) — Sonata for Cello & Piano, Op. 59

Date of Composition: 1993
Date of Premiere: Unknown
Premiered by: Anne Martindale Williams, cello
Approximate Length: 11 min.

Background Information:

Lee Hoiby was one of the most prominent American composers of the twentieth century, particularly in the realm of vocal music. Although he is most known for his large catalog of art songs and his one-act opera, Bon Appetit!, based on an episode of a Julia Child cooking show, he also wrote a fair amount of instrumental chamber works. Notable works include his piano quartet Dark Rhosaleen, a woodwind sextet, and his cello sonata.

Composed in 1993, it's a one-movement work that contains all of the hallmarks of Hoiby's style, vocal-esque melodies and catchy rhythms in an ABA form. Hoiby explores the full range of the cello including a high, singing tessitura.

Brian Hodges (the author) met Hoiby when performing his sonata in the Delaware Valley Chamber Music Festival (after an introduction by Carolyn Steinberg, see other entry). He and wife, pianist Betsi Hodges, performed the sonata numerous times over the next couple of years, enough that Hoiby decided to dedicate the sonata to them.

Edition:
PSNY Publications (Project Schott New York)

Bibliography:
Official website of the composer, Accessed July 7, 2023, http://www.leehoiby.net/

Recordings:
No commercial recording is available

Imogen Holst (1907-1984) — Fall of the Leaf for Solo Cello

Date of Composition: 1963
Date of Premiere: unknown
Premiered by: Pamela Hind o'Malley, cello
Approximate Length: 8 min.

> I. Theme. Andante (1 min)
> II. Vivace (2 min)
> III. Poco adagio (3 min)
> IV. Presto (1 min)
> V. Da capo. Andante molto moderato (1 min)

Background Information:

   Daughter of famed English composer, Gustav Holst, Imogen Holst made a name for herself as both a composer and conductor. She did a lot to help keep her father's legacy intact, writing a biography on him and his music, as well as annotating editions of his music. For years, she worked as assistant to composer Benjamin Britten and acted as director of his Aldeburgh Festival. She still found time to compose in between the work for Britten, preserving her father's musical legacy and conducting. She left behind a catalog of over 100 works of chamber, orchestra and vocal works.

   Fall of the Leaf for solo cello is subtitled "Three short studies for solo cello on a sixteenth-century tune", and is based on a keyboard piece by Martin Peerson found in the Fitzwilliam Virginal Book. It is a beautiful, and slightly haunting, work.

Edition:
Oxford University Press

Bibliography:
Publisher page on the composer, Accessed August 9, 2023, https://www.fabermusic.com/we-represent/imogen-holst
Isserlis, Steven, Liner notes on Holst, Imogen "Elgar & Walton Cello Concertos", Steven Isserlis, cello, Philharmonia Orchestra, Paavo Järvi, cond., Hyperion, 2016.

Recordings:
A couple of commercial recordings have been released, including the aforementioned recording by Steven Isserlis.

John Ireland (1879-1962) — Sonata for Cello & Piano

Date of Composition: 1923
Date of Premiere: April 1924
Premiered by: Beatrice Harrison, cello with Evlyn Howard-Jones, piano
Approximate Length: 21 min.

> I. Moderato e sostenuto (9 min)
> II. Poco largamente (7 min)
> III. Con moto e marcato (5 min)

Background Information:

John Ireland was a prolific British composer at the turn of the twentieth century. He studied with Charles Stanford and was in good company, considering Stanford's other students were a veritable who's who of English composers: Ralph Vaughan Williams, Frank Bridge, Gustav Holst, Arthur Bliss, and others. Later, he would teach at the Royal College where he counted Benjamin Britten as one of his students.

His compositional career took off with his participation in the Walter W. Cobbett Chamber Music Competitions; Ireland was a prize-winner two years in a row, one for his Phantasy Piano Trio, and the other for his violin sonata. Part of the parameters for the competition was the use of the Phantasy, an older, cyclical form that was English in origin. This use of the Phantasy would have a large effect on Ireland, as a good portion of his music utilized that form.
One way Ireland's music has been described is "English Impressionism". The music of Debussy was all the rage in France, and traces of his compositional style was making its way into England; The English were decidedly moving farther and farther from German Romanticism.

Ireland's Cello Sonata is, as expected, in the cyclical Phantasy form as material from the beginning appears again in the third movement. The third movement, with its jagged leaps, was supposedly inspired by the Devil's Jumps, a set of five barrows in Sussex. The final moments contain a tremendous buildup from the two instruments very low in their respective ranges, climbing all the way to a victorious high note in the cello.

Beatrice Harrison, who premiered the work, was pleased with the work, calling it "glorious".
It's hard to not agree with her.

Edition:
Stainer & Bell

Bibliography:
Foreman, Lewis, Liner notes, Ireland, John, "Chamber Music of John Ireland", Karine Georgian, cello, Ian Brown, piano, Chandos, 1995.
Hodges, Betsi. W.W. Cobbett's Phantasy: A Legacy of Chamber Music in the British Musical Renaissance (VDM Verlag Dr. Müller, 2009)
Official website of the composer, Accessed August 16, 2023, https://johnirelandtrust.org/biography/

Recordings:
There are a few commercial recordings made of this piece

Marie Jaëll (1846-1925) — Cello Concerto in F Major

Date of Composition: 1882
Date of Premiere: May 1882
Premiered by: Jules Delsart, cello at the Salle Erard, Charles Lamoureaux conductor
Approximate Length: 17 min.

> I. Allegro moderato (7 min)
> II. Andantino sostenuto (5 min)
> III. Vivace molto (5 min)

Background Information:

Marie Jaëll was a French composer in the nineteenth century. She was a well-known pianist and pedagogue of the day. She not only composed numerous pieces for a wide variety of instrumentation, but she published a book on her piano method after a bout of tendonitis sent her into researching healthy approaches to playing.

For the cello, she composed a sonata and concerto, both for cellist Jules Delsart. The manuscript for the cello concerto fell into relative obscurity, but was recently brought to light thanks to the efforts of cellist Wendy Velasco.

The music is gorgeous and tuneful, reminiscent of Dvorak's mighty concerto, even though it preceded it by a decade.

Edition:
SMP Press (available as a digital download)

Bibliography:
Program notes on the piece, Accessed March 24, 2021, http://www.bruzanemediabase.com/eng/layout/set/print/Works/Cello-Concerto-Marie-Jaell
Program notes on the piece, Accessed August 29, 2023, https://www.cellobello.org/cello-blog/artistic-vision/expanding-the-cello-repertoire-to-include-women-composers/

Recordings:
Xavier Phillips and the Brussels Philharmonic conducted by Herve Niquet (Bru Zane Records, 2016)

Leoš Janáček (1854-1928)   Pohádka for Cello & Piano

Date of Composition: 1st version - 1910, 2nd version - 1912, 3rd version - 1923
Date of Premiere: 1910
Premiered by: Unknown
Approximate Length: 12 min.

> I. Con moto - Andante (5 min)
> II. Con moto - Adagio (4 min)
> III. Allegro (3 min)

Background Information:

Leoš Janáček was one of the most well-known and respected Czech composers of the twentieth century. Seizing inspiration from multiple fronts, he was taken with the folk music of his native land, and studied them extensively. He was also fascinated with Russian culture, basing a number of his works on Russian Literature.

Pohádka (Fairytale) for Cello and Piano was one of those works. It's a twelve minute work based on a poem by VA Zhukovsky entitled "The Tale of Tsar Berendey, about his son Ivan the Tsarevich, about the Acumen of Immortal Kaschei and about the wise Tsarievna Maria, Kaschei's Daughter." (cellists are glad Janáček didn't use the full title). The story that Janáček uses roughly concerns a Prince who falls in love with a Princess, whose father happens to be the King of the Underworld.

The piece is in three movements and highly evokes the magical story it is based on. Janáček uses a variety of colors and textures to suggest a moonlit lake, a chase on horseback, magic spells and of course romance between the two young lovers.

Janáček apparently had a hard time solidifying the work. Following the premiere in 1910, he produced a second revised version in 1912, only to revise it once again in 1923. This final version is the one most cellists play today.

Selected Edition:
Bärenreiter (Urtext)

Bibliography:
Official website of the composer, Accessed August 16, 2023, https://www.leosjanacek.eu/en/leos-janacek/
Isserlis, Steven, Liner notes, Janacek, Leo "Lieux retrouvés", Steven Isserlis, cello, Thomas Adès, piano Hyperion, 2012.

Recordings:
There are a number of commercial recordings available for this work.

Nathalie Joachim (b. 1983) — Dam Mwen Yo for Solo Cello

Date of Composition: 2016
Date of Premiere: 2016
Premiered by: Amanda Gookin
Approximate Length: 7 min.

Background Information:

Nathalie Joachim is a triple threat: flutist, composer and singer. Educated at Juilliard, she was a member of the famed contemporary ensemble Eighth Blackbird, and is now a member of Flutronix, a flute duo with fellow flutist/composer Allison Loggins-Hull (see other entry). She has long embraced her Haitian heritage, weaving it seamlessly into her compositions, incorporating songs, the language and stories. Grammy-nominated, she is an United States Artist Fellow, an Artistic Partner with the Oregon Symphony, and on faculty at Princeton. She has written The Race: 1915 for solo cello and the gorgeous Dam mwen yo for cello and recorded vocals.

Dam mwen yo was commissioned by cellist Amanda Gookin for the Forward Music Project. Joachim writes about the work:

> *Dam mwen yo in Haitian Creole simply translates to "my ladies". In Haiti, the cultural image of women is one of strength. They are pillars of their homes and communities, and are both fearless and loving, all while carrying the weight of their families and children on their backs. As a first generation Haitian-American, these women - my mother, grandmothers, sisters, aunts, cousins - were central to my upbringing and my understanding of what it means to be a woman. In Dantan, Haiti-Sud, where my family is from, it is rare to walk down the countryside roads without hearing the voices of women - in the fields, cooking for their loved ones, gathering water at the wells with their babies. This piece and the voices within it are representative of these ladies - my ladies. And the cello sings their song - one of strength, beauty, pain and simplicity in a familiar landscape.*

Edition:
From the composer's website, backing track included

Bibliography:
Notes from the composer herself in an email exchange, November 2020
Official website of the composer, Accessed July 6, 2023, www. nathaliejoachim.com

Recordings:
Amanda Gookin has recorded this work on her Forward Music Project 1.0.

David H. Johnson (b. 1977) — 5 Melodies for Cello & Piano

Date of Composition: 2008
Date of Premiere: 2009 violin version; 2023 cello version
Premiered by: Steven Taylor, cello with Hue Jang, piano
Approximate Length: 13 min.

I. Allegretto ma con anime (2 min)
II. Moderato (2 min)
III. Adagio cantabile e sostenuto (3 min)
IV. Allegretto molto marcato (3 min)
V. Vivace (3 min)

Background Information:

David H. Johnson is a composer and violinist who teaches at Georgia College State and Southern University. Studying at UCLA, Yale and Indiana, he has also taught at Midwestern State University, University of Puget Sound and the Townsend School of Music in Macon, Georgia.

Johnson has composed works for solo piano, violin, cello, piano trio, orchestra and choir. Due to his prowess on the violin, his writing for strings is especially brilliant.

His Five Melodies for Cello and Piano was first written for violin and piano, but arranged for cello and piano by the composer. About this work, Johnson writes, "5 Melodies was composed with the advanced student in mind. Each movement addresses a different technical issue for the instrument, such as various bowing styles and double stops, all the while focusing on a mix of lyrical and dramatic performance."

Edition:
Available from the composer's website.

Bibliography:
Official website of the composer, Accessed August 18, 2023, https://www.davidhjohnson.com/index.html
Program quote from the composer from an email conversation with the author.

Recordings:
At press time, no commercial recording is available.

Dmitri Kabalevsky (1904-1987)   Cello Concerto No. 1 in G minor, Op. 49

Date of Composition: 1948
Date of Premiere: March 15, 1949
Premiered by: Sviatoslav Knushevitsky, cello and the Moscow Conservatory Youth Orchestra
Approximate Length: 18 min.

I. Allegro (7 min)
II. Largo (6 min)
III. Allegretto (5 min)

Background Information:

    Dmitri Kabalevsky was a twentieth century Russian composer, who in his day enjoyed a bit more widespread fame than his contemporary, Dmitri Shostakovich. He ended up writing a handful of cello works in his career (a second concerto and a sonata most notably), with this first cello concerto being the most well-known.

    Composed while he was a professor at the Moscow Conservatory, he wrote this concerto as part of a trilogy of concerti (one for violin, one for cello, and the other for piano), in which they are written for the young student (the violin concerto, in particular, is very similar in thematic material). Indeed, this first cello concerto is not prohibitively difficult, certainly not on par with the second concerto he wrote for cello, but does have some rather challenging sections.

    The first movement is a quasi-march, lively and bouncy; the orchestra keeping a steady beat, and the cello dancing and swooning over it. The second is based on a Russian folk song and is dedicated to fallen Russian soldiers, while the third is a theme and variations on a different Russian song.

    Despite the minor key, this concerto isn't nearly as heavy in mood as the Shostakovich concerti or the Prokofiev Symphonie Concertante, the other major twentieth century Russian cello concerti written some time after. Structured in a rather traditional compositional style, it was very popular with audiences when it premiered.

Selected Editions:
International
Sikorski

Bibliography:
Fairley, E. Lee, Preface, Kabalevsky Dmitri "Concerto No. 1", New York: International, 1970.
Program notes, Accessed March 15, 2021, https://www.allmusic.com/composition/cello-concerto-no-1-in-g-minor-op-49-mc0002369931

Recordings:
Many commercial recordings are available.

Aaron Kernis (b. 1960) — Colored Field (Cello Concerto)

Date of Composition: 2000
Date of Premiere: 2000
Premiered by: Truls Mørk, cello with Eiji Oue conducting the Minnesota Orchestra
Approximate Length: 40 min.

> I. Colored Field (12 min)
> II. Pandora Dance (6 min)
> III. Hymns and Tablets (22 min)

Background Information:

Aaron Kernis is a Pulitzer-prize winning American composer with an impressive resume. He began composing works when he was a teenager, and before college, he had already won a few BMI Foundation Composing awards, winning the Pulitzer Prize for his String Quartet No. 2 in 1998. His major teachers were John Adams and Charles Wourinen. Renée Fleming, Joshua Bell, the New York Philharmonic and the San Francisco Symphony are among the luminaries that have premiered his works.

In 1994, Kernis was commissioned to write a concerto for English Horn and Orchestra for the San Francisco Symphony. Kernis wrote Colored Field for Julie Ann Giacobassi, the principal English Hornist. Several years later, he turned it into a cello concerto for Truls Mørk and the Minnesota Symphony.
Colored Field was inspired by Kernis' visit to the concentration camps of Auschwitz and Birkenau. During his visit, he was keenly aware of the beauty around him, ironic given the dark history of the sites.
The cello acts as a lone voice against a massive orchestra (the strings are divided on either side of the soloist) representing hope and humanity against a dark evil. It is plaintive, harsh, but ends, much as it begins, in a quiet stillness, the soloist still pleading for peace. One final, brash, discordant outburst from the orchestra–mirroring the opening of the third movement– makes it as if the evil potentially will win if we're not careful.

The cello version of Colored Field won Kernis the Grawemeyer Award in 2000.

Edition:
Associated Music Publishers

Bibliography:
Official website of the composer, Accessed August 16, 2023, https://aaronjaykernis.com/
Milliken Archive on the composer, Accessed August 16, 2023, https://www.milkenarchive.org/artists/view/aaron-kernis
Program notes on the piece, Accessed August 16, 2023, http://www.lcsproductions.net/MusicHistory/MusHistRev/Articles/ColoredField.html

Recordings:
To date, Truls Mørk's premiere recording with the Minnesota Symphony is the one recording available.

Zoltán Kodály (1882-1967) — Sonata in B minor for Solo Cello, Op. 8

Date of Composition: 1915
Date of Premiere: May 7, 1918
Premiered by: Jenö Kerpely, cello
Approximate Length: 26 min.

> I. Allegro maestoso ma appassionato (8 min)
> II. Adagio con gran espressivo (8 min)
> III. Allegro molto vivace (10 min)

Background Information:

Zoltán Kodály became one of the foremost Hungarian composers of the twentieth century. Like Béla Bartók before him, he became fascinated with the folk music of his culture and began to incorporate it into his music (whether intentionally or not).

He had already written a sonata for cello and piano in 1910 which was steeped in folk songs and rhythms, but it would be his epic Sonata in B Minor for Solo Cello that would become the staple of cello repertoire.

It would be hard to imagine anyone composing a work for solo cello and not have Bach's iconic Six Suites for Unaccompanied Cello in mind. It's not entirely clear how much Bach's Suites influenced Kodály in his solo sonata, but there are striking similarities, from the polyphonic textures down to the scordatura tuning. They also reflect a bit of Paganini's Caprices and Ysaÿe's Solo Sonatas for Violin.

The Solo Sonata is a tremendous work consisting of incredibly difficult technique and musicality. Virtually every skill in playing the cello is on display, including an arsenal of extended techniques. Kodály calls for the bottom two strings to be tuned down a half step from G to F# and C to B changing the sonic landscape of the cello considerably.

The work received a lot of attention on its premiere and was quickly picked up by many cellists, including the young János Starker. In much the same way that the Elgar Concerto became strongly associated with Jacqueline duPré, the Kodály Sonata became Starker's standout piece. He recorded it no less than 4 times and earned Kodály's blessing.

Kodály declared that eventually no cellist would be acceptable without performing his solo sonata. While not entirely true, the piece does prove to be a testing ground for the performer. It is not for the faint of heart and remains an exhilarating experience for the player and listener alike, one hundred years after its premiere.

Edition:
Universal Edition

Bibliography:
Starker, János The World of Music According to Starker (Indiana University Press, Bloomington, 2004)
Berger, Melvin Guide to Sonatas (Anchor Books, New York, 1991)

Recordings:
Many commercial recordings have been released, but Starker's recordings remain the gold standard. Which of the four is the best is a matter of personal taste.

Erich Korngold (1897-1957) — Cello Concerto in C Major, Op. 37

Date of Composition: 1946
Date of Premiere: December 29, 1946
Premiered by: Eleanor Aller Slatkin, cello; Los Angeles Philharmonic Orchestra
Approximate Length: 12 min

Background Information:

    Erich Wolfgang Korngold is best known for essentially creating the "sound of Hollywood" in his numerous film scores. A few auspicious premieres of some of his stage work in Hamburg led him to emigrate to the United States and escape the atrocities of the second World War. Through connections, he began composing for films, such as The Sea Hawk and The Adventures of Robin Hood, which won him the second of his Academy Awards for Best Original Score. He did write a large amount of music for the concert hall stage (non-film music), but it has been largely ignored, Korngold being a victim of his own success in the realm of film scoring. However, in recent decades, more and more of his concert hall music has been performed, namely his Violin Concerto.

    His Cello Concerto in C Major occupies a space in between his concert hall works and his film scores. The work was actually written for the film Deception, a 1946 thriller starring Bette Davis, as a pianist involved in a jealous love triangle with a composer and a cellist. The composing and performing of a cello concerto factors into the plot. Korngold wrote a cello concerto for the film score, then fashioned it into a cello concerto separate from the film score.

    It is a work played in one movement and as is befitting the nature of the film, suitably melodramatic. However, the piece does work incredibly well on its own, and a listener without prior knowledge of its origins in the film, can understand and appreciate it.

Edition:
Schott

Bibliography:
Leviton, Lawrence Dana. An Analysis of Erich Wolfgang Korngold's Cello Concerto and Underscore Written for the Film "Deception" dissertation for The University of Wisconsin-Madison, 1998.
Official website of the composer, Accessed August 15, 2023, http://www.korngold.com/
Program notes by the Los Angeles Philharmonic, Accessed August 15, 2023, https://www.laphil.com/musicdb/pieces/1210/cello-concerto-in-c-op-37-from-deception

Recordings:
There are several commercial recordings of this concerto available.

Antonin Kraft (1749-1820) — Cello Concerto in C Major, Op. 4

Date of Composition: Unknown; first published by Breitkopf and Härtel in 1792
Date of Premiere: Unknown
Premiered by: likely either Antonin Kraft, himself, or his son Nikolaus Kraft, both of whom were principal cellists at the orchestra of Prince Joseph Franz on Lobkowitz

Approximate Length: 21 min.

> I. Allegro aperto (9 min)
> II. Andante (Romance) (6 min)
> III. Moderato (Rondo alla Cosacca) (6 min)

Background Information:

Anton Kraft was a virtuoso cellist and member of the Ensemble at the court of Prince Nikolaus Esterházy. As has been well documented, he played under the direction of Franz Joseph Haydn, who was the music director at the court. A composer himself, Kraft studied composition under Haydn, and wrote a fair amount of solo music for cello, including six sonatas and the Concerto in C Major.

Because of their close professional association, the authorship of these pieces was in question for centuries. Many believed that Haydn's Cello Concerto in D Major was, in fact, written by Anton Kraft, and at the very least, Kraft was the cellist who premiered it. Research finally proved that the D Major Concerto was from Haydn's quill, and more recent research has shown that Kraft did not premiere either of Haydn's two cello concerti (it was most likely Joseph Weigl who premiered the C Major Concerto and Joseph Cervetto who premiered the D Major).

Regarding Kraft's own cello concerto, it is a charming concerto rooted in the galant style that was so prevalent in the eighteenth century, even if the ghost of Haydn looms large over the entire work, perhaps unavoidably. The first movement whips along at a brisk speed in virtuosic passages. The second movement is a grand and noble andante, with shades of Beethoven here and there. The third movement is a fun rondo with a very catchy, sing-song melody.

After the death of Nikolaus Esterházy, Kraft moved on, eventually landing in the service of Prince Lobkowitz, who was a strong supporter of Beethoven. Kraft and Beethoven became acquainted, and it was Kraft who performed the cello part in the premiere of Beethoven's Triple Concerto.

He left behind a great legacy, besides his own compositions for cello, his son and grandson were both prominent cellists in their day as well.

Selected Editions:
Breitkopf und Härtel
International

Bibliography:
Stevens, Denis, Liner notes to Haydn, Franz Joseph "Haydn and Kraft Cello Concertos", Anner Bylsma, cello, Tafelmusik, Jean Lamon, cond., Deutsche Harmonia Mundi, 1990.

Recordings:
A few recordings have been made of this concerto, mostly on period instruments.

Édouard Lalo (1823-1892) Cello Concerto in D Minor

Date of Composition: 1876
Date of Premiere: December 9, 1877
Premiered by: Adolphe Fischer, cello
Approximate Length: 29 min.

> I. Prélude: Lento - Allegro maestoso (13 min)
> II. Intermezzo: Andantino con moto - Allegro presto (7 min)
> III. Andante - Allegro vivace (9 min)

Background Information:

Éduard Lalo today enjoys a favorable reputation as a nineteenth century French composer, but it took him quite a while to earn the respect of critics and audiences in his lifetime. Failing to make waves with his compositions, he supported himself by playing violin in local string quartets. Finally, just before he reached the age of fifty, did he start to make a name for himself as a composer. His Violin Concerto and Symphonie Espagnole pushed him even further into the public eye.

In 1876, he wrote his Cello Concerto in D Minor. The impulse to write a cello concerto is not clear, but cellist Adolphe Fischer was apparently a big help to Lalo in the writing of the cello part. After the premiere in 1877, Fischer championed the work, taking it on tour. This helped introduce the piece to other cellists, assisted further by the publication by Bote & Bock in 1878.

The Concerto is in a traditional three-movement format; forgoing the rather trendy method of the three movements played together in one piece (a la Saint- Säens' Cello Concerto written several years earlier).

It makes good use of the D Minor key, particularly in the first movement with its melodramatic and turbulent introduction. The intensity continues in the Allegro maestoso section, but retaining a lyrical line. The tender second theme feels like a lullaby before the intensity returns.

The second movement begins with a slow, dirge-like character, with the cello singing out in sorrow. Suddenly the mood breaks into a Spanish dance, lively and joyous.
Another slow introduction starts the third movement before launching into a raucous Rondo with more shades of Spanish dance and rhythms.

Lalo's concerto now enjoys its place firmly in the canon of the great cello concerti.

Selected Editions:
Barenreiter (Urtext)
G. Henle Verlag (Urtext)

Bibliography:
Dubal, David. The Essential Canon of Classical Music (North Point Press, New York, 2001)
Jost, Peter, Preface, Lalo Edouard "Cello Concerto in D minor", Munich: G. Henle Verlag.

Recordings:
Many of the top cellists have released recordings of this concerto.

Libby Larsen (b. 1950) — Juba for Cello & Piano

Date of Composition: 1986
Date of Premiere: 1986
Premiered by: Janet Horvath, cello; Arthur Rowe, piano at the Schubert Club in Minnesota
Approximate Length: 8 min.

Background Information:

Libby Larsen is one of the most prominent American composers of the late twentieth and early twenty-first centuries. She has amassed a body of over 500 works across all the standard genres. In addition to her considerable compositional output, she co-founded the Minnesota Composer's Forum, which is now the American Composer's Forum.

Her work Juba for cello and piano is one of a couple works she has composed for cello. About this work, she writes:

> *JUBA: a lively dance accompanied by hand clapping. When the Schubert Club commissioned this piece for the London debut concert of cellist Janet Horvath, I thought of the juba, a dance originating in the culture of African-Americans. I wanted to compose a work which carried the rhythmic, improvisatory nature of American music but maintained the formal flow of Western European music. Juba is in rondo form. The rondo theme contains a rhythmic, foot stomping motive and a melodic motive. From these two themes the music for the episodes between rondo statements is taken. The cellist plays the role of the dancer, the piano plays the role of on-looker.*

Edition:
Schirmer

Bibliography:
Official website for the composer, Accessed August 1, 2023, https://libbylarsen.com/works/juba

Recordings:
No commercial recording is available, but there is a recording made by Janet Horvath and Arthur Rowe on Larsen's website.

Luise LeBeau (1850-1927) — Sonata in D Major, Op 17 for Cello & Piano

Date of Composition: 1878
Date of Premiere: Unknown
Premiered by: Unknown
Approximate Length: 19 min.

> I. Allegro molto (6 min)
> II. Andante tranquillo (6 min)
> III. Allegro vivace (7 min)

Background Information:

Luise LeBeau was a talented composer and pianist of the nineteenth century. She was noted by the critics as the first woman to compose large-scale vocal and orchestral works successfully. While this is a stinging blow to the many other skilled woman composers before and contemporary with her, it was a nice endorsement of her abilities for sure. Thanks to the support of her parents, who believed she needed a full, well-rounded education, she achieved success early on. She studied with Clara Schumann, and Joseph Rheinberger, and embarked on a solo career. She eventually halted her concertizing to focus more on composition.

In 1880, the Neue Zeitschrift für Musik (Robert Schumann's publication) hosted a competition for a new cello work. LeBeau sent in her Cello Sonata in D Major, which had been written a couple of years earlier. The pieces were to be submitted without any indication of who was the author, with only a personally chosen quote to identify the work. LeBeau chose a quote from Göethe: "If you do not feel, pursuing it will not help." She didn't win for the sonata (her other submission Three Pieces for Cello and Piano did win a prize however), but the attention got the Sonata published.

The sonata is fresh and generally lighthearted overall. The cello is given strand after strand of gorgeous melodies, very vocal in nature, throughout the piece, over an active and brilliant piano part. A charming and engaging work that should have had a long performance history, were it not for her gender. As to her own efforts to compose music in a man's world, LeBeau once wrote, "It has to be enough to know that one has contributed to building the temple of art to the best of one's knowledge and ability. Even if I was only allowed to add a few pebbles I always tried to fulfill my artistic obligations." Fortunately, more cellists are discovering this beautiful work.

Edition:
Hildegard Publishing Company

Bibliography:
Isserlis, Steven, Liner notes, LeBeau, Luise, "A Golden Cello Decade, 1878-1888", Steven Isserlis, cello, Connie Shih, piano, Hyperion, 2022.
Neuls-Bates, Carol. Women in Music (Northeastern University Press, Boston, 1996.)

Recordings:
At press time, it appears that Steven Isserlis has made the only commercial recording.

Leonardo Leo (1694-1744) 6 Concerti for Cello, Strings & Basso Continuo

Date of Compositions: 1737-1738
Date of Premiere: Unknown
Premiered by: Unknown, but presumably Leo himself.
Approximate Lengths: 13 min average

Concerto No. 1 in A Major (September 1737)
I. Andantino grazioso (3 min)
II. Allegro (3 min)
III. Larghetto a mezza voce (3 min)
IV. Allegro (2 min)

Concerto No. 2 in D Major (September 1737)
I. Andante grazioso (4 min)
II. Con Bravura (3 min)
III. Larghetto, con poco moto - mezza voce (3 min)
IV. Fuga. Per il portamento dell'imitazione del 2do pensiere, o soggetto mi con fervito della riposta d'imitazione (2 min)
V. Allegro di molto (2 min)

Concerto No. 3 in D Minor (August 1738)
I. Andante grazioso (4 min)
II. Con Spirito (3 min)
III. Amoroso - mezza voce (3 min)
IV. Allegro (3 min)

Concerto No. 4 in A Major (August 1738)
I. Andante piacevole (3 min)
II. Allegro (4 min)
III. Larghetto e gustoso (4 min)
IV. Allegro (3 min)

Concerto No 5 in F Minor (undated)
I. Andante grazioso (4 min)
II. Allegro (3 min)
III. Segue il cantabile - Largo gustoso (4 min)
IV. Allegro (3 min)

Sinfonia concertata (Concerto No. 6) in C Minor (October 1737)
I. Andante grazioso (3 min)
II. Presto (2 min)
III. Larghetto (4 min)
IV. Allegro (3 min)

Leonardo Leo (1694-1744)   6 Concerti for Cello, Strings & Basso Continuo

Background Information:

One of the more prominent composers of the Neapolitan School, Leonardo Leo was well-known in his time, but unfortunately largely forgotten in the time since. He was a teacher, organist, conductor as well as composer whose style was firmly rooted in the Baroque, but also foreshadowing the Classical era. Today, he is mostly known for his handful of sacred works and operas, but cellists have these six beautiful concertos to explore.

Written for the Duke of Maddaloni, who was an amateur cellist and a patron of Leo's (not to mention Pergolesi), they are all six gems and dispel the favored conception that the cello took a longer time to become a solo instrument. They were written before the Vivaldian-three-movement concerto pattern of Fast-Slow-Fast had been solidified; they are all in four movements with a Slow-Fast-Slow-Fast format. He also includes some beautifully descriptive movement titles rather than the typical tempo indications, such as 'Andante grazioso', 'Amoroso-mezza voce', and 'Con Bravura', with a fantastic fugue in the fourth movement of the second concerto.

Selected Editions:

There are a handful of editions (Schott, International, etc.) but some are in the incorrect keys. Musicaneo editions online are accurate.

Bibliography:

Bukofzer, Manfred. Music in the Baroque Era (W.W. Norton & Company, New York, 1947).
Scholz, Horst A., Liner notes, Leo, Leonardo, "Six Cello Concertos", Hidemi Suzuki, cello, Orchestra 'Van Wassanaer', Bis records, 1999.

Recordings:

A handful of recordings have been made of these concerti.

Tania Léon (b. 1943) — Four Pieces for Solo Cello

Date of Composition: 1983
Date of Premiere: Unknown
Premiered by: Unknown
Approximate Length: 12 min.

I. Allegro (2 min)
II. Lento doloroso, sempre cantabile (To My Father) (4 min)
III. Montuno (1 min)
IV. Vivo (3 min)

Background Information:

Cuban-born composer Tania Léon is a composer, conductor and educator. The recipient of the Pulitzer Prize for her commissioned orchestral work Stride for the New York Philharmonic, she has been the subject of profiles for PBS, CBS, ABC and CNN and was honored with a lifetime achievement award at the 2022 Kennedy Center Honors.

Her work Four Pieces for Solo Cello was written in remembrance of her father after his death. He had encouraged her to incorporate more Cuban-style music into her own, something she hadn't really done overtly before. This was the first piece where she let that side of her heritage more into her music.

It's a powerful work that involves an entire array of extended techniques, including foot-stamping, and knocking on the fingerboard. Its dynamics range from barely audible to the loudest playing possible (she marks fff in the score on the jolting last note). It is a tour de force and is a powerful tribute to her father.

Edition:
PeerMusic

Bibliography:
Official website of the composer, Accessed August 10, 2023, https://www.tanialeon.com/
Program notes, Accessed August 10, 2023, https://hcommons.org/deposits/objects/hc:20792/datastreams/CONTENT/content

Recordings:
So far, there are no commercial recordings available, however there are several video performances on youtube.

György Ligeti (1923-2006) — Sonata for Solo Cello

Date of Composition: 1948-1953
Date of Premiere: 1953
Premiered: Vera Dénes, for a radio broadcast that was not aired. Cellist Manfred Stiltz performed the first public performance in 1983.
Approximate Length: 8 min.

> I. Dialogo - Adagio, rubato, cantabile (4 min)
> II. Capriccio - Presto con slancio (4 min)

Background Information:

Romanian composer, György Ligeti endured a horrifying early life. His family were captured by the Nazis and taken to Auschwitz, while he was sent to a labor camp. He and his mother were the only two survivors from this incident. After the war, he went to Budapest and studied with Zoltán Kodály at the Franz Liszt Academy, where he became fascinated with Hungarian folk music. He then moved to Cologne where he began to learn about more electronic and experimental music which captured his imagination.

His works that followed involved a technique he termed "microtonality", as well as tone clusters, and pictorial notation. His choral work "Lux Aeterna" for a cappella choir, written in 1966, is a classic example of the techniques he was using and ended up famously being used in the film 2001: A Space Odyssey.

His Sonata for Solo Cello was written in 1948, and was rejected by the Composer's Union, banning the work from being performed in public or published. It wasn't until 1983 when it got its formal premiere and was finally published in 1990. In later years, it was used as one of the chosen pieces for the Rostropovich Cello Competition.

The piece is divided into two sections. The Dialogo was written earlier, when Ligeti was a student, for a cellist in whom he had a romantic interest. He envisioned the first movement as a dialogue, using the different strings of the cello as the different voices in the conversation. The second movement is to be played incredibly fast (does that mean one should play it 'Ligeti-split'?...), and is loosely based on the caprices by Paganini.

Edition:
Schott

Bibliography:
David, Dubal. The Essential Canon of Classical Music (North Point Press, New York, 2001)
Official website for the composer, Accessed August 15, 2023, https://en.gyorgy-ligeti.com/biography
Paul, Steven, Liner notes, Ligeti, Gyorgi "Suites and Sonatas for Solo Cello", Matt Haimovitz, cello, Deutsche Grammophon, 1991.
Publisher page on the piece, Accessed August 15, 2023, https://www.schott-music.com/en/sonate-noc38212.html

Recordings:
Many commercial recordings have been released.

Allison Loggins-Hull (b. 1982) — Stolen for Solo Cello

Date of Composition: 2016
Date of Premiere: unknown
Premiered by: Amanda Gookin, cellist
Approximate Length: 6 min.

Background Information:

Allsion Loggins-Hull is one-half of the Flutronix Duo, a contemporary flute duo. She has composed for a variety of instrumentations and styles, collaborating with artists as diverse as the Cleveland Orchestra, Alarm Will Sound, Hans Zimmer and Lizzo.

About her piece Stolen, she writes on her website:

Stolen (2016) is a sonatine of 3 short movements exploring the journey of a young girl who is sold into marriage. The first movement represents her stolen youth and the lamentation of saying goodbye to childhood...The second movement explores the anxiety and sense of urgency felt about being forced into womanhood...The third movement is her reluctant acceptance of and submission to an undesired life...Today, one third of girls in the developing world are married before the age of 18 and 1 in 9 are married before the age of 15.

Commissioned by Amanda Gookin for The Forward Music Project.

Edition:
Flutronix Publishing

Bibliography:
Official website for the composer program notes, Accessed July 6, 2023, https://www.flutronix.com/shop/stolen-for-solo-cello/

Recordings:
Amanda Gookin has recorded the work on her Forward Music Project 1.0.

Witold Lutosławski (1913-1994) — Concerto for Cello and Orchestra

Date of Composition: 1970
Date of Premiere: October 14, 1970
Premiered by: Mstislav Rostropovich, cello; Edward Downes, conductor; Bournemouth Symphony Orchestra
Approximate Complete Length: 25 min.

>   I. Introduction
>   II. Four Episodes
>   III. Cantilena
>   IV. Finale

Background Information:

   The cello world has Mstislav Rostropovich to thank for a tremendous amount of new works from some of the most celebrated and important composers of the twentieth century (see numerous other entries in this book). Not only was he in high demand to write pieces for, but he in turn sought and chased down composers he felt could write successfully for the cello. Acclaimed Polish composer Witold Lutosławski was one such composer.

   Rostropovich had been badgering Lutosławski for a cello concerto for a couple of decades, before he finally found the time in his schedule to answer the request. The composer, well aware of Rostropovich's freakish talent, didn't hold back in the difficulties of the work, either technical or musical. The piece is fiendishly challenging; Rostropovich said he had to invent new fingerings just to be able to pull off some of the passages.
It also walks a musical tightrope, wavering just on the edge of sanity and complete chaos. The gestures are sometimes interior, other times bombastic, soulful, or virtuosic. Opening with a glib, repeated set of open Ds, and finishing with the pattern transformed into repeated high As (no longer glib, but defiant), in between, there are flighty, skittering passages and other places that are terrifyingly earthbound. It blazes through its four sections without pause, unleashing an entire world of possibilities on the listener, the cello, the grand marshal in this audacious parade.

   It remains one of Lutosławski's most well-known and loved pieces.

Edition:
Chester Music

Bibliography:
Steinberg, Michael. The Concerto: A Listener's Guide (Oxford University Press, New York, 1998)

Recordings:
Many cellists have recorded this work.

James MacMillan (b. 1959) — Sonata No. 1 for Cello & Piano

Date of Composition: 1999
Date of Premiere: May 30, 1999
Premiered by: Raphael Wallfisch, cello with John York, piano
Approximate Length: 26 min.

> I. Face (14 min)
> II. Image (12 min)

Background Information:

James MacMillan is one of the foremost composers from Scotland of the late twentieth and early twenty-first centuries. Many world-class musicians have premiered his works, and he has received both a knighthood and a CBE from Queen Elizabeth II.

His Sonata No. 1 for Cello and Piano is one of a handful of pieces he has written for cello, including a concerto and a second sonata. This sonata is in two movements, one subtitled Face, and the other Image; Image is a mirror image of the first movement Face with the roles of the two instruments reversed in many places, and certain themes played in retrograde.

Face starts off very lyrically in the cello, with the piano rolling ethereal arpeggios underneath. The mood gradually turns more and more sinister, eventually exploding into pounding chords in the lowest register of the piano.

Image begins with the cello, growling away on the low strings, in much the same as the
piano's role earlier. At the very end, the two instruments fade off into nothing.

MacMillan says in his program notes that "The most important element in the Sonata's two movements is the interval of a minor 3rd, from which emerges much of the music's material and which binds the ideas together."(www.boosey.com)

This Sonata was written for Raphael Wallfisch, who has premiered other works of MacMillans.

Edition:
Boosey & Hawkes

Bibliography:
Publisher page on the composer, Accessed August 15, 2023, https://www.boosey.com/composer/James+MacMillan
Publisher page on the piece, Accessed August 15, 2023, https://www.boosey.com/cr/music/James-MacMillan-Cello-Sonata-No-1/2649

Recordings:
A couple of recordings have been made of this work.

Elisabeth Maconchy (1907-1994) — Divertimento for Cello & Piano

Date of Composition: 1941-43
Date of Premiere: 1943
Premiered by: William Pleeth, cello with Margaret Good, piano
Approximate Length: 12 min.

          I. Serenade. Allegro moderato, poco improvisator (3 min)
          II. Golubchik. Allegro (2 min)
          III. The Clock. Allegro ritmico (1 min)
          IV. Vigil. Lento moderato (4 min)
          V. Masquerade. Allegro vigoroso (2 min)

Background Information:

    Elizabeth Maconchy was born in England, but lived most of her formative years in Ireland. She began composing at an early age and studied at the Royal College of Music as a student of Ralph Vaughn Williams. Her composition career got off to a great start with a premiere at the Proms Festival, but a diagnosis of tuberculosis at the age of 25 took her out of the public eye for a time, yet she continued composing.

    She helped form a group called Macnaghtan-Lemare Concerts which were dedicated to playing the works of female composers. Many of Machonchy's works were performed, exposing more of the public to her music. She left behind a vast catalog of 13 string quartets, a number of symphonic works, several operas, art songs and choral works. She received the CBE and later the DBE from Queen Elizabeth II.

    Her Divertimento for Cello and Piano is a collection of five movements or character pieces. From an opening serenade with a groovy, jazzy bassline, to a Russian folk tune, to a clock-like pizzicato, to a mournful song with a sparse piano chordal accompaniment, to a spunky last movement, this whole work showcases the diversity of Maconchy's writing. It shows off both instruments brilliantly and is a thrilling listen.

Edition:
Alfred Lengnick

Bibliography:
Fuller, Sophie. The Pandora Guide to Women Composers: Britain and the United States 1629-Present (Pandora Publishing, 1994)
Program notes on the piece, Accessed August 16, 2023, https://henselproject.wordpress.com/2016/08/05/elizabeth-maconchy-divertimento-1954/

Recordings:
A recording has been made by cellist Lionel Handy and on the Lyrita label, 2019.

Bohuslav Martinů (1890-1959) Sonata for Cello and Piano No. 3, H.340

Date of Composition: 1952
Date of Premiere: 1953
Premiered by: Unknown
Approximate Length: 18 min.

> I. Poco andante-Moderato (7 min)
> II. Andante (6 min)
> III. Allegro, ma non presto (5 min)

Background Information:

Bohuslav Martinů was a prominent and prolific Czech composer of the twentieth century. With a catalog of over 400 works that span instrumental, chamber, symphonic, operas and ballets.

By the time Martinů wrote his three sonatas for cello and piano that took a little over a decade, he had already written two concerti for cello. By 1952 when he wrote his third cello sonata, he was well versed in composing for cello.

The third cello sonata is the one that is generally played most often. It is genial, upbeat, and is brimming with energy. The first movement begins with a tuneful, folk-like introduction before it revs up in a poco vivo section, both instruments flying around their instruments. It is flashy and dazzling. Even the second movement, labeled Andante is incredibly active at the start, before melting into a lyrical second section. The last movement is full of motion with the two instruments passing virtuosic motives back and forth.

Although sometimes Martinů's tonal language veers into some discordant, modern territory, he doesn't stay there for very long. The entire sonata feels welcoming and is an incredibly entertaining work.

Selected Edition:
Bärenreiter (Urtext)

Bibliography:
Dommett, Kenneth, Liner notes, Martinů, Bohuslav "Cello Sonatas", Steven Isserlis, cello, Peter Evans, piano, Hyperion, 1989.
Dubal, David. The Essential Canon of Classical Music (North Point Press, New York, 2001)

Recordings:
There are many commercial recordings available.

David Maslanka (1943-2017)

Remember Me for Cello and Nineteen Players

Date of Composition: 2013
Date of Premiere: February 23, 2014
Premiered by: Paul York, cello; Fred Speck conductor with the Chamber Winds Louisville in Louisville, Kentucky
Approximate Length: 17 min.

Background Information:

David Maslanka was a composer noted for his wind ensemble works. The recipient of numerous awards and honors, he wrote in various genres. For cello, he composed a piece for cello and piano, Cello Songs (1978) and in 2014 he was commissioned to compose Remember Me for cello and Nineteen Players (wind ensemble members).

On Remember Me, Maslanka writes:

Remember Me is not a concerto in the traditional sense, but a single-movement, free-flowing fantasia. This composition was inspired by my reading of a "relatively minor" Holocaust event—the extermination of 5,000 Jews in a small town - in William L. Shirer's Rise and Fall of the Third Reich. ...On reading [about] this, I was deeply drawn in, without knowing where I was going or why. I know that something of this had to be spoken through me in musical sound. Musical vibration heals...The child's life remembered in this way is that life redeemed; it is evil transformed; it is my own life transformed and redeemed.

Edition:
Maslanka Press available from the composer's website.

Bibliography:
Official page on the piece, Accessed July 29, 2023, https://maslankapress.com/shop/remember-me-vc-19tet-sets/

Recordings:
A commercial CD recording was made by cellist Tess Remy-Schumacher and a handful of video performances are available on youtube.

Emilie Mayer (1812-1883) — 12 Sonatas for Cello & Piano

Date of Composition: Various
Date of Premiere: Unknown
Premiered by: Unknown
Approximate Lengths: 20 min.

Background Information:

Generally speaking, when a composer in the nineteenth century has written twelve cello sonatas, they tend to be a known commodity, and usually some, if not all, of the sonatas are performed and recorded. It is frustrating, to say the least, that Emilie Mayer, who lived and composed in the nineteenth century and wrote twelve cello sonatas—not to mention solo piano works, seven violin sonatas, eight piano trios, two piano quartets, seven string quartets, art songs, a piano concerto and eight symphonies—has largely been forgotten.

Details of her biography are sketchy. She studied with Carl Lowe, who admired her work and championed her works. She connected with many of the major musicians in Europe as she traveled around performing. She was known, as was her music. However, after her death, she faded into obscurity. Thankfully, people are rediscovering her works today, although a good majority of her music is still hard to come by.

Her cello sonatas are well worth an investigation. They fit incredibly well into the nineteenth century aesthetic, traces of the Classical style can be heard, as is a more Romantic sensibility. Here's hoping they will become more prominent in the very near future.

Edition:
Hildegard Publishing

Bibliography:
Biography on the composer, Accessed August 16, 2023, https://www.harmonysinfonia.co.uk/post/a-celebration-of-female-composers-emilie-mayer
Cadieux, Marie-Aline. The Cello and Piano Sonatas of Emilie Mayer (1821-1883) dissertation for Ohio State University, 1999.

Recordings:
Thomas Blees has recorded her D Major Sonata on the FSM label.

Missy Mazzoli (b. 1980) — Beyond the Order of Things (After Josquin) for Solo Cello

Date of Composition: 2021
Date of Premiere: November 12, 2021
Premiered by: Matt Haimovitz, cello at St. Mark's Episcopal Church in Palo Alto, California
Approximate Length: 4 min.

Background Information:

According to Bachtrack.com, which charts the number of performances for composers, Missy Mazzoli was the 19th most performed living composer in the world in the year 2022. She is mostly known for her operatic works, but has composed in a wide variety of genres and instrumentations. She has written for major opera companies, orchestras and ensembles and has been nominated for a Grammy. She is currently on the faculty at Bard College and is the founding member of the Luna Composition Lab, a program that encourages and supports young female, non-binary and non-gender-conforming composers.

About Beyond the Order, she writes:

Beyond the Order of Things was commissioned by cellist Matt Haimovitz as part of the 2021 Primavera Project. The work is a response to a 2020 painting by Charline von Heyl, itself a response to Botticelli's Primavera painting from the late 1400's…In composing Beyond the Order of Things I replicated, in music, von Heyl's technique of erasing and recontextualizing source material from the Renaissance. I transcribed a vocal motet, Praeter rerum serium (translation: Beyond the Order of Things) by Botticelli's contemporary Josquin des Prez. Like von Heyl, I reworked this material, repeating fragments and chopping up phrases, to create an entirely new work that is a beautifully corrupted translation of the original.

Edition:
Available as a print-on-demand from Schirmer

Bibliography:
Official website of the composer, Accessed July 7, 2023, https://missymazzoli.com/

Recordings:
Matt Haimovitz has recorded it for his album Primavera II: The Rabbits on his Oxingale Record Label.

Marc Mellits (b. 1966) — Book of Ruth for Solo Cello

Date of Composition: 2010
Date of Premiere: Unknown
Premiered by: Unknown
Approximate Length: 12 min.

I. Chapter 1 (3 min)
II. Chapter 2 (2 min)
III. Jaana's Gift (2 min)
IV. Chapter 3 (2 min)
V. Chapter 4 (3 min)

Background Information:

Marc Mellits is one of the most creative and unique composers in the United States. Educated at the Eastman School of Music, Yale, Cornell University and Tanglewood, he has written for all kinds of instrumental ensembles and voices. Known for he unique and humorous titles for his pieces (Parking Violation, Tight Sweater, and Fruity Pebbles to name a few), his music is anything but, which can be at once, achingly, hauntingly beautiful, while the next moment, full of power-driven and funky rhythms.

Book of Ruth for solo cello is five-movement work which is mostly meditative and lilting, not unlike a lullaby. The typical Mellits rock-inspired rhythms do make an appearance, namely in movement II.

Mellits has a couple of other solo cello works, including a work for cello and string orchestra called Paranoid Cheese, which despite what the title might suggest is a gorgeous work with the strings sustaining harmonies underneath a soaring solo cello.

Edition:
Available from https://www.marcmellits.com

Bibliography:
Official website of the composer, Accessed July 7, 2023, https://www.marcmellits.com/bio

Recordings:
No commercial recording is available, but sound clips are available on the composer's website.

Fanny Mendelssohn (1805-1847) — Zwei Stücke for Cello & Piano

Date of Composition: 1830
Date of Premiere: Unknown
Premiered by: Unknown, but perhaps Paul Mendelssohn-Bartholdy
Approximate Length: 11 min.

I. Fantasia in G minor (4 min)
II. Capriccio in A-flat Major (7 min)

Background Information:

Fanny Mendelssohn was a part of the famous Mendelssohn family. Renowned philosopher Moses Mendelssohn was her grandfather, and of course, her younger brother was composer Felix Mendelssohn. She had a well rounded and supportive education, beginning her musical studies early. She rapidly became known for her piano playing talent, as well as her compositions.

Much can be written about her place in society at that time, and how it played a huge limiting role in her career. While just as talented as her brother Felix, his career skyrocketed, while she remained for the most part in the shadows. Adding insult to injury is the fact that when several of her compositions were first published, they were published under her brother's name, causing confusion as to what she actually wrote. After sorting the attribution out, it's clear she had much more of a voice in composing than originally thought. Today, we have a much better sense of her scope and skill as a composer.

Her Zwei Stücke for Cello and Piano was written around 1830 presumably for her younger
brother Paul, who was a cellist. These two pieces, the Fantasia in G Minor and Capriccio in A-flat Major, are full of character and contrast.

The Fantasia begins with a doleful melody in the piano, with the cello low in its range. The cello takes over with the melody much higher, heartfelt and cantabile. The mood suddenly changes into an energetic, faster section, before cleverly melting back into the opening theme. She closes off with another faster section, light and breezy, all the way to the pizzicato final chord.

The Capriccio begins with what amounts to a song without words, a highly lyrical melody in the cello, with a gently urging piano accompaniment. This opening section fades off nicely, and is immediately followed by a firestorm of Sturm und drang, the piano darting around the piano in brilliant display. It calms down somewhat before the storm whips up again. The storm dies down giving way to the return of the opening theme, this time more confident and assured. It ends calmly and serenely.

Selected Edition:
Breitkopf und Härtel

Bibliography:
Neuls-Bates, Carol. Women in Music (Northeastern Press, Boston, 1996)
Tillard, Françoise. Fanny Mendelssohn (Amadeus Press, Portland, 1992)

Recordings:
There are several recordings available.

Felix Mendelssohn (1809-1847) — Sonata No. 2 in D Major for Piano & Cello, Op. 58

Date of Composition: 1843
Date of Premiere: 1845
Premiered by: Alfred Piatti, cello with Mendelssohn, piano
Approximate Length: 26 min.

I. Allegro assai vivace (8 min)
II. Allegretto scherzando (6 min)
III. Adagio (5 min)
IV. Molto allegro e vivace (7 min)

Background Information:

Placed in the music history timeline between the Classical and Romantic eras, Felix Mendelssohn's music contains elements from both styles. His music bears the influence of Beethoven, with the frequent Sturm und Drang characters throughout, but also contains strong traces of the music of Bach. Mendelssohn spent a fair amount of his career in Leipzig, and was quite taken with his Baroque predecessor.

Both the tempestuous late Classical/early Romantic style and the ordered harmonic world of Bach are in full display in Mendelssohn's second cello sonata. He had written a couple of earlier works–a set of variations and a sonata–for piano and cello (the instrumentation appeared in that order on the score), but the Sonata in D Major, Op. 58 is perhaps the synthesis of Mendelssohn's prodigious compositional skills. Written at an extremely busy time for him–he had at least seven or eight pieces in the works at the same time–the sonata capitalizes on his considerable experience at this point in his life.

The sonata starts out with a driving energy in the piano underneath a soaring cello melody. In true deference to Beethoven, the two instruments are in constant conversation with one another trading material back and forth all throughout. A rather coy and playful Allegretto scherzando follows with the cello playing pizzicato in the main theme. A song-like second theme follows. The third movement is where Mendelssohn's debt to Bach is revealed the most in a lovely chorale-like theme in the piano; the cello melody once again is highly vocal, even mirroring a recitative style in certain moments. The last movement is a lightning-fast romp with an astonishing amount of notes in the piano part (perhaps evidence as to why Mendlessohn listed the piano first on the title page).

The sonata was initially dedicated to his brother Paul, who was a cellist, but later officially dedicated to Count Wielhorsky, a government official and a reported talented cellist (Clara Schumann played with him and referred to him as a true "artist".).

Selected Editions:
Barenreiter (Urtext)
G. Henle Verlag (Urtext)

Bibliography:
Berger, Melvin Guide to Sonatas (Anchor Books, New York, 1991)
Heinemann, Ernst-Günter, Preface, Mendelssohn, Felix "Sonata for Piano and Cello in D major", Munich: G. Henle Verlag, 2001.

Recordings:
Many commercial recordings by prominent cellists are available.

Darius Milhaud (1892-1974) — Cello Concerto No. 1, Op. 136

Date of Composition: 1934
Date of Premiere: June 28, 1935
Premiered by: Maurice Maréchel, cello with Désiré Émile-Inghelbrecht, conductor
Approximate Length: 14 min.

> I. Nonchalant (4 min)
> II. Grave (7 min)
> III. Joyeux (3 min)

Background Information:

Darius Milhaud was a member of a group of French composers in the twentieth century known as Les Six. Francis Poulenc and Arthur Honnegger were two of the other members. These composers were lumped together by a music critic who felt they all had a similar sensibility and approach to composing. These composers moved their music into different directions, away from German Romanticism, but also French stylings of Claude Debussy and Maurice Ravel. Milhaud, in particular, was taken with jazz and incorporated it profusely into his music (jazz greats Dave Brubeck and jazz-influenced pop composer Burt Bacharach were among his students).

His Cello Concerto No. 1 is one of five major cello works that he composed–a second cello concerto, a suite for cello and orchestra, an Elégie, and a sonata for cello and piano round out his cello oeuvre.

Written for cellist Maurice Maréchel, the work perfectly sums up the different elements in Milhaud's typical writing. The first movement starts out with a dramatic cello cadenza full of chunky chords and bellicose playing on the low strings. This makes it seem as if the piece is going to be somewhat harsh and modern sounding, however it suddenly whisks into a casual theme, which sounds like laid-back circus music with its quiet oom-pah accompaniment in the brass.

The second movement has Milhaud utilizing some discordant harmonies throughout creating a dark and dirge-like mood. The cello sings its line above the low-ranged orchestral accompaniment. The strings attempt to bring comfort to the cello, but the brass, in particular, keep the outlook desolate. This movement is perhaps a reflection of the previous year for Milhaud as he was quite ill for some time.

If the mood of the second movement is somber and potentially bleak, the third movement makes an abrupt about-face. Titled Joyeaux, it lightens the character considerably. Different styles of rhythms churn around, from a march to jazz to Spanish. It's a bright whirlwind of energy that finishes up the character with flair.

Edition:
Editions Salabert

Bibliography:
Dubal, David. The Essential Canon of Classical Music (New Point Press, New York, 2001)
Chen, Kuei-Fan. Historical Background and an Analysis of Darius Milhaud's Violoncello Concerto No. 1, Op. 136 dissertation for University of Georgia, 2017

Recordings:
Quite a few commercial recordings are available.

Georg Matthias Monn (1717-1750)   Cello Concerto in G Minor

Date of Composition: between 1740-1750
Date of Premiere: Unknown
Premiered by: Unknown
Approximate Complete Length: 19 min.

I. Allegro (6 min)
II. Adagio (8 min)
III. Allegro non tanto (5 min)

Background Information:
    Georg Matthias Monn was one of a handful of composers who served as links between the Baroque and Classical periods. Employed in Vienna at the Karlskirche, not much is known about his life or compositions. He left behind numerous instrumental works, including some early forms of the symphony and chamber music.
    The cello concerto is one of his most well-known works in large part to an edition and continuo realization by Arnold Schoenberg for Pablo Casals.

Selected Edition:
Edition Kunzelmann

Bibliography:
Friesenhagen, Andreas, Liner notes, "Cello Concertos", Jean-Guihen Queyras, cello, Freiberger Barockorchester, Petra Müllejans, Harmonia Mundi, 2004.

Recordings:
A handful of commercial recordings of this concerto are available.

Jesse Montgomery (b. 1981)   Divided for Cello & String Orchestra

Date of Composition: 2022
Date of Premiere: October 13, 2022
Premiered by: Tommy Mesa, cello; Sphinx Virtuosi; Carnegie Hall
Approximate Length: 12 min.

Background Information:
    Jesse Montgomery is an accomplished violinist and composer. Educated at Juilliard, New York University, and Yale, she was a founding member of the PubliQ and Catalyst String Quartets. She writes frequently for the Sphinx Organization and has been composer-in-residence for the Chicago Symphony Orchestra.

    On Divided, from the composer's website:

Divided for solo cello and orchestra is a response to the social and political unrest that has plagued our generation in the recent past. Specifically, the sense of helplessness that people seem to feel amidst a world that seems to be in constant crisis, whether it is over racial injustice, sexual or religious discrimination, greed and poverty, or climate change…The cello is a voice crying out to be heard, in chorus with a few, passionate and unrelenting, with the orchestra performing a gritty accompaniment.

Edition:
Score and parts available from the composer's website.

Bibliography:
Official website for the composer program notes, Accessed July 6, 2023, https://www.jessiemontgomery.com/work/divided/

Recordings:
No commercial recordings available, although a video of the premiere performance is on youtube.

Dorothy Rudd Moore (b. 1940) — Baroque Suite for Solo Cello

Date of Composition: 1965
Date of Premiere: Unknown
Premiered by: Kermit Moore, cello
Approximate Length: 14 min.

> I. Allegro (4 min)
> II. Molto adagio (6 min)
> III. Allegro vivace (4 min)

Background Information:

    Dorothy Rudd Moore has been a trailblazer in the world of classical music forging a successful path for herself in a predominantly all-male and all-white culture in the arts. She has said, "when I was growing up, I felt that all composers were white, male, and dead." (www.bruceduffie.com) She went on to study at Howard University and with Nadia Boulanger at the American Conservatory at Fontainebleau. A singer as well as a composer, she has written vocal, instrumental, orchestral and operatic works. She has taught at the Harlem School of the Arts and New York University. With her husband, cellist Kermit Moore, she founded the Society of Black Composers.

    Her "Baroque Suite for Solo Cello" was written for her husband. "I was influenced by two things–meeting him, and loving the Bach Suites."(www.bruceduffie.com) It is clear that both had a profound impact on the writing of this work. Using Bach as a jumping off point, Moore captures the feel and style of the Baroque instrumental suite, yet putting her own signature stamp on it. The swinging rhythms and unique meter of 5/8, gives it a more contemporary feel, without destroying the 18th-century construct. The second movement is a moving, expressive adagio, and the allegro vivace that follows is a joyous lilting movement with an infinitely catchy melody and a cheeky ending that brings the suite to a close with a warm smile. This is a wonderful tribute to Bach and the cello.

Edition:
American Composers Alliance

Bibliography:
Biography on the composer, Accessed August 12, 2023, https://composers.com/composers/dorothy-rudd-moore
Interview with Moore, Accessed August 12, 2023, http://www.bruceduffie.com/moore.html

Recordings:
A couple of recordings have been made of this work, including the dedicatee, Kermit Moore on the Performance Records label.

Nico Muhly (b. 1981) — Cello Concerto

Date of Composition: 2012
Date of Premiere: March 16, 2012
Premiered by: Oliver Coates, cello; André de Ridder, conductor; Britten Sinfonia
Approximate Length: 18 min.

> I. Fast (5 min)
> II. Slow (6 min)
> III. Fast (7 min)

Background Information:

Composer Nico Muhly has written for a variety of different mediums and ensembles. With commissions from such major institutions as the Metropolitan Opera, Los Angeles Philharmonic, Carnegie Hall, the Tallis Scholars, and the San Francisco Symphony, he music has become a ubiquitous presence in concert halls. He also has composed scores for a number of films, such as The Reader and Kill Your Darlings.

About his cello concerto, he writes:

When the Barbican asked me to write a concerto for Olly Coates and the Britten Sinfonia, I immediately started making plans. I wanted to write something formally traditional (fast-slow-fast) but with steadily developing content…The concerto ends enigmatically, with foghorn brass and a long, sustained drone from the cello.

Edition:
St. Rose Music Publishing

Bibliography:
Official website of the composer, Accessed July 7, 2023, https://nicomuhly.com/
Publisher page on the piece, Accessed July 7, 2023, https://www.wisemusicclassical.com/work/47277/Cello-Concerto--Nico-Muhly/

Recordings:
Thus far, there is only one commercial recording available performed by Zuill Bailey, cello and the Indianapolis Symphony on the Steinway & Sons label.

Thea Musgrave (b. 1928) — D.E.S.- In Celebration for Solo Cello

Date of Composition: 2016
Date of Premiere: June 17, 2017
Premiered by: Yehudi Hanani, cello
Approximate Length: 3 min.

Background Information:

Scottish-American composer Thea Musgrave has a rich catalog of music to her name, centered on big-scale dramatic works. A student of Nadia Boulanger in Paris, she eventually moved to the United States where she took up a series of teaching positions at schools such as UCLA, and Queens College in City University of New York. She is the recipient of two Guggenheim Fellowships, the Ivor Classical Music Award and a CBE from the Queen of England. Some of her more notable works include Space Play, her viola concerto and her opera Mary Queen of Scots.

D.E.S.-In Celebration for Solo Cello was written for cellist Yehudi Hanani, when he requested a piece for his concert honoring suffragettes. The initials D.E.S. stand for Dame Ethel Smyth, a leading suffragette, as well as composer (see entry on her cello sonata). Musgrave also uses those three letters to designate three different sections of the piece (Desolate, Energized and Stormy) as well as the three last notes (D, E and Eb).

[Musgrave has written a large-scale concerto for cello entitled From Darkness into Light, however, it is still under exclusivity rights by the premiere performer.)

Edition:
Chester Novello

Bibliography:
Official website for the composer, Accessed August 14, 2023, https://www.theamusgrave.com/biography
Publisher page on the piece, Accessed August 14, 2023, https://www.wisemusicclassical.com/work/56910/

Recordings:
No commercial recording has been made, but there are a couple of performances on youtube.

Michael Nyman (b. 1944) — On the Fiddle for Cello & Piano

Date of Composition: 1997
Date of Premiere: Unknown
Premiered by: Unknown
Approximate Length: 15 min.

I. Full Fathom Five (5 min)
II. Angelfish Decay (3 min)
III. Miserere Paraphrase (7 min)

Background Information:

Michael Nyman is a British composer who works in a variety of mediums. Best known for his film score to the film The Piano, which was nominated for Academy and BAFTA Awards for Best Original Score, he has composed symphonies, concerti, chamber music, and operas (such as The Man Who Mistook His Wife for a Hat). Besides The Piano, his other film scores include The Cook, The Thief, His Wife, & Her Lover, Prospero's Books, The End of the Affair, and Gattaca. In 1977, he formed his own ensemble called The Michael Nyman Band dedicated to playing his own works.. He has been awarded the CBE by the Queen of England.

On the Fiddle is a series of three vignettes taken from his score for the film The Cook, The Thief, His Wife, & Her Lover. The original version was for violin and piano; he later made a version for cello and piano.

[In 2007, Nyman wrote a cello concerto entitled Cello Concerto: A New Pavan for Sad Times. At press time, it is only available for rental.]

Editionn:
Chester Music

Bibliography:
Official website of the composer, Accessed August 14, 2023, http://www.michaelnyman.com/
Publisher page on the piece, Accessed August 14, 2023, https://www.wisemusicclassical.com/work/11419/On-the-Fiddle--Michael-Nyman/

Recordings:
The only commercial recording available is the violin and piano version.

Maria Theresia von Paradis (1759-1824) — Sicilienne for Cello & Piano

Date of Composition: Unknown
Date of Premiere: Unknown
Premiered by: Unknown
Approximate Length: 3 min.

Background Information:

Maria Theresia von Paradis was named after Empress Maria Theresia, who was her godmother; her father worked for the Empress' court. The young Paradis was tragically blinded at the age of two, but this didn't stop her from learning piano and composing music herself. She studied with Antonio Salieri and concertized around Europe for some time. In her later years, she founded a school to improve music education for young women.

The attribution of some of her compositions is in question, including this lovely Sicilienne, which was originally for violin and piano. It's possible that it was composed by the first editor, Samuel Dushkin, but it's not entirely clear, however, and he does credit this work to her.

Regardless, it's a graceful and elegant work, with its lilting piano part, and heartfelt cello melody. It is used most often and successfully as an encore piece.

It recently gained a spike in interest when the Sicilienne was performed by Sheku Kanneh-Mason at the royal wedding of Prince Harry and Megan Markle in 2018.

Edition:
Schott

Bibliography:
Neuls-Bates, Carol. Women in Music (Northeastern University Press, Boston, 1996)

Recordings:
There are quite a few recordings of this available.

Arvo Pärt (b. 1935) — Fratres

Date of Composition: 1977
Date of Premiere: Unknown
Premiered by: Unknown
Approximate Length: 11 min.

Background Information:

Fratres is one of the first works Pärt wrote upon coming to the West from his native Estonia. Leaving behind the largely dissonant and harsh style of his earlier works, Fratres embraces his newfound spiritualism and is one of the hallmarks of his tintinnabulation style.

The piece effectively exists in three planes: The melody, reminiscent of medieval chant; the accompaniment, which is often simple blocked chords; and a sustained drone throughout. It is structured as a theme and variations with the melody expanding and contracting in an arch shape over the course of the piece. It is both a meditative and ecstatic work for both the performers and listener.

Pärt first wrote the work without specific instrumentation, but later in 1980 wrote a specific version for violin and piano. Like others of his works (Spiegel im Spiegel, Summa, etc.), there exist numerous versions and instrumentations: string quartet, string orchestra, cello octet, and cello and piano. The cello and piano version doesn't contain the full sustaining drone--it is shared between the two instruments; it is not as omnipresent as in the other versions.

The word Fratres can be translated to brethren. Perhaps he meant it in the union of the three elements of the work, or it has a deeper, more spiritual meaning. It's very likely that both are correct and it's difficult not to hear the work and be moved and transformed by the combination of the static movement and the florid, churning music.

Edition:
Universal Edition

Bibliography:
Hillier, Paul. Arvo Pärt (Oxford Studies in Music) (Oxford Press, London, 1997).

Recordings:
There are a couple of recordings of this work that have been released.

Arvo Pärt (b. 1935)   Pro et Contra (Concerto for Cello & Orchestra)

Date of Composition: 1966
Date of Premiere: November 3, 1967
Premiered by: Toomas Velmet, cello; Neeme Järvi, conductor; Symphony Orchestra of the Estonian National Symphony Orchestra
Approximate Complete Length: 10 min.

> I. Maestoso (5:15)
> II. Largo (:45)
> III. Allegro (3:00)

Background Information:

    Listeners familiar with Arvo Pärt's works from the late '70's and beyond, might be shocked that this piece is from the same composer of such transcendent, contemplative works like Fratres, Spiegel im Spiegel, and Dona Nobis Pacem. Stemming from his earlier style and period, it is a combative, harsh and challenging work, with a good measure of sly humor thrown in as well.

    Pro et Contra, which translates to "For and Against", was commissioned by and dedicated to Mstislav Rostropovich, but premiered by cellist Toomas Velmet (although Rostropovich would perform it himself several months after). It is essentially a study in contrasts, stark sections of differing textures and sounds pitted against one another. One moment, it sits in a hushed whisper, the next, explodes in a fury of cacophony. Framed as a parody of a Baroque concerto grosso, it is scored for solo cello, a smaller concertino group, and orchestra.

    The first movement opens with a somewhat ironic, resounding D Major chord, followed immediately by a flare of blaring dissonance from the orchestra, and then an extended cadenza from the cello, in which the player utilizes various extended techniques: harmonics, sul ponticello, gooey glissandi, scratchy and swishy bow strokes, and percussive knocking on the body of the instrument among the most unique. The soloist and orchestra then trade impassioned, snarky gestures back and forth, with the cello having the last word.

    The second movement is a very brief, transitional, slightly expanded cadential progression posed to set up the third movement which is a feverish perpetual motion. The piece ends in a tongue-in-cheek model of a typical Baroque ending, in all of its pomp and formality.

    Despite the periods where the music sounds as though it is improvised, particularly in the cadenza section of the first movement, Pärt is quite meticulous in his notations and what type of effects he's looking for. It is a fiendishly tricky work that is representative of a style Pärt would soon leave behind for more transcendental things.

Edition:
Hans Sikorski Publishers (Study Score available for purchase; performing parts for rental)

Bibliography:
Hillier, Paul. Arvo Pärt (Oxford Studies in Music) (Oxford Press, London, 1997).
Official page on the piece, accessed June 2020, https://www.arvopart.ee/en/arvo-part/work/577/

Recordings:
There are few recordings of this work available.

Arvo Pärt (b. 1935) — Spiegel im Spiegel

Date of Composition: 1978
Date of Premiere: Unknown
Premiered by: Unknown
Approximate Complete Length: 8 min.

Background Information:

 Spiegel im Spiegel is a tender and beautiful meditation for cello and piano, showcasing Pärt's spiritual and mystical side, and was the last piece he composed before leaving his homeland of Estonia. The title translates as "mirror in the mirror" and is representative of Pärt's tintinnabular (ringing of bells) style, where one voice arpeggiates the tonic triad (in this instance, the piano), while the other moves in a stepwise direction (the cello has a long, drawn out, stepwise melody which both ascends and descends).

 Pärt describes this style as: "Tintinnabulation is an area I sometimes wander into when I am searching for answers – in my life, my music, my work. In my dark hours, I have the certain feeling that everything outside this one thing has no meaning. The complex and many-faceted only confuses me, and I must search for unity. What is it, this one thing, and how do I find my way to it? Traces of this perfect thing appear in many guises – and everything that is unimportant falls away. Tintinnabulation is like this. Here I am alone with silence. I have discovered it is enough when a single note is beautifully played. This one note, or a silent beat, or a moment of silence, comforts me. I work with very few elements—with one voice, with two voices. I build with the most primitive materials—with the triad, with one specific tonality. The three notes of a triad are like bells. And that is why I call it tintinnabulation." (Hillier, pp. 87).

 Originally written for violin and piano, Pärt has created numerous other versions of this work for different instruments.

Edition:
Universal Edition, 1996

Bibliography:
Hillier, Paul. Arvo Pärt (Oxford Studies in Music) (Oxford Press, London, 1997).
Shenton, Andrew, ed. The Cambridge Guide to Arvo Pärt (Cambridge Companions to Music) (Cambridge University Press, Cambridge, 2012).

Recordings:
There are a couple of commercial recordings of the version for cello and piano. Many more exist of the violin and piano version.

Dora Pejačević (1885-1923) — Sonata in E Minor, Op. 35 for Cello & Piano

Date of Composition: 1913
Date of Premiere: unknown
Premiered by: unknown
Approximate Length: 28 min.

> I. Allegro moderato (7 min)
> II. Scherzo allegro (7 min)
> III. Adagio sostenuto (7 min)
> IV. Allegro comodo (7 min)

Background Information:

Hungarian-born Dora Pejačević was a composer and violinist whose heritage was Croatian, her father being a Croatian count. Her mother was a musician and started teaching Dora from a young age. Though largely self-taught, and incredibly well-read, she began composing her first works as a teenager. The majority of works from her oeuvre veer towards chamber music, although her Symphony in F-sharp minor is one her best known works.

Her Cello Sonata in E Minor was written in 1913. It's a gorgeous work bursting at the seams with long lyrical lines. The opening movement soars and dives in passionate exchanges between the piano and cello. The scherzo is light and energetic, with a tender second theme. The third movement Adagio is a soulful, deep movement, with the cello spending most of the beginning section low in its range. The sun comes out for the fourth movement, as it is in the key of E Major, both instruments reveling in the brightness of the tonality.

Edition:
Muzički Informativni Centar

Bibliography:
Biography on the composer, Accessed August 10, 2023, http://www.maudpowell.org/signature/Portals/0/pdfs/New%20Articles/Dora%20Pejacevic%20for%20Signature.pdf
Farny, Natasha. "Worthy of the Canon: Romantic Sonatas by Women" (College Music Symposium, Vol. 61, No. 2, 2021)

Recordings:
A couple of commercial recordings have been released of this sonata.

Krzysztof Penderecki (1933-2020) — Cello Concerto No. 2

Date of Composition: 1982
Date of Premiere: 1983
Premiered by: Mstislav Rostropovich, cello; Krzysztof Penderecki, conductor, Berlin Philharmonic Orchestra
Approximate Length: 33 min.

> I. Andante con moto
> II. Vivo
> III. Tempo 1
> IV. Allegretto
> V. Lento
> VI. Allegretto
> VII. Poco meno mosso
> VIII. Tempo 1
> [played without pause]

Background Information:

Krzysztof Penderecki was a towering composer of Polish descent. His works have been performed all over the world, and inspired numerous orchestras, conductors and performers to commission works from him. Penderecki wrote music featuring a wide variety of extended techniques (his Threnody for the Victims of Hiroshima is a masterclass in extended sounds and colors), atonality and aleatoric elements, but often wove in forms and techniques from early, more traditional styles such as Renaissance, Baroque and Classical.

Penderecki wrote a number of works for the cello, both on the large scale in the form of works with orchestra, as well as smaller, unaccompanied works. Many of his cello works were inspired by the cellist Siegried Palm, as well as Mstislav Rostropovich.

His Cello Concerto No. 2 was premiered in 1983 by Rostropovich and moves beyond the standard three movement format typical of concerti, but rather an 8-section work, played without a break. The concerto is full of Penderecki's favored tonal language: strange, otherworldly, often haunting semi-tones, glissandi, and dramatic outbursts from the orchestra. The music careens through wide-ranging textures from eerie, high-pitched dissonances, to brutal, blaring motives, to yearning, pleading lines in the cello, to skittish, scrambly fast passages bristling with nervous energy. It's a huge work and demonstrates what a powerful composer Penderecki was.

Edition:
Schott Editions

Bibliography:
Biography on the composer, Accessed August 12, 2023, https://www.britannica.com/biography/Krzysztof-Penderecki
Program notes, Accessed August 12, 2023, https://onpolishmusic.com/prog-notes/%E2%80%A2-1999-penderecki-cello-concerto-no-2/

Recordings:
Many cellists have recorded this concerto in commercial releases, notably Rostropovich and Penderecki.

Coleridge-Taylor Perkinson (1932-2004)   Lamentations: Black/Folk Song Suite for Solo Cello

Date of Composition: 1973
Date of Premiere: 1973
Premiered by: Ronald Lipscomb, cello in New York City
Approximate Length: 17 min.

> I. Fuguing Tune (4 min)
> II. Song Form (2 min)
> III. Calvary Ostinato (3 min)
> IV. Perpetual Motion (6 min)

Background Information:

    Coleridge-Taylor Perkinson was named after the famous Black British composer, Samuel Coleridge-Taylor, whom Perkinson's mother greatly admired. Perkinson followed in the footsteps of his namesake and studied music, eventually studying at the Manhattan School of Music and Princeton University. He also studied conducting in Europe.

    In 1965, he co-founded the Symphony of the New World, the first multi-racial orchestra in the United States. He also was artistic director of the Alvin Ailey American Dance Theater. Steeped in the traditional western Classical style, he was equally at home with jazz, blues, and other popular styles; they all found their way into his pieces.

    Lamentations: Black/Folk Suite for Solo Cello is a multi-movement work that, while building on the traditional instrumental suite, also incorporates African American songs into the texture. Perkinson said that, "The common denominator of these tunes is the reflection and statement of a people's crying out." (content.thespco.org)

    The first movement "Fuguing Tune" combines a bluesy-tune into a polyphonic package, a not-so-subtle nod to Bach. "Song-Form" is a languid, slow jazzy movement which repeats the opening sections throughout. The third movement "Calvary Ostinato" is an all-pizzicato movement with a continuous bass groove, and a melody based on a spiritual with the line "Surely He died on Calvary" as its refrain. The last movement is a brilliant perpetual motion with energetic string crossings surrounding a jazzy melody.

Edition:
Lauren Keiser Music Publishing

Bibliography:
Publisher page on the composer, Accessed August 12, 2023, https://www.keisersouthernmusic.com/composers/coleridge-taylor-perkinson
Program notes, Accessed August 12, 2023, https://content.thespco.org/music/concert-library/composition/lamentations-blackfolk-song-suite-for-solo-cello-coleridge-taylor-perkinson

Recordings:
A few commercial recordings have been made, as well as a number of performances on youtube.

Astor Piazzolla (1921-1992) — Le Grande Tango for Cello & Piano

Date of Composition: 1982
Date of Premiere: 1990
Premiered by: Mstislav Rostropovich, cello
Approximate Length: 11 min.

Background Information:

It's hard to think of any one composer who brought the tango—the fiery, yet elegant, dance from Argentina—to the masses like Astor Piazzolla. Certainly, he brought it to the concert hall more than any other composer has done. Piazzolla started his composition journey in a rather traditional way, writing in a more European style. It was his study with Nadia Boulanger who, when she heard the tango in his music, told him, "Here's Piazzolla, don't ever leave him!" (www.wiseclassical.com) Thus, his fate was sealed and the tango, as well as other Argentinian music became the lifeblood of his pieces.

Le Grande Tango is exactly as the title suggests: a grand tango. It's a big piece, one that has several sections, each exploring different sides or shades of the tango. There's the foot-stomping, grounded tango that opens the work, there's the more quiet and sultry tango, there's the singing and rhapsodic tango, and finally the up-tempo, joyous tango. It's evocative music that suggests the dancers and their choreography throughout.

Edition:
Berben

Bibliography:
Publisher page on the composer, Accessed August 15, 2023, https://www.wisemusicclassical.com/composer/4933/Astor-Piazzolla/

Recordings:
Many recordings have been made of this work.

David Popper (1843-1913) Hungarian Rhapsody, Op. 68
for Cello & Piano

Date of Composition: 1893
Date of Premiere: April 4, 1893
Premiered by: David Popper, cello
Approximate Length: 8 min.

Background Information:
In the nineteenth century, pianists had Chopin and Liszt. Violinists had Paganini and later Ysaÿe. Cellists had David Popper as the preeminent virtuoso performer on their instrument.

Hungarian cellist Popper had a brilliant career, playing for and with some of the biggest luminaries in the European music world of the time. He played under Wagner's baton, performed recitals with Johannes Brahms, Clara Schumann, and Béla Bartók. He was in two of the most esteemed professional string quartets, and he was professor of cello at the Franz Liszt Academy for many years.

As a composer, he wrote a huge amount for cello, concerti, sonatas, and all kinds of show pieces. However, his legacy has been cemented by his method book, the Hohe Schule des Violoncellospiels, Op. 73, a collection of 40 etudes. It is not an understatement to say that this method book is the indispensable etude collection of virtually every cellist studying, playing and teaching today. It's entirely fundamental and foundational to the development of a cellist.

It is a bit of a sad note to realize that a huge majority of Popper's vast array of solo pieces is largely ignored, and that most people only know him through his etudes. His Ungarische Rhapsodie, Op. 68 (Hungarian Rhapsody) is one of the few expectations that gets a regular amount of study and performance.

The Rhapsody is in six sections, all linked together with each section based on a different Hungarian folk song or tune. There are incredibly fast sections, slow, expressive sections, cadenzas, thumb position octaves; Popper packs a lot in eight minutes. It's a show-stopping, virtuosic work that puts any cellist through their paces.

It was premiered first in a cello and piano version, but was released with an orchestra accompaniment a number of years later.

Selected Editions:
International Edition
Yuriy Leonovich Critical Edition

Bibliography:
Official page on the composer, Accessed August 18, 2023, https://www.davidpopper.org/
Official page on the piece, Accessed August 18, 2023, https://www.davidpopper.org/ungarische-rhapsodie-hungarian-rhapsody
Biography on the composer, Accessed August 18, 2023, https://www.cellobello.org/cello-blog/artistic-vision/a-biographical-sketch-of-david-popper/

Recordings:
Many commercial recordings have been released of this and other of Popper's solo works.

Nicola Porpora (1686-1768) — 6 Cello Sonatas

Date of Compositions: Unknown
Date of Premiere: Unknown
Premiered by: perhaps Giovanni Batista Constanzi
Approximate Lengths:

Sonata No. 1 in C Major: 10 min
Sonata No. 2 in G Minor: 10 min
Sonata No. 3 in G Major: 10 min
Sonata No. 4 in B Major: 11 min
Sonata No. 5 in C Minor: 12 min
Sonata No. 6 in G Major: 10 min

Background Information:

A key figure in the Neapolitan Baroque music scene, today, Nicola Porpora is known mostly for his extravagant operatic works and being the teacher of the famed castrato, Farinelli. However, he did leave behind a fair amount of instrumental works, which suggests that chamber music was not overlooked in the predominantly theatrical Italian cities of that time period.

Porpora wrote one cello concerto and six sonatas for cello, violins and basso continuo. Even though they are listed as sonatas for cello, they are actually written more as duos for cello and violin, with the cello taking on a slightly more prominent solo role. The manuscript also attributes the composition to cellist Giovanni Batista Constanza, but most scholars think he was only in an advisory role, and not necessarily creating any of the actual musical content. The six sonatas are charming chamber works, predating the more overtly soloistic Vivaldi sonatas, that show the cello rapidly emerging into a solo instrument.

Selected Editions:
The London edition of all six sonatas published in the eighteenth century is available on imslp.org
Musedita

Bibliography:
Bukofzer, Manfred F. Music in the Baroque Era (W.W. Norton & Company, Inc., 1947).
Fiore, Carlo, Liner notes, Porpora Nicola, "6 Cello Sonatas", Adriano Maria Fazio, cello, Brilliant Classics, 2016.

Recordings:
There are a couple of recordings available mostly on period instruments.

Francis Poulenc (1899-1963) — Sonata for Cello & Piano, FP. 143

Date of Composition: 1948
Date of Premiere: May 18, 1949
Premiered by: Pierre Fournier, cello; Francis Poulenc, piano
Approximate Length: 23 min.

I. Allegro - Tempo di Marcia (6 min)
II. Cavatine (7 min)
III. Ballabile (4 min)
IV. Finale (6 min)

Background Information:

Despite being quoted as saying that he preferred woodwinds to stringed instruments, composer and pianist Francis Poulenc still ended up composing both a sonata for violin and a sonata for cello. The idea for a cello sonata had apparently been with Poulenc for some time, as sketches for a cello piece showed up as early as 1940. The subsequent World War II put a lot of his compositions on hold, including that of the cello sonata.

He finally got serious about it in 1948, but sensing his limitations at writing for an instrument he wasn't overly familiar with, he turned to cellist Pierre Founier for assistance in crafting the cello part. Fournier would go on to premiere the work with Poulenc at the piano, as well as be the dedicatee of the piece.

The sonata is in four movements beginning with a jaunty march in the first movement, a tender slow movement with beautiful, elegant singing lines, a delightful scherzo, and a majestic finale. There are numerous touches throughout that are typical, quirky Poulenc, as well as echoes of other twentieth-century French composers Debussy, Ravel and Satie.

Edition:
Heugel Edition

Bibliography:
Berger, Melvin Guide to Sonatas (Anchor Books, New York, 1991).

Recordings:
Many of the major cellists have made commercial recordings of this sonata.

Paola Prestini (b. 1975) — To Tell a Story for Solo Cello & Electronics

Date of Composition: 2019
Date of Premiere: 2019
Premiered by: Amanda Gookin, cello
Approximate Length: 12 min.

Background Information:

    Italian-born, American composer Paolo Prestini is a dynamic and bold composer of music that transcends boundaries. She has written operas, film scores, symphonic, choral and chamber works. Often incorporating visual or electronic elements into her music, this highlights her other interests from the environment to the cosmos. She is the co-founder and artistic director of National Sawdust, and started the Hildegard Commission to support women and marginalized composers.

    To Tell a Story was commissioned by Amanda Gookin for her Forward Music Project 2.0 which consisted of soliciting music from five female composers to write multimedia works for solo cello that elevate the issue of female empowerment.

    From an interview about this piece, Prestini says:

When Amanda asked me to create this work for her, it was right around the time of the Kavanaugh hearings. Like most people, I was unable to focus and began thinking about the value of truth, and how Blasey Ford's truth had been manipulated violently into fiction. I began to think about whose voice, steadying and calm, could guide me through the difference between story and fiction, and quite naturally, fell upon an interview with Susan Sontag from 1983 where the interviewer had asked her about the power of storytelling…I began to structure the interview as an outline to the work, cutting apart the sound file and sampling excerpts of the interview…The woman's voice instigates points of departure, her breaths resulting from cutting out all the speaking during the talk and just leaving her remaining breaths, while the cello tells the story in the abstract way that society has continued to require of women."

Edition:

https://www.paolaprestini.com/compositions/to-tell-a-story

Bibliography:

Official website of the composer, Accessed August 3, 2023, https://www.paolaprestini.com/
Biography on the composer, Accessed August 3, 2023, https://www.forwardmusicproject.com/20-biographies/paola-prestini

Recordings:

Amanda Gookin recorded this work, as well as the other commissioned works from her Forward Music 2.0 project, and released it on the Bright Shiny Things label.

Florence Price (1887-1953) — Adoration for Cello & Piano

Date of Composition: 1951/Cello arr. 2020
Date of Premiere: Unknown
Premiered by: Unknown
Approximate Length: 4 min.

Background Information:
Florence Price was a trailblazer in many ways during her life. As an African-American woman living in the south, she faced many hardships due to her gender and her race. She started music lessons at a young age from her mother, and excelled at the piano, later learning to play the organ and the violin. She ended up studying keyboard as well as composition at the New England Conservatory in Boston. After graduation (in which she earned her double degree in just three years), she returned to her hometown in Arkansas where she began teaching. To escape the racial tensions prevalent in the south, she moved to Chicago.

Once in Chicago, her composition career really moved forward. She continued to study, working with composers such as Carl Busch and Leo Sowerby. To make ends meet, she played organ during silent movies. In 1932, her big break came when she won first and third place in the Wanamaker Foundation Awards for her Symphony in E Minor and her piano sonata. The following year, the Chicago Symphony performed her Symphony, making it the first major orchestra to perform a symphonic work by a African-American woman composer.

After her death in 1953, only a handful of her pieces were known, but in 2009, a large collection of her music scores were found in an abandoned summer house she had once used. This greatly transformed her legacy, proving that she had composed far more than people had realized. The breadth and quality of her writing was made readily apparent and she is now becoming more and more part of the standard canon.

Her work Adoration—one of the lost scores rediscovered in 2009–was originally for organ, but later was arranged for violin and string orchestra. Since then, numerous transcriptions have been made, including one for cello and piano. It's a sweet and enchanting work. Although it's not known what precisely inspired the title, since its origin was a piece for organ, it's quite possible it has spiritual implications.

Edition:
Schirmer

Bibliography:
Fuller, Sophie. The Pandora Guide to Woman Composers: Britain and the United States 1629-Present (Pandora Books, 1994).
Official website of the composer, Accessed August 19, 2023, https://florenceprice.com/

Recordings:
To date, there doesn't seem to be commercially released recordings of the cello and piano version, although there is of the violin transcription. There are, however, quite a few performances of the cello version on youtube.

Gabriel Prokofiev (b. 1975) — Cello Multitracks

Date of Composition: 2011
Date of Premiere: May 17, 2011
Premiered by: Peter Gregson, cello (and recorded backing tracks)
Approximate Length: 17 min.

> I. Outta Pulsor (5 min)
> II. Jerk Driver (3 min)
> III. Float Dance (4 min)
> IV. Tuff Strum (4 min)

Background Information:

Gabriel Prokofiev is the grandson of famed Russian composer, Sergei Prokofiev. His compositional style veers quite a ways from his famous relative often combining electronics and manipulated elements with live acoustic instruments.

In 2011, he wrote a work entitled Cello Multitracks for solo cello and pre-recorded 8-part cello ensemble. About the piece, Prokofiev writes:

The solo cellist is the only live human in this ensemble; he/she plays live and in concert alongside a virtual cello ensemble of 8 loud-speakers which playback multitrack recordings of eight cello parts…'Cello Multitracks' is a dance suite for cello nonet; originally conceptualized as a multitrack work to be recorded by just one cellist.

He has also written a concerto in 2013 for Cello, Orchestra and Turntables, however, at press time, it is only available to rent by special request from the publisher.

Edition:

Chester Music Publications (Note: the score comes with parts for the 8 accompanying cello parts for the option of playing them with live players. Otherwise upon request, the backing tracks originally recorded by Peter Gregson are available.)

Bibliography:

Official website for the composer, Accessed August 3, 2023, https://www.gabrielprokofiev.com/cello-multitracks-2011

Recordings:

Peter Gregson has released a recording on the Nonclassical label. In addition, it includes a number of remixes of the individual movements.

Sergei Prokofiev (1891-1953) — Sinfonia Concertante for Cello and Orchestra, Op. 125

Date of Composition: 1950
Date of Premiere: 1952
Premiered by: Mstislav Rostropovich, cello; Sviatoslav Richter, conductor, Moscow Youth Symphony. Revised, final version premiered in 1954 with Rostropovich and Thomas Jensen conducting the Danish State Radio Symphony.
Approximate Length: 40 min.

I. Andante (11 min)
II. Allegro (18 min)
III. Andante con moto - Allegretto - Allegro marcato (11 min)

Background Information:

Sergei Prokofiev wrote his famous Symphony-Concerto for Cello after hearing the great Russian cellist, Mstislav Rostropovich perform live. He wrote a cello sonata with Slava in mind and shortly following wrote this epic work for him. There exists an earlier cello concerto in Prokofiev's catalog, however, for most people, this is the only cello concerto that Prokofiev wrote. Originally known as Concerto No. 2, or the Symphony-Concerto, it's better known as the Sinfonia Concertante today.

Written and tailored specifically for Rostropovich's prodigious talent at the cello, it's an epic work. The cello part is, naturally, incredibly soloistic, but given the piece's length, scope and the solo part's integration into the orchestral part, it earned the name of Symphony-Concerto.

This concerto is largely considered one of the (if not, *the*) most difficult pieces written for the cello. Rostropovich apparently told Prokofiev that many cellists had complained about the severity of the work and suggested that maybe he could rewrite some of the more difficult passages to make it a little more manageable. "He said he would do it, of course, but he would make a point of marking the corresponding places in the piano score, not with the word ossia which means "alternative" but facilitazione, meaning "simplified". When I asked him what he meant by that, he replied, "Surely no self-respecting musician would want to play a 'simplified' version." (Schlifstein)

It would be one of the last major pieces he worked on before his death in 1953.

Edition:
Boosey & Hawkes

Bibliography:
Schlifstein, S. Sergei Prokofiev: Autobiography, Articles, Reminiscences (University Press of the Pacific, Hawaii, 2000)

Recordings:
Numerous commercial recordings by some of the great cellists are available, however, Rostropovich's recordings are the paradigm.

Sergei Prokofiev (1891-1953) — Sonata in C Major, Op. 119 for Cello & Piano

Date of Composition: 1949
Date of Premiere: March 1, 1950
Premiered by: Mstislav Rostropovich, cello; Sviatoslav Richter, piano
Approximate Length: 23 min.

> I. Andante grave (11 min)
> II. Moderato (5 min)
> III. Allegro, ma non troppo (7 min)

Background Information:
Famed Russian composer Sergei Prokofiev had a long and fruitful collaborative relationship with famed Russian cellist Mstislav Rostropovich yielding several major works for cello including a solo sonata and concerto (see entry on his Sinfonia Concertante). Before meeting Slava, he had written a couple of smaller works for cello as well as an earlier cello concerto, but after attending a performance of Rostropovich, he became newly inspired to write for the instrument (as well as Rostropovich). At the performance, Prokofiev mentioned to Rostropovich that he was writing a cello sonata and would send it to him. A short while later, Slava received an invitation to come to Prokofiev's home to read through the sonata. He did, with Prokofiev at the piano.

Slava remembers, "I was very much surprised to see how quickly he had forgotten his own music–he played the accompaniment as if he had never seen it before." Apparently this was a common occurrence with the composer, rapidly forgetting what he had only recently written. Only after a number of repeated times playing through the piece would it start to become familiar again.

On the occasion of his fiftieth birthday, Prokofiev outlined the five qualities he claimed were to be found in his music: classicism, innovation, motor element, lyricism and the grotesque. All of these (and more) can be found throughout the cello sonata.

Working within the standard sonata-allegro template, Prokofiev infuses the music with highly lyrical melodies, fits of extreme virtuosity and an overall good-natured spirit. The cello and the piano complement one another as if they were two old friends embroiled in a deep philosophical conversation long into the night.

Prokofiev writes incredibly idiomatically for the cello, no doubt helped by Rostropovich's input, and the whole sonata is a tour de force for both instruments. It remains one of the quintessential sonatas of the twentieth century.

Selected Editions:
Sikorski Edition
Peters Edition
International Publications

Bibliography:
Berger, Melvin Guide to Sonatas (Anchor Books, New York, 1991).
Schlifstein, S. Sergei Prokofiev: Autobiography, Articles, Reminiscences (University Press of the Pacific, Hawaii, 2000)

Recordings:
Most of the major cellists have released commercial recordings, however the Rostropovich recordings (he made a couple) are the best place to start.

Blaž Pucihar (b. 1977) — Summer Sonata for Cello & Piano, Op. 8

Date of Composition: 2005
Date of Premiere: Unknown
Premiered by: Igor Mitrović, cello; Blaž Pucihar, piano
Approximate Length: 9 min.

Background Information:

    Slovenian composer and pianist Blaž Pucihar composes dynamic and highly lyrical pieces heavily steeped in jazz. His wife, flutist Ana Kavčič Pucihar, has inspired from him a wealth of flute compositions and they have collaborated on a children's book together entitled "Luna's Magic Flute".

    His Summer Sonata for Cello and Piano was composed in 2005 and contains several interlocking sections. The mood of the piece is warm and inviting, contrasted with episodes of quippy, jaunty rhythms clearly influenced by jazz.

Edition:
Available as a download from the composer's website

Bibliography:
Official website of the composer, Accessed August 8, 2023, https://puciharmusic.net/about-blaz/

Recordings:
A commercial recording is available from cellist Nikolaj Sajko.

Kevin Puts (b. 1972) — Air for Cello & Piano

Date of Composition: 2004
Date of Premiere: September 2004
Premiered by: Andres Diaz, cello; Kevin Puts, piano
Approximate Length: 8 min.

Background Information:
      Kevin Puts is one of the most celebrated American composers working today. Winner of the Pulitzer Prize for his opera Silent Night, not to mention various Grammy awards, he has received major commissions, most notably from the Metropolitan Opera and the Philadelphia Orchestra for an opera adaptation of The Hours which was released to great acclaim.

      In 2004, he wrote a collection called Four Airs for four different solo instruments and piano with the movement for cello and piano being the second of the group. It has been published, and thus performed, on its own as a standalone piece.

Edition:
Aperto Press

Bibliography:
Official website of the composer, Accessed August 3, 2023, https://www.kevinputs.com/works/air

Recordings:
A recording has been released by the Bridgehampton Chamber Festival on their own label, bcmf records.

Sergei Rachmaninoff (1873-1943)

Sonata in G Minor, Op. 19 for Cello & Piano

Date of Composition: 1901
Date of Premiere: December 2, 1901
Premiered by: Anatolly Brandukov, cello; Sergei Rachmaninoff, piano
Approximate Length: 34 min.

> I. Lento - Allegro moderato (13 min)
> II. Allegro scherzando (6 min)
> III. Andante (6 min)
> IV. Allegro mosso (9 min)

Background Information:

Sergei Rachmaninoff was one of the titans of the piano in the early twentieth century. Known for his incredible technique at the instrument, his own compositional works for the instrument were tailor-made for him. They are virtuosic, make no mistake, but never at the expense of expression. They are highly Romantic, in every sense of the term.

Where Rachmaninoff was initially less successful was his works not involving the piano. Upon release of his First Symphony in 1897, the reception was very unfavorable, sending him into a deep depression. Seeking psychiatric help, he eventually found the mental and emotional strength to continue composing. He came back with a triumph in the form of his Second Piano Concerto which received universal acclaim, eventually becoming one of the most famous piano concertos of all time.

His next piece would be the cello sonata. It's not entirely clear what inspired him to compose this piece; he wrote no other instrumental chamber sonatas. More than likely it was his close friendship with cellist Anatolly Brandukov who premiered the piece and received the dedication.

When premiered, the sonata was a success, and quickly entered into the canon of cello sonatas. As expected, the piano part is considerable, often regarded as one of the most difficult cello sonata accompaniments (as well as inspiring criticisms that the work is highly unbalanced in favor of the piano). However, the cello is not just a passenger along for the ride to enjoy the view. The piano does introduce virtually all of the main themes, but the cello part is substantive and carries a lot of the musical weight of the work.

The first movement soars and winds around in long phrases, set off by a near-obsession with the minor second interval, which occurs incessantly throughout. The second movement is a blustery, dark night scherzo that explodes with mounting tension at various points, contrasted with a dolce second theme. The last movement is an epic finale, triumphant and dazzling, a real tour de force for both instruments.

The true highlight, though, is the third movement Andante, which is about as heart-melting and tender as music can get. It's operatic, consoling, and beautiful, and we cellists should be forever thankful Rachmaninoff wrote this movement for us to play.

Editions:
International Music Company
Boosey & Hawkes

Bibliography:
Berger, Melvin Guide to Sonatas (Anchor Books, New York, 1991).

Recordings:
Many commercial recordings by some of the great cellists have been released.

Kaitlyn Raitz (b.1989) — Not So Simple for Solo Cello

Date of Composition: 2022
Date of Premiere: Unknown
Premiered by: Kaitlyn Raitz, cello
Approximate Length: 5 min.

Background Information:

Kaitlyn Raitz is a cellist, composer, and singer-songwriter. Her background and interests have allowed her to combine her traditional, foundational training, with a more pop-indie sensibility of improv and style. She has written a large collection of music for cello, whether solo, duo or cello ensemble. Regular features include song-like melodies, shimmery harmonics, and folksy plucking.

Her solo work Not So Simple was written in 2022. Commissioned by the Lotus Chamber Music Collective, it is Raitz's own set of variations on the Shaker song "Simple Gifts".

Edition:
Available from the composer's website

Bibliography:
Official website of the composer, Accessed August 8, 2023, https://www.kaitlynraitz.com/sheetmusic/not-so-simple-solo-cello

Recordings:
No recording has been made as of press time.

Shulamit Ran (b. 1949) — Fantasy Variations for Solo Cello

Date of Composition: 1979 (revised 1984)
Date of Premiere: Unknown
Premiered by: André Emelianoff, cello
Approximate Length: 14 min.

Background Information:

Israeli-born composer, Shulamit Ran has carved out a highly successful composing career writing across all genres. Winning the Pulitzer Prize in 1991 for her Mass, she has been commissioned by some of the top ensembles and artists in the world, including a seven-year stint as the composer-in-residence for the Chicago Symphony. She has been professor of composition at the University of Chicago since 1973.

Her work "Fantasy Variations" for Solo Cello is her second work for cello to involve the word 'fantasy' in the title. An earlier work, "Three Fantasy Pieces" exists in a version for cello and piano, and later in a cello and orchestra version.

"Fantasy Variations" was commissioned by cellist André Emelianoff. It is a twelve minute work that includes both standard and modern notation, taking the cello from its lowest note to its highest registers. It's a technically ferocious and powerful work that takes both the performer and the audience on a riotous journey before ending on an ethereal chord made up of harmonics.

Edition:
Theodore Presser

Bibliography:
Faculty biography page on the composer, Accessed August 4, 2023, https://music.uchicago.edu/people/shulamit-ran
Guzzo, Anne M. Liner notes, Ran, Shumalit "Fantasy Variations", Peabody Trio, New World Records, 2002.

Recordings:
A commercial recording was made by members of the Peabody Trio on the New World Records in 2002.

Max Reger (1873-1916) — Three Suites for Solo Cello, Op. 131c

Date of Composition: 1914
Date of Premiere: Unknown
Premiered by: Unknown
Approximate Length: 19 min. (average of the three)

I. Suite No. 1 in G Major (13 min)
Präludium. Vivace
Adagio
Fuga. Allegro
II. Suite No. 2 in d minor (20 min)
Präludium. Largo
Gavotte. Allegretto
Largo
Gigue. Vivace
III. Suite No. 3 in a minor (22 min)
Präludium. Sostenuto
Scherzo. Vivace
Andante con variazioni finale

Background Information:

Max Reger's music occupies a space between the old and the new. Fascinated with the forms and technique from the Baroque and Classical period, he was also a man of his time, using the harmonic language of the day in his music as well. In that regard, he possesses a connection to Johannes Brahms who approached composition from a similar place, although Brahms never went as far in his choice of harmony.

Reger, most known for his enormous output for the organ and piano, wrote a fair amount of music for strings as well. It isn't apparent what prompted Reger to write the three unaccompanied suites for solo cello, however, they are part of a trilogy of sorts; Reger wrote a set of solo pieces for violin and for viola around the same time. Although each of the cello suites are dedicated to a different cellist (1: Julius Klengel, 2: Hugo Becker and 3: Paul Grümmer), there isn't clear information on who premiered them and when. They were published in 1915.

The influence of J.S. Bach's Cello Suites are obvious, especially in the first suite, with its slight paraphrasing of the famous opening of the G Major Prelude. The keys of Reger's suites almost completely match those of the first suites of Bach's: Suite 1 G Major, Suite 2 D Minor,--instead of C Major for the third suite like Bach's, Reger goes to the relative minor. As he goes through each suite, they seem to get less and less overly dependent on Bach, although the Suite-structure is still there. Each suite opens up with a Prelude followed by some Baroque dances common to suites, with other types of movements thrown in.

Selected Edition:
G. Henle Verlag (Urtext)

Bibliography:
Dubal, David. The Essential Canon of Classical Music (North Point Press, New York, 2001)
Shigihara, Susanne, Preface, Reger, Max "Three Suites for Solo Cello", Munich: G. Henle Verlag, 1992.

Recordings:
A number of cellists have made commercial recordings of these suites.

Ottorini Respighi (1879-1936)

Adagio con Variazione for Cello & Orchestra

Date of Composition: 1921
Date of Premiere: Unknown
Premiered by: Unknown
Approximate Length: 13 min.

Background Information:

If ever a composer captured the sights and sounds of Italy, it was Ottorino Respighi. Famous for his programmatic orchestral works, I Pini di Roma, (The Pines of Rome), and Le Fontane di Roma (The Fountains of Rome), Respighi became known for his ability to paint imagery with the instruments of the orchestra (something he no doubt picked up from his teacher, Rimsky-Korsakov).

Respighi had written a cello concerto in the early years of the century, however, for some reason, it remained unpublished. Some twenty years later, he came back to the concerto, focusing and ultimately releasing the slow movement on its own.

The Adagio con Variazione, while not as dazzling and spectacular as his orchestral tone poems, it is, nevertheless, a beautiful work, with a tender, operatic theme. The variations all flow from this opening theme, generally retaining the lyrical feel to it, with an extended English horn solo included. Although there are some mildly virtuosic passages for the cello, it mostly is in full cantabile mode throughout.

Selected Editions:
International
Masters Music Publications

Bibliography:
Dubal, David, The Essential Canon of Classical Music (North Point Press, New York, 2001)
Johnston, Guy, Liner notes, Respighi, Ottorino, "Tecchler's Cello", Guy Johnston, cello, Hyperion, 2017.

Recordings:
There are a number of recordings of this work that have been released.

George Rochberg (1918-2005) Ricordanza Soliloquy for Cello & Piano

Date of Composition: 1972
Date of Premiere: Unknown
Premiered by: Perhaps Michael Rudiakov, for whom this work is dedicated.
Approximate Length: 12 min.

Background Information:

    George Rochberg belonged to a group of composers who moved against the typical experimental and atonal works of the mid-to-late twentieth century. His early pieces were written squarely in the serialist vein, but after his son died, Rochberg realized that serialist music was incapable of expressing the heartache he felt over losing his son. His works then turned to a more "neo-Romantic" style, a term he didn't necessarily agree with, but didn't dismiss outright either.

    His Ricordanza Soliloquy for Cello and Piano is a collage, a blend of Beethoven's Cello Sonata No. 4 in C Major and Rochberg's own music. The piece is in an ABA format, with the middle section featuring extensive quotes from Beethoven's sonata. The outer sections are lyrical and certainly of a romantic spirit, with nary a serialistic element to be found. It displays its emotions clearly and plainly without any sense of irony, just pure expression. It's a stunning work that creates a sense of magic from the opening notes, through the Beethovenian middle section, to the cello cadenza towards the end. The return of the A section is exceptionally sublime, a heart-melting, tender and special moment.

    This piece is particularly effective performed just after the Beethoven Sonata from which it borrows liberally.

Edition:
Theodore Presser

Bibliography:
Biography on composer, Accessed August 20, 2023, https://www.milkenarchive.org/artists/view/george-rochberg
Interview with Rochberg, Accessed August 20, 2023, http://www.bruceduffie.com/rochberg.html

Recordings:
There are only a couple of commercially released recordings of this work.

Joaquin Rodrigo (1901-1999) — Concierto in modo galante for Cello & Orchestra

Date of Composition: 1949
Date of Premiere: November 4, 1949
Premiered by: Gaspar Cassadó, cello with Ataulfo Argenta conducting the Orquesta Nacional de España
Approximate Length: 27 min.

> I. Allegretto grazioso (11 min)
> II. Adagietto (10 min)
> III. Rondo giocoso (6 min)

Background Information:

Spanish composer Joaquin Rodrigo used the sounds of his native land to great success in his music. Blinded at the age of three, he nevertheless forged ahead as a composer. He shot to fame with his guitar concerto Concierto de Aranjuez in 1939 with its famous slow movement. He received commissions from such famous musicians as James Galway and Andrés Segovia. Although he is most known for his concerti, he composed works for orchestra, wind ensemble and choir, solo piano and numerous solo guitar works.

His Concierto in modo galante for Cello and Orchestra was commissioned by cellist Gaspar Cassadó. Cassadó, a composer in his own right (see entry), was pleased with the work, saying, "an excellent work and a significant addition to the cello/orchestra repertoire ... its instrumentation is so economical as to make this one of the few scores in which the solo cello is never drowned out by the weight of the orchestra."

It's a delightful work full of life and character. Upbeat rhythms and gestures abound, mixed with plenty of tuneful melodies. As bright and colorful as music can get, it is an incredibly entertaining work, one that a listener would be hard pressed not to hum along or dance to.

Rodrigo would later write another cello concerto for Julian Lloyd Webber called Concierto como un divertimento in 1981.

Edition:
Schott

Bibliography:
Official website of the composer, Accessed August 19, 20203, https://www.joaquin-rodrigo.com/index.php/en/
Miura, Enrique Martínez, Rodrigo, Joaquin, "Complete Orchestral Works, Vol. 3", Asier Polo, cello, Naxos, 2002.

Recordings:
A couple of commercial recordings are available of this work.

Bernhard Romberg (1767-1841) — Sonata No. 1 in E Minor, Op. 38 for Cello & Piano

Date of Composition: Unknown, but first published in 1825
Date of Premiere: Unknown
Premiered by: Unknown, but presumably Romberg himself
Approximate Length: 14 min.

I. Allegro non troppo (4 min)
II. Allegro grazioso (4 min)
III. Rondo allegretto (6 min)

Background Information:
What does it say about the confidence level of a cellist, who, when Beethoven offered to compose a cello concerto for him, demurred and said they preferred their own compositions. Bernhard Romberg's boldness is the cello world's loss, but you have to give the man applause for his incredible conviction in himself.

Regardless of his faux pas with Herr Beethoven, he is widely considered to be the father of the German school of cello playing. He had a brilliant career around Europe, and had a long connection with the aforementioned Beethoven. He played in a string trio with Beethoven, and a string quartet that premiered several of Beethoven's early quartets. As for his own compositions, he was a prolific composer, leaving behind a large catalog of chamber music and solo cello works.

In addition to his legacy as a performer and composer, he was instrumental in transitioning the cello into the nineteenth century. He lengthened the fingerboard for higher access, flattened the part of the fingerboard underneath the C string for more clearance for the string to vibrate. His system for notating fingerings and thumb position is the accepted system we use today.

His Sonata in E Minor for Cello and Piano is just one of his solo cello works, but it's probably his best known. It's a highly lyrical and tuneful work that possesses very little of the ferocious energy Beethoven usually employs. It's generally laid back and galant in its scope with its style leaning mostly into the Classical character.

Selected Editions:
International
Schott

Bibliography:
Article on Romberg's influence, Accessed August 20, 2023, https://cellomuseum.org/7-ways-bernhard-romberg-influences-the-cello-world-today/
Campbell, Margaret. The Great Cellists (Trafalgar Square Books, Vermont, 1988)
Ginsberg, Lev. History of the Violoncello (Paganiniana Publications, New Jersey, 1983)

Recordings:
There are a few commercial recordings that have been released.

Daniel Bernard Roumain (b. 1971) — Why Did They Kill Sandra Bland for Solo Cello

Date of Composition: 2020
Date of Premiere: October 2020
Premiered by: Arlen Hlusko, cello
Approximate Length: 5 min.

Background Information:

Daniel Bernard Roumain, often known simply as DBR, is an electrifying violinist and composer. Combining elements of African-American music influences, electronic music, traditional classical music with social commentary, his music is both challenging and thrilling–not to mention you can dance to many of his pieces. He has collaborated with the most prominent artists from the Classical world, as well as the pop world, and has composed solo, chamber, orchestral and operatic works. He is Artistic Catalyst for the New Jersey Symphony, and the Artist Activist-in-Residence at the Longy School.

Why Did They Have to Kill Sandra Bland for Solo Cello was commissioned by Arlen Hlusko, the cellist best known for her involvement with the Bang On a Can ensemble. Hlusko cultivated a program of cello works, interpolated with spoken word and dance that was live streamed in the fall of 2020. It has since been recorded and released as an album.

Roumain's work is a powerful commentary on the events of 2020, sobering, yet hopeful. The work of reckoning is dedicated to Sandra Bland and Breonna Taylor, two Black women who were needlessly and unjustly killed. Roumain writes,

"Black women deserved more, continue to suffer, and continue to be victimized. I pledge to listen more, defend more, and call attention to their trauma, brilliance, and truth. What will you do?." The piece has the inscription: *"For Sandra Bland, rest in power…"*

Edition:
Available from the composer's website.

Bibliography:
Official website of the composer, Accessed August 9, 2023, https://www.danielroumain.com/
Official website of the cellist who commissioned the work, Accessed August 9, 2023, https://www.arlenhlusko.com/
Program notes, Accessed August 9, 2023, https://www.ffdnorth.com/programs/inverse?/tab/track-list

Recordings:
Arlen Hlusko has recorded and released it on her album [in]verse

Christopher Rouse (1949-2019) — Morpheus for Solo Cello

Date of Composition: 1975
Date of Premiere: Unknown
Premiered by: Carey Miller, cello
Approximate Length: 9 min.

Background Information:

    Christopher Rouse was a prominent American composer, whose list of commissions is a who's-who of Classical music greats. Virtually every major orchestra, soloist and conductor performed works by him. He won the Pulitzer Prize in 1993 for his Trombone Concerto, not to mention a Grammy Award for best Classical Contemporary Composition in 2002. He was on the composition faculty of the University of Michigan, the Eastman School of Music and the Juilliard School. Additionally, he served as composer-in-residence for the New York Philharmonic, the Baltimore Symphony, the Aspen and Tanglewood Music Festivals.

    Known for his big symphonic works (he wrote six symphonies), and concerti (he wrote a dozen), he also composed small, intimate works. Morpheus for Solo Cello may not be his most known work, but it's a beautiful tribute to the sound of the cello and the Cello Suites by Johann Sebastian Bach. Many composers have written solo cello works inspired by the Bach Suites, either using it as an inspiration point, or including actual sections of the Suites. Rouse does the latter, basing Morpehus on material from the Cello Suite No. 2 in D Minor.

    Right from the start, we get the exact opening of the D Minor Prelude–note for note– for a few measures, before it starts to deviate, and slip into new material. Elsewhere he quotes passages in the Sarabande, ending the whole piece with it. Throughout, Rouse includes harmonics, trills and pizzicato to embellish and thread the work, before a Bach quote appears again. It's Bach as seen through a fractal lens, as if we're hearing Bach from different angles. It's a lovely work on its own, but also is a nice companion piece to Bach's second Suite.

Edition:
Schott

Bibliography:
Homuth, Donald Cello Music Since 1960 (Fallen Leaf Press, Berkeley, 1994)
Publisher biography on the composer, Accessed August 12, 2023,
    https://www.boosey.com/pages/cr/composer/composer_main?composerid=2720&ttype=BIOGRAPHY

Recordings:
No commercial recording has been released, but there are a number of performances on youtube.

Kaija Saariaho (1952-2023) Sept Papillons for Solo Cello

Date of Composition: 2000
Date of Premiere: September 2000
Premiered by: Anssi Karttunen, cello
Approximate Length: 13 min.

> I. Papillons No. 1- Dolce, leggiero, libero (2 min)
> II. Papillons No. 2 - Leggiero, molto espressivo (2 min)
> III. Papillons No. 3 - Calmo, con tristezza (2 min)
> IV. Papillons No. 4 - Dolce, tranquillo (2 min)
> V. Papillons No. 5 - Lento, misterioso (2 min)
> VI. Papillons No. 6 - Sempre poco nervoso, senza tempo (2 min)
> VII. Papillons No. 7 - Molto espressivo, energico (1 min)

Background Information:

Kaija Saariaho is one of the foremost composers from Finland. For her entire career, she expanded the boundaries of music into a musical language uniquely her own. Often incorporating electronics, or extended techniques, her works are ethereal, poignant and seem to come from another time and place, yet current at the same time. She has written solo, chamber, orchestral and operatic works. Many of the major orchestras and performers in the world have performed her works.

In 2000, Saariaho was working on her opera L'amour de loin which was a huge undertaking. Acting as a kind of palette cleanser, she began work on Sept Papillons for solo cello, which was worlds away from the grand production of the opera.

Each movement is an exploration of what Saariaho says is "the ephemeral–the butterfly". Imploring extended techniques such as harmonics, sul ponticello, and extremes in bow pressure, the seven vignettes create a crystalline sound world. Even visually, the rapid oscillation of the cellist's left hand in the numerous trills imitates the fluttering of a butterfly's wings.

Edition:
Chester Music

Bibliography:
Official website of the composer, Accessed August 12, 2023, https://saariaho.org/
Program notes on the piece, Accessed August 12, 2023, http://saariaho.org/works/sept-papillons/

Recordings:
There have been a few commercial recordings released, as well as numerous videos of live performances on youtube are available.

Camille Saint-Säens (1835-1921)   Cello Concerto No. 1 in A Minor
Op. 33

Date of Composition: 1872
Date of Premiere: January 19, 1873
Premiered by: Auguste Tolbecque, cello with Édouard Deldevez conducting
Approximate Length: 20 min.

> I. Allegro non troppo (6 min)
> II. Allegretto con moto (5 min)
> III. Tempo primo (9 min)
> [The three movements are played without pause]

Background Information:

    Camille Saint-Säens was one of the most prominent French composers in the nineteenth century. He was also an organist, pianist, conductor, critic, amateur astronomer, and teacher (Gabriel Fauré was one of his top students).

    He was an established part of the French musical scene when he wrote his Cello Concerto No. 1 in 1872. He was most likely inspired to write the work by his connection with cellist August Tolbecque, who received the dedication and premiered the work.

    Right from the start, it forgoes standard concerto practice (particularly in the Romantic era) of a lengthy orchestral introduction. The orchestra blasts one confident chord, and the cello comes in right away with its theme of rolling triplets. The overall mood of the first movement is fairly intense with a tender, cantabile middle section.
The second movement has a sweet, plaintive and slightly playful character. The mood turns more melancholy as the movement progresses

    A recap of the first movement opens the third movement before launching into lightning fast scales up and down the instrument. The concerto ends in A Major with a sunny, warm coda.

    The concerto was fairly well received upon its premiere and its popularity has only increased in the years since. It is played often by top professionals with major orchestras around the world, but is also technically accessible to advanced students as well.

    Perhaps due to its high popularity, Saint-Säens' other solo cello works tend to all but be ignored. A second concerto followed in 1902, and two cello sonatas were written as well.

Selected Editions:
G. Henle Verlag (Urtext)
International

Bibliography:
Schonberg, Harold C. The Lives of the Great Composers (Norton, New York, 1981)
Jost, Peter, Preface, Saint-Saens, Camille "Concerto in A Minor", Munich: Henle, 2002.

Recordings:
Essentially, every major cellist has recorded this work. There are innumerable recordings available.

Camille Saint-Säens (1835-1921)   Le Cygne (The Swan) from Le Carnaval des animaux for Cello & Piano

Date of Composition: 1886 orchestral version/1887 piano version
Date of Premiere: March 3, 1886
Premiered by: Charles Lebouc, cello
Approximate Length: 3 min.

Background Information:

Next to the Prelude from the G Major Suite by J.S. Bach, The Swan is one of the most popular and recognizable pieces for cello. As part of the larger work Le Carnaval des animaux, it is three minutes of pure cello heaven.

Camille Saint-Säens had a career full of ups and downs. Major successes seemed to be followed by disastrous premieres. In 1885-1886, he was on a tour of Germany that did not go well at all. He was devastated from this experience, and retreated to the countryside where he began work on a suite of vignettes for orchestra centering around animals. Primarily acting as a distraction, Saint-Säens was taken with the fact that it was simply entertaining, something that kept his mind off his recent professional disappointments.

Most composers of the Romantic period were preoccupied with writing programmatic music, often in the form of symphonic tone poems. Saint-Säens didn't normally write programmatic works like his colleagues, so this was a rare occasion.

The overall tone of the work is comical, which is why it's most often performed on children's concerts, with Saint-Säens cleverly using the different instruments in the orchestra and motives to represent the various animals (double bass for the elephant, clarinet for chickens, xylophones for skeletal bones). The mood becomes the most serious in the Le Cygne section with a solo cello playing the part of the swan against a two-piano accompaniment.

The cello theme mirrors the gliding of the swan across the water in long, drawn-out phrases, smoothly traveling up and down the instrument. The piano accompaniment is in the form of rolling arpeggiated patterns, continuously flowing underneath the seamless cello part. It is one of the most endearing pieces that Saint-Säens ever composed. He knew this movement was something special as it was the only one he would allow to be played apart from the whole work, making a cello and (one) piano version a year later.

Selected Editions:
G. Henle Verlag (Urtext)
International

Bibliography:
Program notes on the piece, Accessed August 20, 2023, https://www.laphil.com/musicdb/pieces/248/carnival-of-the-animals
Wells, Dominic, Liner notes, Saint-Saens, Camille "Works for Cello and Orchestra", Gabriel Schwabe, cello, Naxos, 2017.

Recordings:
Numerous recordings have been made, both within the original Carnival of the Animals work, and on its own.

Aulis Sallinen (b. 1935) — Cello Concerto

Date of Composition: 1976
Date of Premiere: September 1977
Premiered by: Arto Noras, cello; with Jorna Panula, conducting the Finnish Radio Symphony Orchestra
Approximate Length: 25 min.

> I. Moto variabile - quasi marcia funebre (20 min)
> II. Allegro - Presto - Prestissimo (5 min)

Background Information:

Next to Jean Sibelius, Aulis Sallinen is one of the most famous Finnish composers. Early studies on violin and piano led to him studying at the Sibelius Academy (he would eventually teach there) and composing. His works gained rapid attention to the point where the Finnish government awarded him the honor of being Professor of Arts for life, which gave him the freedom to concentrate solely on his composing. Known for his big orchestral scores, namely his eight symphonies, he has concentrated on instrumental music within the last twenty years. He composed a well-received cello sonata in 2005, as well a couple of other smaller works for cello.

His Cello Concerto was written in 1976 with the premiere the following year in 1977. It is in two movements, the first a long, expansive movement which is almost four times the length of the second movement. The first movement is a set of variations ending with a cello cadenza. The second movement is a rapid, jaunty romp with the cello, at first playing pizzicato alone, then fast, scherzo-like passages. The whole piece ends incredibly fast and triumphant.

Edition:
Novello

Bibliography:
Publisher biography on the composer, Accessed August 9, 2023, https://www.wisemusicclassical.com/composer/1356/Aulis-Sallinen/

Recordings:
There are a few commercial recordings of this concerto, including the premiere cellist, Arto Noras on the Finlandia label.

Alfred Schnittke (1934-1998) — Sonata No. 1 for Cello & Piano

Date of Composition: 1978
Date of Premiere: January 23, 1979
Premiered by: Natalia Gutman, cello with Vasilyi Lobanov, piano
Approximate Length: 22 min.

> I. Largo (4 min)
> II. Presto (6 min)
> III. Largo (12 min)

Background Information:

Alfred Schnittke went through several stylistic periods and influences throughout his career. He had a connective relationship with serialism, but ultimately felt it was too impersonal for him. Along with a couple of other composers, he perpetuated "polystylism" in his music, which is the blending and contrasting of different styles of music, such as jazz against quotes of Bach or Beethoven. He eventually toned his polystylism down to where the disparate parts blended together a bit more homogeneously.

His Cello Sonata No. 1 contains various styles of music, but the seams are much better hidden, representing his more evolved sense of polystylism. It begins with a cello cadenza, lonely and questioning. The piano eventually comes in, offering slight comfort. Throughout the movement, the cello part never seems settled, flitting between tonality and atonality, constantly seeking for purpose and meaning.

The second movement, which begins right after the first, is a twitchy, nervous, terrifying juggernaut, with the cello chugging along in non-stop eighth notes, the piano adding punctuation every so often. The two instruments eventually meet and each dance around each other in furious energy. It all comes crashing together, leading into the third movement.

Picking up where the second movement left off, with its breathless energy, the third movement begins with the cello wailing, pleading even, in one its highest registers. The music wanders around, before fading into the ether, never resolved, still seeking.

The spirits of Prokofiev and Shostkovich hover around in this sonata; the grotesque brutalism of Prokofiev in the second movement, the bleak, despondency of Shostakovich in the third movement. But it's Schnittke's music through and through as he takes the performers and listeners on a journey, through darkness and light.

Editions:
Sikorski
Universal Edition

Bibliography:
Fairclough, Pauline, Schnittke, Alfred, "Shostakovich and Schnittke Cello Sonatas", Alban Gerhardt, cello, Steven Osborne, piano, Hyperion, 2006.
Kleinmann, Johannes. Polystylistic Features of Schnittke's Cello Sonata (1978) dissertation for University of North Texas, 2010.
Official website of the composer, Accessed August 21, 2023, https://schnittke.org/en/index.html

Recordings:
There are a number of recordings of this work, including a recording made by the premiere cellist, Natalia Gutman.

Franz Schubert (1797-1828) — Sonata in A Minor, D. 821 Arpeggione

Date of Composition: November 1824
Date of Premiere: late 1824
Premiered by: Vinzenz Schuster, arpeggione, and Franz Schubert, keyboard
Approximate Length: 25 min.

> I. Allegro moderato (12 min)
> II. Adagio (4 min)
> III. Allegretto (9 min)

Background Information:

The arpeggione is an instrument that has a curious and unique history. When the so-called modern string instruments (violin, viola, cello, and bass) were being developed in the 17th century, there were numerous hybrid instruments in different shapes, sizes, ways to hold the instrument, number of strings, and tunings. By the time the arpeggione was created in the 19th century, the existence of these hybrid instruments had effectively died down, with the four modern string instruments firmly established as well as standardized.

It's quite likely that many would never have heard of the arpeggione--described as a cross between a guitar and a cello--had it not been for Schubert's sonata. He was approached by Johann Georg Stauffer, an instrument maker, to compose a piece to showcase his new instrument. Schubert obliged and composed this sonata for the guitar virtuoso Vinzenz Schuster, a musician Schubert was already familiar with. Reportedly, he and Schubert premiered the piece in late 1824, but the work, like most of Schubert's catalog, wouldn't be published until much later, in 1871.

The sonata is a gorgeous, moody work exploiting the full range of the arpeggione, which had six strings. Since the arpeggione is not a common instrument (Schubert's masterful work failed to ignite an arpeggione renaissance), the work is most often performed on the cello, with versions also for viola and double bass. In fact, when the piece was first published, a cello and viola part were wisely included, with the arpeggione part included in the piano score only.

Due to the limited range of the modern four-string instruments of today, this piece is incredibly difficult, with the melodic tunes often soaring into the stratospheric higher positions. Some have chosen to play it on a 5-string cello, which is a successful alternative.

Selected Editions:
Barenreiter (Urtext)
G. Henle Verlag (Urtext)
International

Bibliography:
Sieffert, Wolf-Dieter, Preface notes, Schubert, Franz, "Sonata in A Minor Arpeggione", Munich: Henle, 1995.

Recordings:
Numerous commercial recordings are available.

Robert Schumann (1810-1856) — Concerto in A Minor, Op. 129

Date of Composition: 1850
Date of Premiere: June 9, 1860
Premiered by: Ludwig Ebert, cello; Julius Rcitz, conductor; Gewandhaus Orchestra
Approximate Complete Length: 24 min.

> I. Nicht zu schnell (11 min)
> II. Langsam (5 min)
> III. Sehr lebhaft (8 min)

Background Information:

One of the first major concertos for cello written in the Romantic period, the Cello Concerto written by Robert Schumann fits the persona of the Romantic artist, and thus the cello, very well. Prone to more introspection than extroversion, reflection to melodrama, the music reveals the soul of the tortured composer who was in the height of his mental and emotional struggles.

Schumann had some experience with the cello, studying it in his youth, and brings the warm, earthy sound of the cello to great effect as it gives voice to his emotional unrest. He was reported to have been dismayed at the lack of repertoire for the cello; it's not clear for whom or what purpose he composed the concerto, dashing it down in the span of two weeks.

His wife Clara was quite fond of the work after she had initially played through the score: "It pleases me very much and seems to me to be written in true violoncello style...The romantic quality, the vivacity, the freshness and the humor, also the highly interesting interweaving of violoncello and orchestra are indeed wholly ravishing, and what euphony and deep feeling one finds in all the melodic passages!"

Sadly, the work didn't see the light of day while he was alive. He put it through a series of revisions before his inner turmoil got the best of him, and he made an attempt at ending his life. He was sent immediately to an asylum where he spent the rest of his days, dying a couple years later. The cello concerto would receive a posthumous premiere, and wouldn't catch on as one of the staples of the Romantic cello literature until the beginning of the next century.

In a change from typical concertos of the time, rather than having a long orchestral introduction, the cello enters in the second measure, the orchestra laying down a murmuring heartbeat for the cello's melody to rest upon. What follows throughout the entire work is music capturing the highs and lows, the joys and sorrows of life, itself. The movements run seamlessly together with no pause, something that would become more of the norm within the next decade or so.

The solo part is deceiving, as it neither looks or sounds difficult, but in fact, is quite challenging. The soloist must not betray this fact to the audience, letting the music speak for itself, allowing Schumann's heart and soul to grab the listener's ear.

Selected Editions:
Breitkopf & Härtel (Urtext)
International

Bibliography:
Ostwald, Peter. Schumann: The Inner Life of a Musical Genius (Northeastern University Press, Boston, 1985)
Steinberg, Michael. The Concerto: A Listener's Guide (Oxford University Press, New York, 1998)
Program notes, Accessed August 4, 2023, https://interlude.hk/schumann-cello-concertopremiered-today-1860/

Recordings:
Numerous commercial recordings have been released.

Robert Schumann (1810-1856) — Fünf Stücke im Volkston, Op. 102 for Cello & Piano

Date of Composition: 1849
Date of Premiere: June 8, 1850
Premiered by: Andreas Grabau, cello with Clara Schumann, piano
Approximate Length: 17 min.

I. Mit humor, "Vanitas vanitatum (3 min)
II. Langsam (4 min)
III. Nicht schnell, mit viel Ton zu spielen (4 min)
IV. Nicht zu rasch (2 min)
V. Stark und markiert (4 min)

Background Information:

Robert Schumann wrote his Fünf Stücke im Volkston (Five Pieces in a Folk Style) for Cello and Piano in a sweep of instrumental chamber music. Just prior to the composition of this piece, he had written the Adagio und Allegro and the Fantiestücke for clarinet and piano, and the Romanzen for oboe. He followed it with two violin sonatas and the Märchenbilder for viola and piano.

The five pieces that make up this work are not based on specific folk songs, but rather, original ones that Schumann crafted to reflect qualities of folk tunes. Only the first song bears a creative, quasi-programmatic title Vanitas vanitatum, which is either a quote from Ecclesiastes or from Goethe (or perhaps both). The rest have Schumann's typical descriptive but to-the-point movement headings.

The first "With humor, 'vanity of vanities'" has a slightly pompous theme, but only in a light-hearted way. The humor comes from the obstinate repetition of the phrase in a subito forte dynamic.

The second movement sounds very much like a lullaby, to which Brahms' Wiegenlied (Cradle Song) has a passing resemblance.

"Nicht schnell" that opens the third movement is a moderate scherzo, dance-like movement that suddenly opens up into a beautiful passage played in double-stops up in thumb position.

The fourth piece begins in a declamatory mood, then softens into a mildly unsettled section. The polar personalities of Florestan (impetuous and extroverted) and Eusebius (gentle and introspective) are the most present here.

Again, the dual sides of Schumann's fractured mind are at play here, with a "strong and marked" opening theme, contrasted by a more merciful second theme. The stodgy triplets also seemed to have inspired Brahms, as it sounds similar to the third movement of his Cello Sonata in E Minor.

This work was first performed at a celebration for Schumann's 40th birthday. Clara wrote about them in her diary, "…the pieces in folk style, they absolutely beguiled me with their freshness and originality." Four years later, his mental and emotional anguish would take its toll on him, and he would attempt to drown himself in the Rhine, dying in a mental asylum at the age of 46.

Selected Edition:
G. Henle Verlag (Urtext)

Bibliography:
Hettrich, Ernst, Preface, Schumann, Robert, "Five Pieces in Folk Style", Munich: Henle, 2010.
Program notes on the piece, Accessed August 21, 2023, https://www.schumann-portal.de/grabau-andreas.html

Recordings:
There are many commercial recordings of this work.

Caroline Shaw (b. 1982) — In manus tuas for Solo Cello

Date of Composition: 2009
Date of Premiere: 2009
Premiered by: Hannah Collins, cello
Approximate Length: 10 min.

Background Information:

Caroline Shaw is rapidly becoming one of the most prominent composers of the early twenty-first century. She is the youngest recipient of the Pulitzer Prize for her vocal work Partita for 8 Voices, not to mention numerous grammy awards and high profile commissions. She has composed for many different ensembles, traditional and non, and has worked with members of rock bands The National and Arcade Fire, as well as Kanye West. Shaw likens her compositional process to a quilter–someone who takes different pieces of cloth and sews them together to make something brand new. She likes to combine different sounds and textures, mixing them in unusual ways, loving the sound of things in the music breaking apart, then coming back together again.

In manus tuas is a contemplative work that involves creating different extended sounds from the instrument, calling for the cellist to sing/harmonize with their own playing.
Shaw's own notes on the piece says:

In manus tuas is based on a 16th century motet by Thomas Tallis. While there are only a few slices of the piece that reflect exact harmonic changes in Tallis' setting, the motion (or lack of) is intended to capture the sensation of a single moment of hearing the motet in the particular and remarkable space of Christ Church in New Haven, Connecticut. In manus tuas was written in 2009 for cellist Hannah Collins, for a secular solo cello compline service held in the dark, candlelit nave.

Edition:
Caroline Shaw Editions: https://caroline-shaw-editions.myshopify.com

Bibliography:
Program notes on the piece, Accessed July 7, 2023, https://caroline-shaw-editions.myshopify.com/collections/small-plates/products/in-manus-tuas

Recordings:
There are a couple of commercial recordings available, including one by the premiere cellist, Hannah Collins, as well as numerous video performances on youtube.

Bright Sheng (b. 1955) — Seven Tunes Heard in China for Solo Cello

Date of Composition: 1995
Date of Premiere: 1995
Premiered by: Yo-Yo Ma
Approximate Length: 19 min.

I. Seasons (Qinghai) (2 min)
II. Guessing Song (Yunnan) (1 min)
III. The Little Cabbage (Hebei) (2 min)
IV. The Drunken Fisherman (Classical) (4 min)
V. Diu Diu Dang (Taiwan) (2 min)
VI. Pastoral Ballade (Mongolia) (5 min)
VII. Tibetan Dance (3 min)

Background Information:

In 2001, the MacArthur Foundation described Chinese-American composer Bright Sheng as an "innovative composer who merges diverse musical customs in works that transcend conventional aesthetic boundaries," and that he "will continue to be an important leader in exploring and bridging musical traditions." He has been nominated for a Pulitzer prize twice and has a vast catalog of solo, chamber, orchestra, opera and ballet works, many of which fuse western and eastern musical styles.

His work Seven Tunes Heard in China for solo cello was written for Yo-Yo Ma. Each of the seven tunes of the title is based on folk songs native to China. In his notes on the work, Sheng writes: "[Bartok, Kodaly, and Stravinsky] were the ones who began a new approach to using roots music. Before them, composers just harmonized folk melodies. They didn't convey the roughness, the savageness of this music. I use [folk melodies] as a point of departure for my inspiration, and I take a lot of freedom. I'm searching for a new idiom that doesn't belong to preconceived categories."

Edition:
G. Schirmer

Bibliography:
Official website of the composer, Accessed August 11, 2023, http://brightsheng.com/works.html
Pan, Xiao-Qiang "A study of 'Seven Tunes Heard in China' by Bright Sheng" dissertation (University of Northern Colorado Greeley, 2003)
Program notes on the piece, Accessed August 11, 2023, https://www.wisemusicclassical.com/work/24860/Seven-Tunes-Heard-in-China--Bright-Sheng/

Recordings:
There have been a few commercially released recordings of this work, notably Yo-Yo Ma's premiere recording on the Sony Classical label.

Dmitri Shostakovich (1906-1975) — Concerto No. 1 for Cello & Orchestra, Op. 107

Date of Composition: 1959
Date of Premiere: October 4, 1959
Premiered by: Mstislav Rostropovich, cello; Yevgeny Mravinsky, conductor; Leningrad Philharmonic
Approximate Complete Length: 30 min.

I. Allegretto (7 min)
II. Moderato (11 min)
III. Cadenza (7 min)
IV. Allegro con moto (5 mi)

Background Information:

One wouldn't know that Shostakovich was experiencing a relatively carefree and uneventful period in his life preceding the writing of the cello concerto. The political situation in Russia was fairly peaceful, but the concerto doesn't do much to convince otherwise. It's filled with echoes of Stalinist Russia and his crushing regime during the war. Pain, anguish, rage, sorrow, tension, fear, resolve and ultimately triumph all make an appearance throughout the half hour long work.

The work was written with the great cellist Rostropovich in mind, who, as legend tells, learned and memorized the score in mere days, performing it with piano four days after he had received the score. Playing to Rostropovich's strengths, the work is blisteringly difficult, and emotionally rich. It's an exhausting work both for the performer and audience, but in the best possible way. Shostakovich leaves no stone unturned in his quest to channel fury and sorrow through the conduit of the cello.

It begins with a rather plucky cello motive (which he would later quote in his String Quartet No. 8), which very soon transforms into something more aggressive. The orchestra and the cello battle for supremacy throughout, with the horn and woodwinds putting up most of a fight. It's a relentless movement that kicks the whole work off with a bang.

The second movement seems distant and removed from the pounding urgency of the first movement. Woeful, and at times, weary, it bears the weight of the world, in all its chaos and destruction, despairing over loss and grief. The ending of the movement is incredibly magical with the cello intoning the main melodic material in harmonics accompanied by the celeste. It's eerie, otherworldly, and yet, calming and soothing at the same time.

The third movement is a cadenza, expanded out into its own movement. The cello in this soliloquy ruminates on themes and ideas heard earlier in the piece, wrestling with the implications of its meaning. Eventually, the music and ideas come faster and faster, building to whizzing scales flying up and down, which then plunges without pause into the finale.

The last movement feels somewhat parallel to the first movement in mood and tone, but everything has been kicked into overdrive. It's a fast and furious movement, with just a twinge of humor and sarcasm. The opening material from the first movement returns, but this time in a slightly mocking form (thanks largely to the mutated version blasted out by the horns). The ending is both celebratory and gritty, suggesting that even in victory, there's still a price to pay.

This is one of the greatest works for cello, the result of a brilliant friendship between the composer and cellist. We owe them a debt of gratitude.

Editions:
International Edition
Sikorski Edition

Dmitri Shostakovich (1906-1975) — Concerto No. 1 for Cello & Orchestra, Op. 107

Bibliography:
Steinberg, Michael. The Concerto: A Listener's Guide (Oxford University Press, New York, 1998)
Wilson, Elizabeth. Rostropovich: The Musical Life of the Great Cellist, Teacher and Legend (Ivan R. Dee Publishing, 2007)

Recordings:
Numerous recordings have been made by a good majority of the top cellists. Rostropovich's premiere recording is a good place to start however.

Dmitri Shostakovich (1906-1975) — Sonata in D Minor, Op. 40 for Cello & Piano

Date of Composition: 1934
Date of Premiere: 1934
Premiered by: Viktor Kubatsky, cello; Dmitri Shostakovich, piano
Approximate Length: 25 min.

> I. Allegro non troppo (9 min)
> II. Allegro (3 min)
> III. Largo (8 min)
> IV. Allegro (5 min)

Background Information:

In the time surrounding the writing of this sonata, Shostakovich was being slandered in the press (anonymously, but thought to be by Stalin himself) about his opera Lady Macbeth of Mtsensk. Soldiering on, despite the hurtful, and potentially dangerous, criticism, Shostakovich finished the piece and premiered it with his friend, cellist Viktor Kubatsky.

Despite the sonata being written in the first part of the twentieth century, it harkens back to the more disciplined and structured Classical style, at least in form. It follows the traditional Sonata-allegro form used for virtually every instrumental work from that era. Much like his colleague, Sergei Prokofiev, Shostakovich loved to work within traditional parameters using them for many of his instrumental works.

Although Shostakovich's music tends to fall into either an aggressive and brutal character, or a deeply sorrowful and bleak character, the cello sonata traverses many different moods and emotions, although it certainly does contain his more typical temperaments. It begins in a rather breezy, very lyrical melody line from the cello, with the piano gently coaxing underneath. It veers into pathos up and down, before ending incredibly softly (with a hint of something sinister in the piano).

The second movement explodes with energy in a manic kind of dance. It is elegant as well as belligerent, but all within a spectrum of humor. In stark contrast to the bombastic opening, a highlight is the second section with the cello gliding up the strings in thumb position harmonics creating a giddy, otherworldly sound.

The third movement takes the mood and energy way down into the depths of a mournful dirge. Moving at a glacial pace, its power is contained and controlled within the slow, plodding tempo.

The last movement again brings back some of the humor especially in the opening theme, which is like an inebriated carouser stumbling around the streets at night. It then charges forward into fits of hearty virtuosity from both instruments. Dancing in and out of the shadows, he finally ends it with his tongue firmly in his cheek.
The sonata has become a standard for cellists.

Selected Editions:
Boosey & Hawkes
Sikorski

Bibliography:
Berger, Melvin Guide to Sonatas (Anchor Books, New York, 1991)
Program notes on the piece, Accessed August 4, 2023, https://www.laphil.com/musicdb/pieces/3473/sonata-in-d-minor-for-cello-and-piano-op-40

Recordings:
Many of the major cellists have made commercial recordings of this sonata.

Jean Sibelius (1865-1957) — Malinconia, Op. 20 for Cello & Piano

Date of Composition: 1900
Date of Premiere: March 12, 1900
Premiered by: Georg Schnéevoigt, cello with Sigrid Schnéevoigt, piano
Approximate Length: 11 min.

Background Information:

Jean Sibelius is one of the most successful Finnish composers of the late nineteenth century. Known for big symphonies and tone poems such as Finlandia, and his violin concerto, he did write smaller works as well.

In early 1900, Sibelius' daughter died from typhoid fever, a devastating blow. Shortly after, he composed this work Malinconia for Cello and Piano. The title referring to 'melancholy' or 'sadness' can be inferred to be a response to the loss of his daughter, however, he wasn't explicit about the title, thus, it remains only conjecture.

The work is fraught with emotion and intensity. It opens with a cello soliloquy before the piano comes in with rolling chords, like waves crashing up onto the shore. These opening sections return at various points throughout the piece, interjecting between episodes where the two instruments come together to share in the intense sorrow. There is rarely any letup in the emotion, the cello singing through the despair. It ends dark and despondent, the end of a beautiful, cathartic journey through grief.

Editions:
Breitkopf & Härtel (Urtext)
Schirmer

Bibliography:
Dubal, David The Essential Canon of Classical Music (North Point Press, New York, 2011)
Whitehouse, Richard, Liner notes, Sibelius, Jean "Works for Cello and Piano", Rohan de Saram, cello, Benjamin Frith, piano, First Hand Records, 2014.

Recordings:
There are quite a few available commercial recordings of this work.

Alvin Singleton (b. 1940)   Argoru II for Solo Cello

Date of Composition: 1970
Date of Premiere: December 11, 1970
Premiered by: Ronald Crutcher
Approximate Length: 13 min.

Background Information:

    New York-born composer Alvin Singleton has had a prestigious and varied career. Educated at New York University and Yale, he then studied in Europe on a Fulbright Scholarship. Upon return to the United States, he embarked upon a series of high-profile composer-in-residence positions, namely the Atlanta Symphony Orchestra and the Detroit Symphony Orchestra. He also taught at the Yale School of Music for many years. His catalog encompasses solo, chamber, orchestra, theater and ballet and his music shows a variety of influences and styles.

    Argoru II is part of a series of pieces he composed over the course of twenty-two years. Each Argoru is for a different solo instrument, the cello one being the second of the series. The word Argoru is a word that means "to play" in the Twi language, which is spoken in Ghana. Over the course of 13 minutes, Singleton runs the cello through extremes of dynamics and range, also using a wide variety of extended techniques. The work could almost be a theater piece, which is not too much of a stretch given Singleton's background of writing for the theater. It is a challenging piece, but a fascinating journey into the sound world of the cello.

Edition:
Schott Music

Bibliography:
Official website of the composer, Accessed August 11, 2023, https://www.alvinsingleton.com/
Program notes on the piece, Accessed August 11, 2023, https://www.eamdc.com/psny/composers/alvin-singleton/works/argoru-ii/

Recordings:
A recording of this work has been made by Seth Parker Woods on his album A Difficult Grace on the Cedille Records label.

Derrick Skye (b. 1982) — Hum for Solo Cello

Date of Composition: 2020
Date of Premiere: August 2020
Premiered by: Giovanna Moraga Clayton, cello
Approximate Length: 4 min.

Background Information:

Los Angeles Chamber Orchestra Artistic Director, Derrick Skye, is an award-winning composer and conductor. His education consisted of both traditional Classical training, but also West African music and dance, Persian music theory, Hindustani music, as well as Balkan music theory. All of these elements can be heard in his music, which has been performed by the Chicago Sinfonietta, Rochester Philharmonic, Los Angeles Master Chorale, and the Sphinx Virtuosi.

His piece Hum for Solo Cello was written in 2020 and a ruminative work. He describes it as "a piece that imitates the human voice. It is a personal meditation, meant to sound as if one is improvising a song in an intimate moment."

Edition:
Available from the composer's website

Bibliography:
Official website of the composer, Accessed August 8, 2023, https://www.derrickskye.com/

Recordings:
No commercial recording has been released. There is a video performance of Giovanna Moraga Clayton performing the work on youtube.

Ethel Smyth (1858-1944) — Sonata in A Minor, Op. 5 for Cello & Piano

Date of Composition: 1887
Date of Premiere: Unknown
Premiered by: Julius Klengel, cello
Approximate Length: 19 min.

> I. Allegro moderato (7 min)
> II. Adagio non troppo (7 min)
> III. Allegro vivace e grazioso (5 min)

Background Information:

Dame Ethel Smyth was a force for change, both in the musical world and outside of it. British-born in the Victorian era, she pushed against society's restrictions as to what a woman could do by composing, conducting, and writing. She was a fierce advocate for social change, being on the front lines of the suffragette movement, and was even jailed for a time for throwing stones at politician's homes.

She was well-connected with the musical elite at the time; she came across Tchaikovsky, Dvorak, Grieg, Clara Schumann, and Brahms, with whom her music is often compared.

During her studies at the Leipzig Conservatory, she met the cellist Julius Klengel. She admired him greatly and wrote this sonata for him. While not as flashy or technically demanding as other cello pieces, Smyth seems to focus on the cello's singing abilities, giving it long melodies across the entire range of the instrument. Sometimes the cello is in its dark and low register, other times, it's singing high and vulnerable.

The first movement begins with dark and turbulent energy, traded back and forth between the piano and cello. The music explores the entire range of the cello from its low and dark register to its higher, and more vulnerable octaves. The stormy energy gives way to a tender second theme, and ends quietly resigned.

The second movement brings the piece into a much darker landscape. The cello sings and sighs over gloomy chords in the piano. Despite the melancholic nature, Smyth still pulls beauty out of the sorrow. This is a gorgeous and passionate movement.

The third movement takes the ruminative mood from the first movement and the somber energy of the second movement and kicks it into overdrive. It's a scampering, tumultuous movement which charges forward with determination, even amid moments of quiet repose. The sonata ends triumphantly.

Although it shares some shades and colors with Brahms' two cello sonatas, this work is all her own. It's a beautiful, grand work and shows off Smyth's prowess as a composer. It's about time this work is getting its due after all this time.

Edition:
Edition Silvertrust

Bibliography:
Fuller Sophie The Pandora Guide to Women Composers: Britain and the United States 1629-Present (Pandora, Great Britain, 1994)
Official website of the composer, Accessed August 13, 2023, https://www.ethelsmyth.org/
Vysin, Elizabeth The Cello Sonatas of Dame Ethel Smyth: A Musical Analysis with Social and Feminist Commentary, dissertation for the University of Hartford, 2023.

Recordings:
There are a couple of commercial recordings available.

Sarah Kirkland Snider (b. 1973)   The Reserved, The Reticent for Solo Cello

Date of Composition: 2004
Date of Premiere: April 30, 2004
Premiered by: Hrant Parsamian, cello
Approximate Complete Length: 10 min.

Background Information:

Sarah Kirkland Snider was educated at the Yale School of Music and at Wesleyan University, studying with such distinguished composers as Aaron Jay Kernis, David Lang and Christopher Rouse. She has been commissioned by the New York Philharmonic, Detroit Symphony, San Francisco Symphony, Eighth Blackbird, and Roomful of Teeth, among others. She has won numerous awards, and has been composer-in-residence for many prestigious ensembles around the world. In addition to composing, she runs a record label for new music, and directed a new music festival set in art galleries called the Look & Listen Festival.

She writes about The Reserved, The Reticent:

I wrote this piece in my first year of graduate study at Yale. I wanted to create a lyrical, ruminative, single-movement narrative for solo cello, an instrument I had studied as a child and often longed to play. The music was inspired by this passage from "As One Put Drunk Into the Packet-Boat," a poem by John Ashbery.

"…The night sheen takes over. A moon of Cistercian pallor
Has climbed to the center of heaven, installed.
Finally involved with the business of darkness.
And a sigh heaves from all the small things on earth,
The books, the papers, the old garters and union-suit buttons
Kept in a white cardboard box somewhere, and all the lower
Versions of cities flattened under the equalizing night.
The summer demands and takes away too much,
But night, the reserved, the reticent, gives more than it takes."

Edition:
Schirmer

Bibliography:
Program notes on the piece, Accessed September 14, 2020, https://www.sarahkirklandsnider.com/works/the-reserved-the-reticent

Recordings:
In 2019, Caitlin Sullivan recorded the work on her album "A Page From" on the New Amsterdam Windmill label.

Carl Stamitz (1745-1801) — Cello Concerti for the King of Prussia

Date of Composition: 1786 (?)
Date of Premiere: Unknown
Premiered by: Unknown
Approximate Length: 20 min.

Background Information:
   Son of composer Johann Stamitz, Carl Stamitz followed in his father's footsteps and became a successful composer in his own right. The elder Stamitz was the founder of the so-called Mannheim School, the famed type of playing associated with the court at Mannheim, which was very disciplined and incorporated effects such as gradual crescendos from the whole orchestra.
   Stamitz traveled all over Europe, making connections with all of the prominent musicians of the day, not to mention various members of royalty. King Friederich Wilhelm the II, a cellist himself, was one such member of the nobility, for who Stamitz would write his first three cello concerti.
   The concerti are all in three movements: I. Allegro con spirito, II. Romance: Andantino or Andante poco moderato, and III. Rondo. Each concerto starts with a sizable orchestral introduction laying out all of the themes before the cello finally makes its entrance. The second movements are heartfelt and tender, and the third movements are sprightly fun. Technically, they're not quite on a difficulty level with the Haydn concerti, or Boccherini for that matter, however, they still give the player plenty to do. Full of grace and elegance, not to mention the Mannheim crescendos, the music never strays far from Stamitz's influences, namely that of his father. They are lovely gems from the Classical era.

Selected Edition:
Bärenreiter

Bibliography:
Upmeyer, Walter, Preface, Stamitz, Carl, "Cello Concerto in G Major", Kassel: Barenreiter, 1970.

Recordings:
A few commercial recordings are available of these pieces.

Carolyn Steinberg (b. 1956) A Wintry Mix: Of Ice and Snow for Cello & Piano

Date of Composition: 2008
Date of Premiere: May 2008
Premiered by: Brian Hodges, cello and Betsi Hodges, piano; University of Texas at San Antonio, San Antonio, Texas
Approximate Length: 5 min.

Background Information:

Carolyn Steinberg is a flutist and composer based out of New York. Educated at Juilliard, the Manhattan School of Music, and the University of North Texas, her main composition teachers were Lucio Berio, Franco Donati and Brian Ferneyhough. Carolyn composes in a variety of styles: contemporary, neo-Baroque and Latin Jazz. She is a regular performer with La Banda Ramirez with her husband, percussionist Chacho Ramirez.

Steinberg is the niece of Mary Ruth Leonard, a prominent cello teacher in San Antonio for decades. Mary Ruth taught Brian Hodges (the author) in his formative years from 4th grade to when he graduated high school. In 2007, Mary Ruth commissioned Carolyn to write a work for him which was finished and premiered in the spring of 2008.
A Wintry Mix: Of Ice and Snow is inspired by the winters of Narrowsburg, New York. Steinberg uses different extended techniques and textures to represent the different types of precipitation that is prominent during the winters: ice, snow, freezing rain, and hail. It is a highly atmospheric work that creates a wondrous sonic landscape.

Edition:
Available by contacting the composer via her website.

Bibliography:
Official website of the composer, Accessed July 7, 2023, http://www.carolynsteinberg.com/home.html

Recordings:
No commercial recording is available.

John Steinmetz (b. 1951)   Possessed for Solo Cello

Date of Composition: 1988-90
Date of Premiere: Unknown
Premiered by: Unknown
Approximate Length: 21 min.

Background Information:

    John Steinmetz is a composer, bassoonist and essayist. His bassoon playing has been heard in numerous chamber ensembles, orchestras, and film soundtracks, including Jurassic Park. He has taught at the Herb Alpert School of Music for many years. He has written numerous articles on Classical Music, and his essay on How to Enjoy a Live Concert was distributed by Naxos Records. His compositions are varied and often have a theatrical element to them, not to mention humor.

    Possessed for Solo Cello is a journey into the mind of a performer when they're onstage. The cellist is called not only to perform the written music, but narrate their thoughts (scripted in the music). The internal monologue races around from thoughts on a harrowing upcoming passage in the music, to nagging comments from their mother, to predicting the sobering review of a critic. It is deftly hilarious and startlingly accurate, with just a twinge of hitting too close to home. It is a tour de force work and a real crowd pleaser.

Edition:
Available from the composer's website: johnsteinmetz.org

Bibliography:
Official website of the composer, Accessed August 20, 2023, https://www.johnsteinmetz.org/
Faculty biography on the composer, Accessed August 20, 2023, https://schoolofmusic.ucla.edu/people/john-steinmetz/

Recordings:
At press time, there are no commercial recordings, but some performances are on youtube.

William Grant Still (1895-1978) — Mother & Child for Cello & Piano (transcription)

Date of Composition: 1943
Date of Premiere: Unknown
Premiered by: Timothy Holley, cello
Approximate Length: 8 min

Background Information:

William Grant Still was known as the "Dean of African-American Composers" for his incredible career and contributions to the world of Classical music. His lifetime accomplishments are a catalog of firsts: the first African-American to have a symphony performed by a major symphony orchestra in 1931 by the Rochester Philharmonic, the first African-American composer to have an opera produced by the New York City Opera, the first African-American to conduct a major symphony orchestra, the Los Angeles Philharmonic in 1936, on a concert of his own works, the first African-American composer to have an opera, A Bayou Legend, of his broadcast on television. His Symphony No. 1 "Afro-American" was one of the most performed American symphonies in the twentieth century.

Still did have a background with the cello; it was one of the instruments he studied as a teenager, however, most of what he wrote for cello ended up in his larger ensemble works. Fortunately, cellist Timothy Holley has made arrangements of some of his works for violin and piano for cello, including Summerland and Mother and Child.
Mother and Child comes from his Suite for Violin and Piano, a three-movement work. Each movement is inspired by a different painting by a black artist. Mother and Child, the second movement, was taken from Sargent Claude Johnson's drawing depicting a mother comforting her young child. The popularity of this movement saw Still creating different arrangements of this movement alone, namely for string orchestra. According to his daughter, out of everything he composed, this was his favorite.

[NB: there is a wonderful photograph of William Grant Still playing the cello, housed in the UCLA Digital Library Collection. It is available to view on their website: https://digital.library.ucla.edu/catalog/ark:/21198/z1709jm5]

Edition:
William Grant Still Music Edition, available from the composer's official website

Bibliography:
Official website of the composer, Accessed August 11, 2023, http://www.williamgrantstillmusic.com/
Program notes on the piece, Accessed August 11, 2023, https://www.kcsymphony.org/wp-content/uploads/2021/05/PROGRAM-NOTES-May-9-Classical.pdf

Recordings:
There are few commercial recordings available.

Richard Strauss (1864-1949)   Sonata in F Major, Op. 6 for Cello & Piano

Date of Composition: 1883
Date of Premiere: December 6, 1883
Premiered by: Hanuš Wihan, cello; Hildegard von Keonigs, piano
Approximate Length: 26 min.

> I. Allegro con brio (9 min)
> II. Andante ma non troppo (8 min)
> III. Finale - Allegro vivo (9 min)

Background Information:

It seems odd given what we know about Richard Strauss and his compositions, that he would have a cello sonata in his catalog. His signature style being massive, epic symphonic tone poems, which barely seem to contain all of the ideas he puts in them, a duo sonata for two instruments seems vastly microscopic in comparison. However, this cello sonata is youthful Strauss, written at the age of 19, before he became the conductor and purveyor of large-scale orchestral works.

Inspired by his friendship with cellist Hanuš Wihan, the piece was written and dedicated to him. Strauss revised the sonata before the premiere, composing an entirely new third movement to replace the original one.

In contrast to his later, bolder symphonic tone poems, this sonata holds to traditional instrumental sonata practices and forms. The harmonious language is also less adventurous than it would be in his latter works, and the mood of the work is bright and convivial, no doubt inspired by his friendship with Wihan, showcasing Strauss' gift for melody throughout.

The second movement is a lovely andante which strongly hints at the mature works to come. It is perhaps the third movement that points the way to his future most clearly, with the themes and motives very reminiscent of themes to come.

Strauss continued to favor the cello, writing a Romanze, and later, the famous Don Quixote for cello and orchestra (see other entry), not to mention the myriad of melodies given to the cellos in his tone poems.

Selected Editions:
G. Henle Verlag (Urtext)
International
Universal

Bibliography:
Berger, Melvin Guide to Sonatas (Anchor Books, New York, 1991)

Recordings:
While maybe not quite as ubiquitous as some of the other major Romantic-era cello sonatas, there are plenty of commercial recordings of this sonata.

Richard Strauss (1864-1949)   Don Quixote, Op. 35 for Cello & Orchestra

Date of Composition: 1897
Date of Premiere: March 8, 1898
Premiered by: Friedrich Grützmacher, cello; Franz Wüllner, conductor
Approximate Length: 45 min.

Background Information:
　　One of Richard Strauss' many gifts was his ability to use the instruments of a symphony orchestra to tell a story. The majority of his pieces fall into the category of symphonic tone poems, where the themes, motives and tonal colors of the instruments create narrative elements and images, from a philandering Don Juan, to a pagan god straight out of Nietszche, to death and the afterlife.
　　In Don Quixote, the full title being "Don Quixote: Fantastic Variations on a Theme of Knightly Character for Cello and Orchestra", the work is less a standard concerto, than a tone poem with the cello featured playing the titular character.
　　Sprawling over the course of ten variations, Strauss expertly lays out the story of the rather hapless, but earnest knight, Don Quixote and his patient squire Sancho Panza. Each variation depicts a different episode in his adventures, from battles, to traveling, to quiet conversations between the two heroes. The music is heroic, comedic and tragic, and shows Strauss at the height of his powers.

Selected Editions:
Breitkopf und Härtel
International
Ludwig Masters

Bibliography:
Dubal, David The Essential Canon of Classical Music (North Point Press, New York, 2001).

Recordings:
Many of the major cellists have recorded this work.

Igor Stravinsky (1882-1971)

Suite Italienne for Cello & Piano
(after Pulcinella, trans. Piatigorsky)

Date of Composition: 1932
Date of Premiere: Unknown
Premiered by: presumably Gregor Piatigorsky, who helped with the transcription
Approximate Length: 18 min.

>   I. Introduzione. Allegro moderato (2 min)
>   II. Serenata. Larghetto (3 min)
>   III. Aria. Allegro alla breve (6 min)
>   IV. Tarantella. Vivace (2 min)
>   V. Minuetto (Moderato) e Finale (Molto vivace). (5 min)

Background Information:

Igor Stravinsky became internationally famous in the early part of the twentieth century for his massive ballet scores such as, L'Oiseau de feu (The Firebird) and Le sacre du printemps (The Rite of Spring) with an expanded orchestra and huge blocks of sound. However, after the outbreak of World War I, funds were scarce, causing him to strip down his music's huge ideas and size. Transferring his music into smaller ensembles would enable his music to disseminate easier to more audiences.

At the same time, he became fascinated with music of earlier times, channeling into the works of this period, often known as his neoclassic period, spearheaded by his ballet Pucinella, which borrowed heavily from the music of Giovanni Battista Pergolesi.

Pulcinella proved to be quite popular, inspiring transcriptions. A violin suite was created from the score called Suite Italienne, and later, a version for cello and piano. The great cellist, Piatigorsky, assisted Stravinsky in the creation of the cello transcription.

The suite (even the name comes from a traditional Baroque piece) contains many standard features of a Baroque work: ornamentation, phrase structure, and cadential patterns. It begins with a formal march in the first movement followed by an operatic serenade in the second movement in a lilting meter. The third movement Aria, is less a heartfelt, emotional aria than a characterful, humorous buffa aria. The Tarantella is a Spanish dance with a brisk tempo and the last movement begins with an elegant minuet combined with a big show-stopping finale.

Edition:
Boosey & Hawkes

Bibliography:
White, Eric Walter. Stravinsky: The Composer and his Works, Second Edition (University of California Press, Berkeley, 1979).
Program notes on the piece, Accessed August 21, 2023, https://vanrecital.com/2014/03/program-notes-yo-yo-ma-kathryn-stott/

Recordings:
There have been a number of commercial recordings made of this work.

Mark Summer (b. 1958) — Julie-O for Solo Cello

Date of Composition: 1988
Date of Premiere: Unknown
Premiered by: Mark Summer
Approximate Length: 4 min.

Background Information:

Cellist Mark Summer is one of the most versatile cellists, combining improvisation, jazz, and folk into this classically-trained technique. As one of the founding members of the famed Turtle Island String Quartet, he was able to push the boundaries of what was expected for a cellist. The ensemble, a Grammy-award winning quartet, have consistently explored different genres of music and weaving them into a cohesive whole for the concert hall.

Julie-O began from an improvisation that Summer performed that eventually worked its way into a piece. Keeping to the improv feel, it was a long time before Summer actually notated it, always performing (and changing it each time) from his head. The popularity of the piece convinced Summer to finally write it down, eventually getting published. It's a joyous work that can be as simple or challenging as the player wishes to make it. Many different cellists have added all kinds of extended elements and techniques, including beatboxing.

Editions:
A digital download can be purchased from Summer's website
In print form, there is an edition published by Shar Music, and can be found in Volume 5 of the "Solos for Young Cellists" series by Carey Cheney

Bibliography:
Official website of the composer, Accessed 8, 2023, http://www.marksummer.net/

Recordings:
Summer has recorded the work commercially a couple of times on Turtle Island albums, but there is a vast array of recordings to be found on youtube, with Summer himself, or other cellists.

John Tavener (1944-2013)   The Protecting Veil for Cello & Orchestra

Date of Composition: 1988
Date of Premiere: September 1989
Premiered by: Steven Isserlis, cello with Oliver Knussen conducting the BBC Symphony Orchestra
Approximate Length: 47 min.

I. The Protecting Veil (9 min)
II. The Nativity of the Mother of God (6 min)
III. The Annunciation (3 min)
IV. The Incarnation (4 min)
V. The Lament of the Mother of God at the Cross (11 min)
VI. The Resurrection (3 min)
VII. The Dormition (7 min)
VIII. The Protecting Veil (4 min)
[played without pause]

Background Information:

John Tavener was a British composer who excelled in choral music and music with a spiritual side to it after he converted to Orthodox Christianity in the late 1970's. Many of his works, choral or not, have some kind of spiritual tether giving them their expression and color.

The Protecting Veil is a meditative, reflective, and powerful work depicting the miracle where Mary appeared to the Greeks as they were facing impending slaughter by the Saracens. In the vision, she appeared floating above them, her veil outstretched protecting them. Mary and her song of love is represented by the cello, which plays almost non-stop through the entire 45 minute work.

In almost a literal depiction of Mary high above the terrified army, the cello spends the majority of its time in its highest range, soaring above the orchestra in long, drawn-out lines, seemingly in slow motion. The cello and orchestra rarely share any of the same material. The eight sections, played without pause, travel through the various stages and icons connected with the life of Mary. Tavener said that this was his "attempt to make a lyrical ikon in sound, rather than in wood." It ends in a representation of her tears over the state of the world.

This piece is highly emotional and grand. There are moments of sublime serenity, joyous, exultant outbursts, and it seems to exist out of time. It's a towering work that is infinitely powerful and profound.

Edition:
Chester Music

Bibliography:
Official website of the composer, Accessed August 15, 2023, http://johntavener.com/inspiration/icons-in-sound/the-protecting-veil/
Stewart, Michael, Liner notes, Tavener, John "The Protecting Veil", Steven Isserlis, cello, Virgin Classics, 1992.

Recordings:
There are few recordings of this work available, but a starting place should be Isserlis' premiere recording.

Piotr Illych Tchaikovsky (1840-1893)   Variations on a Rococo Theme for Cello & Orchestra

Date of Composition: December 1876
Date of Premiere: December 18, 1877
Premiered by: Willhelm Fitzenhagen, cello; Niolai Rubenstein, conductor; Russian Musical Society
Approximate Complete Length: 20 min.

Background Information:

    The Rococo Variations by Tchaikovsky are a favorite of cellists and audiences alike, but it has a checkered past that has clouded the history of this fantastic work. The piece exists effectively in two versions, one that was heavily amended by cellist Wilhelm Fitzenhagen, and Tchaikovsky's original version, the former being the one that everyone knows.

    Tchaikovsky wrote the piece for Fitzenhagen, who was the cello professor at the Moscow conservatory and principal cellist of the Orchestra of the Imperial Russian Music Society. They were friendly, and Fitzenhagen premiered many of Tchaikovsky's chamber works.

    Showing the variations to Fitzenhagen before he sent it to the publisher must have seemed like an invitation, as Fitzenhagen felt emboldened to go beyond the usual minor editorial markings, and do a full-scale overhaul of the piece. Fitzenhagen made copious changes, moving the order of variations around and excising one all together. There is some confusion as to what degree Tchaikovsky was agreeable to the changes. Some accounts have him initially furious at the liberties Fitzenhagen took, but other sources dispute this and claim that Tchaikosky was aware and permissive the entire time.

    Certainly, it has been well documented that Tchaikovsky struggled with insecurity and depression for most of his life; he constantly second-guessed himself and would often become anxious to the point of being ill when composing. It's not too much of a stretch to believe that he would relinquish control of the variations to Fitzenhagen, who not only was a first-rate cellist, but a composer himself.

    Whatever the case may be, the work has been firmly entrenched in the cello canon for the majority of its existence. Using the Rococo style as the basis for the main theme, Tchaikovsky takes the cellist through variations that exploit all aspects of the cello and the player's technique. While not as epic, and perhaps musically substantive as his violin concerto, nonetheless, the variations are a masterpiece that are a true testing ground for cellists, and delight the listener at the same time.

    Both versions of the piece have been published so cellists can now choose which one they prefer.

Selected Editions:
International Edition
Peters (Urtext-Tchaikovsky's original version)

Bibliography:
Program notes on the piece, Accessed October 10, 2020, http://en.tchaikovsky-research.net/pages/Variations_on_a_Rococo_Theme
Program notes on the piece, Accessed October 10, 2020, https://www.musicandpractice.org/volume-4/the-history-of-tchaikovskys-variations-on-a-rococo-theme-and-the-collaboration-with-fitzenhagen/
Steinberg, Michael. The Concerto: A Listener's Guide (Oxford University Press, New York, 1998).

Recordings:
Most of the major cellists have recorded this work.

Augusta Read Thomas (b. 1964) — Cantos for Slava for Cello & Piano

Date of Composition: 2007
Date of Premiere: September 21, 2009
Premiered by: Matt Haimovitz cello with Geoffrey Burleson, piano
Approximate Length: 10 min.

Background Information:

Augusta Read Thomas is one of the most performed living composers in the twenty-first century. A finalist for the Pulitzer Prize, she has won many awards and accolades, writing works for some of the major artists and ensembles in the world. She is currently Professor of Composition at the University of Chicago, after previously teaching at the Eastman School of Music and Northwestern University. She has been the longest composer-in-residence with the Chicago Symphony for nine years. Her works span all genres, and recordings of her pieces have earned numerous Grammy awards.

Mstislav Rostropovich, arguably one of the greatest cellists of the twentieth century, passed away in 2007. Thomas was inspired by not only his technical prowess as a musician, but also his spirit and generosity. Cantos for Slava was written as a tribute after his death.

There are four cantos that make up the work played without pause. The piece exists in two versions with a different order of the movements (Fast, Slow, Fast, Slow or Slow, Fast, Slow, Fast). The music vacillates between sparse melancholy and spiky energy. The jazzy pizzicato cantos has also been published as a stand-alone piece entitled Bebop Riddle II.

Edition:

https://classicalondemand.com/incantation-cello.html

Bibliography:

Official website program notes on the piece, Accessed August 4, 2023, https://www.augustareadthomas.com/composition/cantos.html

Recordings:

Matt Haimovitz and Geoffrey Burleson recorded this piece on their album "Odd Couple".

Joan Tower (b. 1938)   Très lent (Hommage à Messiaen) for Cello & Piano

Date of Composition: 1994
Date of Premiere: 1994
Premiered by: André Emelianoff, cellist; Joan Tower, piano
Approximate Length: 8 min.

Background Information:

Joan Tower is one of the most recognized and decorated American composers of the late twentieth and early twenty-first centuries. Recipient of multiple-Grammy awards, honorary doctorates and other prestigious awards, she has been named Composer of the Year by Musical America, and honored by the League of American Orchestras. Her works have been commissioned and performed by some of the world's most illustrious orchestras and performers. Her career has spanned over sixty years as an educator, conductor, and composer.

Throughout her career, she has written a few works featuring the cello, including a celebrated Cello Concerto in 2021. Her Trés lent for cello and piano is a homage to Olivier Messiaen, the brilliant composer of the seminal work Quatuor pour la fin du temps (Quartet for the End of Time), with its heart-stopping middle movement Louange à l'Éternité de Jésus (Praise to the eternity of Jesus) for cello and piano. That movement is marked "infinitely slow" and is a masterpiece exploiting the mystical properties of time and space.

Tower writes: "I grew to love the many risks Messiaen took — particularly the use of very slow "time," both in tempo and in the flow of ideas and events. Trés lent is my attempt to make "slow" music work." (www.wisemusicclassical.com)

Editions:
Schirmer

Bibliography:
Fuller, Sophie The Pandora Guide to Women Composers: Britain and the United States 1629-Present (Pandora, Great Britain, 1994)
Neuls-Bates, Carol Women in Music: An Anthology of Source Readings from the Middle Ages to the Present (Northeastern University Press, Boston, 1996)
Publisher page on the piece, Accessed August 13, 2023, https://www.wisemusicclassical.com/work/23909/Tres-Lent-Hommage-a-Messiaen--Joan-Tower/

Recordings:
The premiere duo of Andre Emelianoff and composer Joan Tower have recorded the work on the New World label.

Jean Balthasar Tricklir (1750-1813)   13 Cello Concerti

Date of Compositions: published in 1782
Date of Premiere: Unknown
Premiered by: Unknown, but presumably Tricklir himself.
Approximate Lengths: Approximately 19 min.

Background Information:

Jean Balthasar Tricklir was a renowned cellist in the late eighteenth century. He studied in Mannheim, and toured around Europe for a time, cementing his reputation. Eventually, he landed in Paris where he performed at the Concert Spirituel, before going back to Germany, taking a position at the Elector of Saxony.

Tricklir was not just a cellist/composer, he also wrote a couple of treatises and even invented a device that was concerned with the effect of fluctuations in temperature on stringed instruments. In addition, he left behind a wealth of cello music in the form of a number of sonatas and 13 concerti. His fourth concerto was performed by Jean Louis Duport at the Concert Spirituel, who later edited and published it.

Tricklir clearly was an accomplished cellist. The concerti are full of virtuosic passages that run the entire range of the cello. Delightful and flashy, they are prime examples of the early Classical period.

Edition:
Original published editions are available on imslp.org

Bibliography:
Walden, Valerie, One Hundred Years of Violoncello: A History of the Technique and Performance Practice (1740-1840) (Cambridge Press, 1998).

Recordings:
A recording of four of the concerti is available from Alexander Rudin on the Cello Classics label.

Peteris Vasks (b. 1946) — Cello Concerto

Date of Composition: 1993/94
Date of Premiere: November 26, 1994
Premiered by: David Geringas, cello; Arturo Tamayo conductor with the Deutsches Sinfonieorchester Berlin
Approximate Length: 32 min.

> I. Cantus I (3 min)
> II. Toccata I (6 min)
> III. Monolighi (7 min)
> IV. Toccata II (5 min)
> V. Canto II (6 mn)

Background Information:

Composer Peteris Vasks is one of the most decorated Latvian composers in history. His music can be highly lyrical although not afraid to embrace more experimental elements. He says his music is often about the battle between the dark and the light, and is fascinated by nature, particularly that of bird songs. He has written for some of the most highly regarded musicians in the world including Gidon Kremer, Sol Gabetta, the Hilliard Ensemble, and the Kronos Quartet.

Although Vasks has written for a multitude of different instruments and voices, he claims that the cello is his favorite instrument. His first Cello Concerto was written and dedicated to cellist David Geringas. About the concerto, Vasks felt that it was a summary of his work up until that point. He says, "I wanted to tell in music of the persistence of a personality against crude, brutal power; about the sources of the strength which helped us to endure it all…and how, above all, we are to carry on with our lives. All of this I have experienced, nothing had to be invented."

He has since written a second cello concerto as well as a solo cello work entitled, The Book.

Edition:
Schott

Bibliography:
Official website of the composer, Accessed August 8, 2023, https://peterisvasks.lv/en/
Kehoe, John, Liner notes, Vasks, Peteris, "Vasks Cello Concerto", David Geringas, cello, Conifer Classics, 1996.

Recordings:
A couple of commercial recordings have been released, namely David Geringas, the dedicatee and premiere cellist.

Ralph Vaughan Williams (1872-1958)

Six Studies in English Folk Song for Cello & Piano

Date of Composition: 1926
Date of Premiere: June 4, 1926
Premiered by: May Mukle, cello; Anne Mukle, piano
Approximate Length: 8 min.

I. Adagio ('Lovely on the Water') (2 min)
II. Andante sostenuto ('Spurn Point') (1 min)
III. Larghetto ('Van Diemen's Land') (1 min)
IV. Lento ('She Borrowed Some of Her Mother's Gold') (1 min)
V. Andante tranquillo ('The Lady and the Dragon') (2 min)
VI. Allegro vivace ('As I Walked Over London Bridge') (1 min)

Background Information:

The turn of the twentieth century saw a renaissance in classical composers from England. In the previous century, the majority of concert hall music was imported from other parts of Europe, leading many to believe that England would lose its identity in music. Steps were taken to amend this problem with many philanthropists setting up major competitions to inspire English composers, in many cases requiring the candidate to write their submitted piece in a purely English form such as the phantasy. Many composers mined England's past and included English folk songs into their music.

Ralph Vaughan Williams was one of those composers who moved English music forward by looking back at the past. In pieces such as Fantasia on a Theme by Thomas Tallis, and his song cycle On Wenlock Edge, Vaughan Williams brought a pure English sensibility and style to his music.

Six Studies in English Folk Song continues his fascination with England's past, namely through folk tunes. Each movement is based on a different folk song, with Vaughan Williams treating each song with reverence and care. He doesn't just present them in the original state, but builds the songs into lovely little vignettes.

This collection of folk songs has been transcribed for other solo instruments and piano, however, the original version was written for cello and piano, which the cellist May Mukle (see Rebecca Clarke Sonata entry) premiered in 1926.

Edition:
Galaxy Music Corporation

Bibliography:
Burn, Andrew, Liner notes, "Vaughan-Williams, Ralph "Chamber Music", Paul Watkins, cello, Hyperion, 2022.
British Library biography on the composer, Accessed August 15, 2023, https://www.bl.uk/people/ralph-vaughan-williams

Recordings:
There are a handful of recordings made of the cello version; numerous other recordings have been released of the transcriptions for other instruments.

Heitor Villa-Lobos (1887-1959) — Concerto No. 2 for Cello & Orchestra, W165

Date of Composition: 1953
Date of Premiere: February 5, 1955
Premiered by: Aldo Parisot, cello; Walter Hendl conducting the New York Philharmonic
Approximate Length: 19 min.

> I. Allegro non troppo (7 min)
> II. Molto andante cantabile (5 min)
> III. Scherzo (vivace) (4 min)
> IV. Allegro engerico (3 min)

Background Information:

Heitor Villa-Lobos is one of the most prominent composers from South America. Born in Brazil, his father, an amateur cellist himself, taught Heitor cello when he was a child; he continued to play it into adulthood. He would go on to have an international career composing for many celebrated performers and ensembles, and his tours around the world brought him much fame and recognition. His music contains characteristics of his native Brazil, but mixes with more traditional classical style elements.

In 1953, famed cellist Aldo Parisot met Villa-Lobos after the string quartet he was a part premiered some of Villa-Lobos' string quartets. The two got along well, and Parisot asked him to write a concerto for him. Villa-Lobos agreed, and the two worked together on the piece, trying out different sections so that he could tailor the piece to fit Parisot.

The Concerto No. 2 was written in the last several years of his life, and was one of a group of 9 concerti that he wrote in that time period. They all fall into the four-movement template, whereas typical concerti, even in the twentieth century follow the three-movement model. Although not overtly indicated, the work contains many folk and rhythmic influences from Brazil.

Villa-Lobos would go on to write other works for cello, most famously his Bachianas Brasileiras No. 5 for soprano and cello choir, as well as two other works for cello and orchestra, a sonata with piano, smaller incidental works, such as the Pequena Suite, and other cello ensemble works.

Edition:
Max Eschig Publications

Bibliography:
Aquino, Felipe José. Villa-Lobos' Cello Concerto No. 2: A Portrait of Brazil (dissertation, Eastman School of Music, 2000)
Publisher page on the composer, Accessed August August 10, 2023, https://www.wisemusicclassical.com/composer/1640/Heitor-Villa-Lobos/

Recordings:
There are numerous commercial recordings available, namely the premiere recording made by Aldo Parisot on the Westminster label.

Antonio Vivaldi (1678-1741)   9 Sonatas for Cello & Basso Continuo, RV 39-47

Date of Composition: 1709-1730
Date of Premiere: Unknown
Premiered by: Unknown
Approximate Length: 12 min.

> I. Largo (4 min)
> II. Allegro (3 min)
> III. Largo (3 min)
> IV. Allegro (2 min)

Background Information:

    Antonio Lucia Vivaldi was one of the foremost composers of the Baroque era, particularly in the realm of instrumental music. Taking his cues from Arcangelo Corelli, Vivaldi explored the potential of stringed instruments in the form of solo concerti (not the least of which were his over 200 concertos for the violin), concerti grossi, and sonatas. Vivaldi himself was a virtuosic violinist, but it was also his teaching position at the Ospedale della Pieta, the all-girls orphanage, that gave him a place to compose so much music. (see entry on Vivaldi concerti).

    The 9 Sonatas for Cello and Basso Continuo were written over the course of a decade and seem to have been written for different scenarios or patrons. A collection of six of the sonatas were published in Paris around 1740, and the others turned up in manuscript form (eventually in print) in a couple of places in Italy. They have since been brought together into the set of 9 that are to be found today. It is possible that he wrote more sonatas, however, thus far, these are the ones that have survived and can be attributed with certainty (a 10th sonata is thought to be by him, but isn't fully verified).

    They are all within the same format commonly attributed to the sonata da chiesa, or church sonata: I. Largo II. Allegro III. Largo IV. Allegro. The accompaniment was most likely written for a keyboard instrument (such as a harpsichord or chamber organ), and may have been intended to include a second cello and/or plucked instrument (such as a theorbo or lute).

    While certainly not the only sonatas to be written for the cello in this time period, they exist as prime examples of cello chamber writing in the Baroque era.

Selected Editions:
Barenreiter (Urtext)
Wiener Urtext Edition (Urtext)

Bibliography:
Berger, Melvin Guide to Sonatas (Anchor Books, New York, 1991)
Kolneder, Walter Antonio Vivaldi: His Life and Work (University of California Press, Berkeley, 1970)
Landon, H.C. Robbins Vivaildi: Voice of the Baroque (The University of Chicago Press, Chicago, 1993)

Recordings:
Many commercial recordings have been released, both on modern set-up and on period instruments.

Antonio Vivaldi (1678-1741)   27 Concerti for Cello & Orchestra, RV 398-409

Date of Compositions: Between 1703 and 1740
Date of Premiere: Unknown
Premiered by: Unknown
Approximate Length: 10 min. (average)

> I. Allegro (3 min)
> II. Andante (4 min)
> III. Allegro (3 min)

Background Information:

Antonio Lucia Vivaldi, the so-called Il Prete Rosso (The Red Priest) was an innovative and brilliant composer of the Baroque period. The main position he held for the majority of his adult career was instructor at the Ospedale della Pieta, an all-girls orphanage in Venice, Italy. The Pieta was renowned for its musical program, and people from all across Europe came to hear these young girls perform.

Part of Vivaldi's responsibilities was not only to instruct the girls on their respective instruments, but also to compose music for them. He mainly used the relatively new genre of the solo concerto as a means of expanding their technique and artistry. As the violin was the primary solo instrument used in concerti, not to mention the instrument he was closely associated with, the bulk of the concerti were written for violin (over 200 have survived). However, he wrote concerti for a vast array of instruments in the ensemble–including bassoon, viola d'amore, trumpet, flute, and cello–at a time when solo pieces for many of these instruments were quite rare.

The twenty-seven concerti for cello represents one of the largest collections of concerti written for the cello from this time period. They range from intermediate level to highly virtuosic, anticipating the even further technically advanced concerti of Boccherini and Haydn to come. They all tend to fall in the standard Italian format for concerti: I. Allegro II. Andante III. Allegro, with a few exceptions here and there, and shows off the cello's gift for sonorous melodies, as well as more dazzling technique.

Selected Editions: (Most are sold individually, but a few collected editions are available)
Walhall Editions (Urtext)
Edition Kunzelmann
Ricordi

Bibliography:

Kolneder, Walter Antonio Vivaldi: His Life and Work (University of California Press, Berkeley, 1970)
Landon, H.C. Robbins Vivaildi: Voice of the Baroque (The University of Chicago Press, Chicago, 1993)

Recordings:
Many commercial recordings are available, both of individual concerti or compilations.

George Walker (1922-2018) — Sonata for Cello & Piano

Date of Composition: 1957
Date of Premiere: Unknown
Premiered by: Unknown; first recorded performance was by Janos Starker in 1976
Approximate Length: 16 min.

I. Allegro passionato (7 min)
II. Sostenuto (6 min)
III. Allegro (3 min)

Background Information:

  George Walker is an American icon. A brilliant pianist, in addition to composing, he studied at the Oberlin Conservatory, and the Curtis Institute of Music, becoming the first person of color to graduate from there. He then earned his Doctorate from the Eastman School of Music, once again, being the first African-American man to receive a doctoral degree, as well as an Artist diploma on piano from the school.

  He was the first African-American composer to receive the prestigious Pulitzer prize for his work Lilacs for Voice and Orchestra, and received commissions from many of the top ensembles and artists in the field, such as the New York Philharmonic, Eastman School of Music, Kennedy Center for the Performing Arts, Boston Symphony, and the Cleveland Symphony. With a catalog of over 100 works, a couple of them are written for the cello, including a Concerto, (see other entry) and his Cello Sonata.

  The Cello Sonata reflects a number of influences from traditional classical to blues to jazz. It contains some difficult contrapuntal rhythms between the two instruments, but never strays from a profound sense of melody and lyricism.

  Given that Walker was a gifted pianist himself, the piano part is considerable and a strong partner to the cello part. Despite some tricky, challenging sections (Walker doesn't waste any time, a precarious thumb position/double-stop passage appears at the very beginning of the piece), the sonata is very well-written for the cello.
The first movement is full of rhapsodic lines in the cello with undulating rhythms in the piano. The second movement is a heartbreaking, tender poem ending on a question mark. The third movement, with its spiky rhythms and propulsive energy is a rush until the very end.

  It sits extremely well with the other late-twentieth century American cello sonatas, and is rapidly becoming a staple of cello recitals around the world.

Edition:
Lauren Keiser Music Publishing

Bibliography:
Official website of the composer, Accessed August 12, 2023, https://georgetwalker.com/index.html
Program notes, Accessed August 12, 2023, http://georgetwalker.com/program_notes/notes_sonata_for_cello_and_piano.html
Article on the sonata by Seth Parker Woods, Accessed August 11, 2023, https://stringsmagazine.com/george-walkers-sonata-for-cello-and-piano-deserves-a-place-in-the-standard-cello-repertoire/

Recordings:
A few commercial recordings have been made notably one on the Albany Records label with the composer at the piano. [N.B. For those interested, there is a fantastic video discussion among cello luminaries talking in great depth about this sonata. It can be found in two different sessions on the cellobello.org website.]

George Walker (1922-2018) — Movements for Cello & Orchestra

Date of Composition: 1976, revised in 2012
Date of Premiere: 1976/Oct. 6, 2012
Premiered by: Concerto: Lorne Monroe, cello with Lorin Maazel conducting the Cleveland Orchestra / Movements: Dmitri Kouzov, cello with Ian Hobson conducting the Sinfonia da Camera at Illinois State University
Approximate Length: 24 min.

> I. Risoluto (12 min)
> II. Doloroso (5 min)
> III. Fuocoso (7 min)

Background Information:

George Walker led a distinguished and decorated career, both as a virtuoso pianist and as a composer. Winning the Pulitzer Prize in Music in 1996 (the first African-American composer to be awarded this honor) for his work Lilacs for Voice and Orchestra, his catalog of over 100 works spans solo piano works, chamber music, orchestral and choral works. He wrote another major work for cello in the form of his Cello Sonata (see other entry).

The Movements for Cello and Orchestra has an intriguing path. It was originally titled Concerto and was commissioned by the Cleveland Orchestra for Lorne Monroe, who premiered the work. Later, Walker revised the work, now calling it Dialogus for Cello and Orchestra (which was nominated for a Pulitzer). This still didn't seem to satisfy him, so he revised once again in 2012 with the final title of Movements for Cello and Orchestra.

About the revised version, Walker wrote: "Its three movements incorporate significantly revised material from an earlier work. The ascending motive that begins the introduction of the first movement becomes an integral and unifying connection within the movement."

Edition:
Lauren Keiser Music Publishing

Bibliography:
Official website of the composer, Accessed August 12, 2023, https://georgetwalker.com/
Liner notes, Walker, George, "Orchestral Works, Vol. 3", Dmitri Kouzuv, cello, Albany Records, 2011.

Recordings:
Thus far, there appears to be one commercially released recording: Dmitri Kousov on the Albany Records label.

Gwyneth Walker (b. 1947)   By Land and by Sea for Cello & Piano

Date of Composition: 2005
Date of Premiere: Unknown
Premiered by: Unknown
Approximate Length: 17 min.

I. Setting Forth (6 min)
II. One if by Land, Two if by Sea–Choices (3 min)
[Interlude–piano only]
III. Homecoming (7 min)

Background Information:

    Gwyneth Walker is an American composer with over 400 commissioned works to her name. Studying at Brown University and the Hartt School, she taught at the Oberlin Conservatory for many years before leaving to focus solely on composing. Writing in all different kinds of genres, she often incorporates aspects of Americana, folk songs and poetry into her music.

    By Land and by Sea is a three movement work for cello and piano. It was inspired by a road trip Walker took across America and contains references to different modes of transportation one can take when making a cross-country trek.

    The first movement is about embarking on a journey. The second movement concerns the different types of terrain across America. The title of the movement is taken from "Paul Revere's Ride", a poem by Henry Wadsworth Longfellow. And the last movement closes the sonata–after a brief piano-only interlude–with an ode to the return to home after a long trip.

Edition:
The sonata is available from the composer's website.

Bibliography:
Official website of the composer, Accessed August 10, 2023, https://www.gwynethwalker.com/

Recordings:
No commercial recording is available; there is, however, a live performance on youtube.

William Walton (1902-1983) — Cello Concerto

Date of Composition: 1956
Date of Premiere: January 25, 1957
Premiered by: Gregor Piatigorsky, cello; Charles Munch, conductor; Boston Symphony Orchestra
Approximate Complete Length: 30 min.

I. Moderato (9 min)
II. Allegro appassionato (7 min)
III. Tema con improvvisazioni (14 min)

Background Information:
Walton's unmistakeable legacy to British music in the twentieth century includes three exceptional concertos for string instruments: the iconic viola concerto, the violin concerto, and the cello concerto. In each case, they were written for legendary soloists, Lionel Tertis, Jascha Heifetz, and Gregor Piatigorsky, respectively.

The cello concerto was begun at Piatigorsky's request after he heard the violin concerto. After a couple of years finishing other works on his agenda, Walton completed the work. During the writing, he corresponded with Piatigorsky, receiving input and ideas for the work, much like he did with the other string concertos.

While Piatigorsky was pleased overall with the work, he was dissatisfied with the ending. He felt that Walton's original ending was too understated and that it deserved a bigger, more exciting finish. Walton agreed and ended up composing two new endings, the final one twenty years after finishing the original work. Piatigorsky finally was appeased with the third and final ending, but illness prevented him from ever performing the third version. The original ending is the one that has stuck and is the one cellists play today.

The concerto follows in the same footsteps as his other two string concertos in that it opens with a slower movement, rather than a faster movement. The brisker movement comes in the 2nd movement with lots of virtuosic displays from the cello, contrasting with the soulful, slightly esoteric melodic material in the first movement. The third movement is titled Tema con improvvisazioni, which would suggest some improvisation is involved, but it's actually a set of variations based on a central theme. The movement encapsulates the entire concerto's mood with alternating episodes of virtuosity and mellow reflective material.

The Walton concerto joins the Elgar Cello Concerto and Britten Cello Symphony as a major contribution to the cello repertoire from an English composer.

Edition:
Oxford University Press, 1957, reprinted in 2010

Bibliography:
Steinberg, Michael. The Concerto: A Listener's Guide (Oxford University Press, New York, 1998).

Recordings:
There are a handful of commercial recordings of this work available.

Mary D. Watkins (b. 1939)   Bus Stop for Cello & Piano

Date of Composition: 2000
Date of Premiere: Unknown
Premiered by: Unknown
Approximate Length: 3 min.

Background Information:

Mostly known for her operas Dark River and Queen Clara , American composer Mary D. Watkins has composed across a wide spectrum of genres, vocal, symphonic and instrumental, and many film scores.

Educated at Howard University, she navigated the difficult world of composing Classical-style music as an African-American woman at a time when that was not the norm. For many years, she worked as a jazz pianist and arranger, appearing on several albums of jazz works, and notably worked for Olivia Records Collective, an all-female recording label. Her music is often a fusion of jazz, spirituals, and a more traditional classical style.

Bus Stop for cello and piano was composed in 2000. It is one of a few pieces she has written for cello, including Focus and The Medium.

Edition:
Hildegard Publishing Company as part of the "Black Women Composers: 20th Century Music for Piano and Strings

Bibliography:
Official website of the composer, Accessed August 8, 2023, https://marydwatkins.com/

Recordings:
To date, there are no recordings of this work.

Anton Webern (1883-1945)   Drei Kleine Stücke, Op. 11 for Cello & Piano

Date of Composition: 1914
Date of Premiere: Unknown
Premiered by: Unknown
Approximate Length: 3 min.

                               I. Mäßige Achtel (1 min)
                               II. Sehr Bewegt (1 min)
                               III. Äußerst Ruhig (1 min)

Background Information:
    Anton Webern, the third member of the Second Viennese School with Arnold Schoenberg and Alban Berg, was a master of brevity. Distilling his pieces to their bare essence, no note, no dynamic or expressive marking is wasted. Everything has a purpose, there is no filler. His pieces are the definition of brief–his entire catalog can be performed in about three hours, while at the same time expanding the possibilities of the 12-tone system of composing.
    Webern had a connection with the cello, studying it when he was younger, composing a sonata and an earlier set of two pieces for cello and piano. His Drei Kleine Stücke for Cello and Piano perfectly encapsulates his approach to music–the entire work is three minutes–yet a lot is contained within.
Sparse and spacious, the music is made up of single gestures back and forth between the two
instruments. Some notes are barely audible in wispy harmonics, while the next note bursts out of the texture, full-voiced.
    These are challenging works, pushing the two performers to create meaning out of such small elements and translating that to the audience. It is a unique experience for players and listeners and is unforgettable.

Edition:
Universal Edition

Bibliography:
Biography page on the composer, Accessed August 12, 2023, https://www.britannica.com/biography/Anton-Webern

Recordings:
Numerous cellists have made commercial recordings of this work.

Paul Wiancko (b.1983)   Microsuite for Solo Cello

Date of Composition: 2022
Date of Premiere: November, 2022
Premiered by: Alexander Hersh, cello
Approximate Length: 5 min.

Background Information:

Paul Wiancko is an incredibly versatile and creative cellist/composer. Crossing genres right and left, he successfully fuses all types of musical genres and styles in his playing and composing. He studied at the Colburn School of Music and was put into the international spotlight when he tied for second place in the Lutosławski International Cello Competition. Early on, he began producing and working with singer/songwriters and pop musicians.

He is currently the cellist in the world-famous Kronos Quartet as well as the founding member of the Owls Quartet, a unique ensemble with a violin, viola and two cellos. He has composed for a variety of instruments and ensembles, in addition to arranging music and playing with artists such as Arcade Fire, Wye Oak and Norah Jones.

His piece Microsuite for Solo Cello was commissioned by the Pro Musicas Foundation for their International Award competition, using it as one of the required pieces for the finals. Cellist Alexander Hersh won, performing it in a program that also included the sonatas by Debussy and Benjamin Britten.

About the work, Wiancko writes: "It is exhilarating to discover music that unlocks something in us. As a young cellist, my first plunge into the rich darkness of Bach's Fifth Suite for Solo Cello was deeply formative. I will also never forget the thrill of stepping into the worlds of Lutoslawski, Chick Corea, or Mahsa Vahdat for the first time. As I composed Microsuite, I channeled the thrill of these moments of discovery, and in the process enjoyed a renewed appreciation for the cello music that impacted me in my youth. I hope this little piece might serve as a reminder that there is always potential to gain a deeper understanding of ourselves simply by stumbling onto something new."

Edition:
Available from Wiancko Editions from the composer's website

Bibliography:
Official website of the composer, Accessed August 9, 2023, http://www.paulwiancko.com/
Program notes on the piece, Accessed August 9, 2023, https://nyconcertreview.com/reviews/pro-musicis-presents-alexander-hersh-in-review/

Recordings:
At press time, no recording is available, although there is a clip of Wiancko playing the piece on his social media.

John Williams (b. 1932) Elegy for Cello & Piano

Date of Composition: 1997
Date of Premiere: February 24, 2002
Premiered by: Yo-Yo Ma, cello with the Los Angeles Philharmonic
Approximate Length: 6 min.

Background Information:

Although most know composer John Williams for his incredibly famous film scores, such as Star Wars, Indiana Jones, E.T., Jaws, Jurassic Park, Schindler's List, Superman, and Harry Potter, he has also written a fair amount of music for the concert hall. These include a number of works for solo cello, including a cello concerto (that was recently revised in 2022), and a trio of pieces for unaccompanied cello. Sadly, none of these scores are available, however, the lone exception being his Elegy for Cello and Piano.

In 1997, John Williams wrote the score for the film Seven Years in Tibet, based on the real life of Heinrich Harrer, a mountain climber who ended up forming a friendship with the young Dalai Lama. The film, directed by Jean-Jaques Annaud, is big and epic, with Williams rising to the occasion by composing one of his most lushest and grandest scores, which is saying a lot.

Williams enlisted frequent collaborator Yo-Yo Ma to perform all of the cello solos, which run throughout the score. In one of the final cues of the score, titled "Regaining a Son", Williams wrote a beautiful and touching melody, which stayed in the back of his mind, perhaps to be expanded some time later.

A short while later, a violinist friend of Williams' tragically lost two of her children. For the memorial service, Williams was to write a short piece to be performed. He remembered this theme from the Tibet score and expanded it into an Elegy for cello and piano, performed by cellist John Walz at the service. Williams later orchestrated it, which Yo-Yo Ma premiered thereafter. (Only the version with piano accompaniment is available.)

The Elegy is a stunning, gorgeous lament, full of anguish, questioning, searching, reminiscing, reflection and acceptance. The accompaniment acts as comforter and support, with the cello weaving all around, struggling to find any kind of solid ground. It's heartbreaking for sure, but Williams (as he so deftly did in his score for Schindler's List) never gives into pity or self-indulgence. It ends in a prayer-like resignation, the cello soaring high in its tessitura. One would be hard pressed to listen to this work and not be moved– it is a stunning work of remembrance.

Edition:
Hal Leonard Publications, 1998

Bibliography:
Williams, John, Liner notes, Williams, John, "Yo-Yo Ma Plays the Music of John Williams", Yo-Yo Ma, cello, Sony Classics, 2022.

Recordings:
The cello and orchestra version can be heard on the recording "Yo-Yo Ma Plays the Music of John Williams" on Sony Classics, 2002.

John Williams (b. 1932) — Theme from Schindler's List for Cello & Piano

Date of Composition: 1993
Date of Premiere: Unknown
Premiered by: Unknown
Approximate Length: 4 min.

Background Information:

In a career full of highlights, not to mention becoming one of the most famous and well-known composers of all time, John Williams reached a new high in December of 1993 with his score for Schindler's List. Fresh off his record-breaking film Jurassic Park, released 6 months earlier, director Steven Spielberg released one of his most personal films to date. A film about the atrocities of the Holocaust and one man's path to trying to save as many Jewish lives as possible. The film was a milestone for both Spielberg and his long-time collaborator Williams, winning Best Picture and Best Original Score, among others, at that year's Academy Awards.

Striving to bring the humanity out of such gut-wrenching material, Williams turned to legendary violinist Itzhak Perlman to perform all of the violin solos throughout the score. It brings the emotion to a personal level through the persona of the lone violin, bringing even more power and meaning to the music, and thus, the film.

Like many of Williams' scores, the music from Schindler's List has taken on a life outside of the film score. He has arranged different parts of the score for other instruments and formats. In the opening notes to the cello edition, Williams writes, "For many years, I thought that cellists might also bring their own particular magic to this music, and I am proud to offer this adaptation that I have made expressly for them." It is a special gift that Williams has given cellists from a very special score.

Edition:
Hal Leonard Publications

Bibliography:
Williams, John, Preface, Williams, John "Theme from Schindler's List for Cello and Piano", Milwaukee: Hal Leonard Publications, 1993.

Recordings:
There is, of course, the legendary original soundtrack recording to the film with Itzhak Perlman's wonderful performance that is available. Yo-Yo Ma plays an arrangement of three themes from the film with the New York Philharmonic and conducted by Williams on their "A Gathering of Friends" recording from 2022. Gautier Capuçon has recorded the main theme with orchestra on his "Sensations" recording from 2021.

John Williams (b. 1932)
Three Pieces from Memoirs of a Geisha for Cello & Piano

Date of Composition: 2005
Date of Premiere: 2005
Premiered by: Yo-Yo Ma, cello
Approximate Length: 9 min.

I. Sayuri Theme (4 min)
II. A Dream Discarded (2 min)
III. Going to School (3 min)

Background Information:

    John Williams, best known for his epic orchestral soundtracks for such films as Star Wars, Indiana Jones, and Jaws, has composed more than a few scores for quieter, dramatic films. One of those was Memoirs of a Geisha which is a film based on the best-selling novel by Arthur Goldstein.

    The score heavily features cello solos for which Williams employed legendary cellist Yo-Yo Ma. Williams said that, "I decided to feature the cello to portray the character of Sayuri, the beautiful young geisha in the story." The story is told from Sayruri's eyes with the music of the cello shadowing her all throughout the film.
After the film's release, Williams arranged six of the segments from the score into a suite for cello and orchestra, which was then released in a suite of three pieces for cello and piano.

Edition:
Hal Leonard Publications

Bibliography:
Williams, John, Preface, Williams, John, "Suite from Memoirs of a Geisha for Cello and Piano", Milwaukee: Hal Leonard Publications, 2005.

Recordings:
Aside from the original soundtrack featuring Ma, the suite for cello and orchestra has not been recorded.

Luna Pearl Woolf (b. 1973) — Helter Skelter arr. for Solo Cello

Date of Composition: 2012
Date of Premiere: 2012
Premiered by: Matt Haimovitz, cello
Approximate Length: 5 min.

Background Information:

Luna Pearl Woolf is fascinated with music as a means to tell a story. She achieves this both in her abstract music, and in works with voice or narrator. For her works, she is the recipient of Grammy awards and has been commissioned by major artists in the Classical field. With husband, cellist Matt Haimovitz, they have created the Oxingale recording label, which has been expanded to include publishing, not only her works, but works of other composers.

Because of her connection with Haimovitz, she has written a number of works for cello, including a handful of solo cello works, a piece for cello and string orchestra, and quite a few chamber works that feature the cello.

Despite the wealth of cello music she's written thus far–and it's all well worth checking out–it's her electrifying arrangement of the Beatles' "Helter Skelter" that is a real showstopper. Based on the raucous song by Paul McCartney from their album The White Album, Woolf captures all of the raw energy and power of the original song. It's a five-minute knockout full of sul ponticello, knocking on the fingerboard, wispy harmonics, crazy glissandi, with a bit of amplification.

Edition:
Available from Oxingale Press

Bibliography:
Official website of the composer, Accessed August 11, 2023, https://lunapearlwoolf.com/

Recordings:
The piece is included on Haimovitz's album Orbit on the Oxingale label.

Alexander Zemlinsky (1871-1942)   Sonata in A Minor for Cello & Piano

Date of Composition: 1894
Date of Premiere: 1894
Premiered by: Friedrich Buxbaum, cello with Alexander Zemlinsky, piano
Approximate Length: 26 min.

>   I. Mit Leidenschaft (11 min)
>   II. Andante (8 min)
>   III. Allegretto (8 min)

Background Information:
  Alexander Zemlinsky, was an Austrian composer contemporaneous with Johannes Brahms, who was a great supporter and champion of Zemlinsky's music. Zemlinsky got his works published by the esteemed publisher Simrock thanks to Brahms' recommendation. He eventually became an important figure as both a composer and conductor, as well as teaching–Arnold Schoenberg was a student of his. After the rise of Nazism, Zemlinsky fled to America where he remained for the rest of his life. Zemlinsky left behind a catalog of art songs, chamber music, symphonic and choral works.
  His Cello Sonata was written and premiered in 1894 at the Weiner Tonküntslerverin, which was a program that supported emerging composers in Vienna (Brahms was one of the main figures in this organization). Some time after the premiere, the manuscript was thought lost, as it disappeared from public performance, but later reemerged and was given to pianist Peter Wallfisch. Wallfisch is the father of famed cellist Raphael Wallfisch, who with the help of Zemlinsky scholar, Antony Beaumont, prepared the work, still in manuscript form, for publishing. Wallfisch made the premiere recording in 2006.

Edition:
Ricordi

Bibliography:
Biography on the composer, Accessed August 9, 2023, http://orelfoundation.org/composers/article/alexander_zemlinsky
Program notes on cellist Raphael Wallfisch's website, Accessed August 9, 2023, http://www.raphaelwallfisch.com/?p=384

Recordings:
This sonata has a number of commercial recordings available, namely Raphael Wallfisch's premiere recording on Nimbus Records.

Ellen Taaffe Zwillich (b. 1939) — Cello Concerto

Date of Composition: 2020
Date of Premiere: March 5, 2020
Premiered by: Zuill Bailey, cello; Sebrina María Alfonso conductor with the South Florida Symphony Orchestra
Approximate Length: 19 min.

I. (6 min)
II. (7 min)
III. (6 min)
(performed without pause)

Background Information:

As the first woman to receive the Pulitzer Prize in music, as well as a host of other awards, including an Academy Award, Ellen Taaffe Zwilich has been at the forefront of composing for decades. She describes her music as music with "fingerprints", as it has her distinctive personality and voice imbued throughout. Her musical style tends to incorporate atonality yet with a sense of romanticism. She is one of the most widely-performed living composers today.

Her Cello Concerto was written in 2020. It is dedicated to the premiere artists, cellist Zuill Bailey and conductor Sebrina María Alfonso, with an extended dedication to legendary cellists Leonard Rose and Mstislav Rostropovich.

Before writing this concerto, Zwilich said that writing a cello concerto was high on her list of pieces to compose. She says, "One of the things I love about the cello is that it covers virtually the entire range of the human voice…My Cello Concerto engages both the lyrical, singing nature of the instrument and its technical possibilities." (Zwilich)

Edition:
Theodore Presser Company

Bibliography:
Official website of the composer, Accessed August 8, 2023, https://www.zwilich.com/
Zwilich, Ellen Taaffe, Liner notes, Zwilich, Ellen Taaffe "Cello Concerto & Other Works", Zuill Bailey, cello, Delos Records, 2022.

Recordings:
Zuill Bailey released a commercial recording of the concerto on the Delos label in 2002.

Appendix A

Unaccompanied

Alberga, Eleanor	Ride Through for Solo Cello
Alexander, Eric	Symmetry of Trees for Solo Cello
Bach, J.S.	Six Suites for Unaccompanied Cello, BWV 1007-1012
Britten, Benjamin	Three Suites for Solo Cello
Canzano, Nicola	Partita No. 1 for Solo Cello
Casarrubios, Andrea	Seven for Solo Cello
Cassadó, Gaspar	Suite for Solo Cello
Corigliano, John	Fancy on a Bach Air for Solo Cello
Crumb, George	Sonata for Solo Cello
Dall'Abaco, Giuseppe	11 Capricii for Solo Cello
Dessner, Bryce	Tuusula for Solo Cello
Esmail, Reena	Perhaps for Solo Cello
Frank, Gabriella Lena & David Fetherolf	Serenata for Solo Cello
Gabrielli, Domenico	Ricercari per violoncello solo
Glass, Philip	Orbit for Solo Cello
Glass, Philip	Partita No. 1 for Solo Cello (Songs & Poems)
Gubaidulina, Sofia	Ten Preludes for Solo Cello
Hailstork, Adolphus	Draw the Sacred Circle Closer for Solo Cello
Hindemith, Paul	Sonata for Solo Cello, Op. 25, No. 3
Holst, Imogen	Fall of the Leaf for Solo Cello
Hughes, Chad "Sir Wick"	First Suite for Solo Cello
Joachim, Nathalie	Dam Mwen Yo for Solo Cello
Kodály, Zoltán	Sonata for Solo Cello, Op. 8
Larsen, Libby	Juba for Solo Cello
León, Tania	Four Pieces for Solo Cello
Loggins-Hull, Allison	Stolen for Solo Cello
Ligeti, György	Sonata for Solo Cello
Mazzoli, Missy	Beyond the Order of Things (After Josquin) for Solo Cello
Mellits, Marc	Book of Ruth for Solo Cello
Moore, Dorothy Rudd	Baroque Suite for Solo Cello
Musgrave, Thea	D.E.S.-In Celebration for Solo Cello
Perkinson, Coleridge Taylor	Lamentations from Black Folk Song Suite for Solo Cello
Prestini, Paola	To Tell a Story for Solo Cello and Electronics
Prokofiev, Gabriel	Cello Multitracks
Raitz, Kathryn	Not So Simple for Solo Cello
Ran, Shalumit	Fantasy Variations for Solo Cello
Reger, Max	Three Suites for Solo Cello, Op. 131c
Roumain, Daniel Bernard	Why Did They Kill Sandra Bland? for Solo Cello
Rouse, Christopher	Morpheus for Solo Cello
Saariaho, Kaija	Sept Papillons for Solo Cello
Singleton, Alvin	Argoru II for Solo Cello
Shaw, Caroline	In manus tuas for Solo Cello
Sheng, Bright	Seven Tunes Heard in China for Solo Cello
Skye, Derrick	Hum for Solo Cello
Snider, Sarah Kirkland	The Reserved, The Reticent for Solo Cello

Steinmetz, John	Possessed for Solo Cello
Summer, Mark	Julie-O for Solo Cello
Wiancko, Paul	Microsuite for Solo Cello
Woolf, Luna Pearl	Helter Skelter arranged for Solo Cello

With Piano

Ades, Thomas	Lieux retrouvés for Cello and Piano
Auerbach, Lera	24 Preludes for Cello and Piano, Op. 69
Auerbach, Lera	Cello Sonata
Bach, J.S.	Three Sonatas for Viola da Gamba and Keyboard, BWV 1027-1029
Baker, David	Cello Sonata
Balentine, James	A Wiser Man for Cello and Piano
Barber, Samuel	Sonata for Cello and Piano in C Minor, Op. 6
Barriere, Jean-Baptiste	Sonatas for Cello and Basso Continuo
Beach, Amy	Five Compositions for Cello and Piano (transcription)
Beamish, Sally	Cello Sonata
Beethoven, Ludwig van	Three Sets of Variations for Piano and Cello, WoO 45, 46, Op. 66
Beethoven, Ludwig van	Sonatas for Piano and Cello Op. 5, No. 1 and No. 2
Beethoven, Ludwig van	Sonata for Cello and Piano No. 3 in A Major, Op. 69
Beethoven, Ludwig van	Sonatas for Cello and Piano Op. 102, No 1 and No. 2
Biedenbender, David	Light Over Mountains for Cello and Piano
Bloch, Ernest	Prayer from Jewish Life, sketches for Cello and Piano
Boccherini, Luigi	Six Cello Sonatas
Bonis, Melanie Helene	Sonata for Cello and Piano in F Major, Op. 67
Boulanger, Lili	Nocturne for Cello and Piano (transcription)
Boulanger, Nadia	Three Pieces for Cello and Piano
Brahms, Johannes	Sonata for Cello and Piano No. 1 in E-flat Major, Op. 38
Brahms, Johannes	Sonata for Cello and Piano No. 2 in F Major, Op. 99
Bridge, Frank	Sonata for Cello and Piano in D Minor, H. 125
Britten, Benjamin	Sonata for Cello and Piano, Op. 65
Bunch, Kenji	Broken Music for Cello and Piano
Carter, Elliott	Sonata for Cello and Piano
Casals, Pablo	Song of the Birds for Cello and Piano
Chopin, Frédéric	Introduction et polonaise brillante, Op. 3
Chopin, Frédéric	Sonata for Cello and Piano in G Minor, Op. 65
Clarke, Rebecca	Sonata for Cello and Piano
Coleridge-Taylor, Samuel	Variations in B Minor for Cello and Piano
Day, Kevin	Sonata for Cello and Piano
Debussy, Claude	Sonata for Cello and Piano in D Minor (1915)
Dunphy, Melissa	Baroque Variations on "The Frail" for Cello and Piano
Fàbregas, Elisenda	Colores Andaluces for Cello and Piano
Farrenc, Louise	Cello Sonata
Faure, Gabriel	Èlègie for Cello and Piano, Op. 24
Faure, Gabriel	Sonata for Cello and Piano No. 2 in G Minor, Op. 117
Fine, Vivian	Cello Sonata (1986)
Foss, Lukas	Capriccio for Cello and Piano
Franck, Cèsar	Sonata for Cello and Piano in A Major

Ginastera, Albert	Pampeana No. 2 for Cello and Piano, Op. 21
Granados, Enrique	Intermezzo (from Goyescas) for Cello and Piano
Grieg, Edvard	Sonata for Cello and Piano in A Minor, Op. 36
Hidgon, Jennifer	Nocturne for Cello and Piano
Hoiby, Lee	Cello Sonata
Ireland, John	Sonata for Cello and Piano in G Minor
Janáček, Leoš	Pohádka for Cello and Piano
Johnson, David H.	5 Melodies for Cello and Piano
LeBeau, Luise	Cello Sonata
MacMillan, James	Sonata No. 1 for Cello and Piano
Maconchy, Elizabeth	Divertimento for Cello and Piano
Martinů, Bohuslav	Sonata for Cello and Piano No. 3, H. 340
Mayer, Emilie	12 Cello Sonatas
Mendelssohn, Fanny	Zwei Stücke for Cello and Piano
Mendelssohn, Felix	Sonata for for Cello and Piano No. 2 in D Major, Op. 58
Nyman, Michael	On the Fiddle for Cello and Piano
Paradis Maria Theresia von	Sicilienne for Cello and Piano
Pärt, Arvo	Spiegel im Spiegel for Cello and Piano
Pärt, Arvo	Fratres for Cello and Piano
Pejačević, Dora	Cello Sonata in E Minor, Op. 35
Piazzolla, Astor	Le Grand Tango for Cello and Piano
Popper, David	Hungarian Rhapsody, Op. 68 for Cello and Piano
Porpora, Nicola	Six Cello Sonatas
Poulenc, Francis	Sonata for Cello and Piano, FP 143
Price, Florence	Adoration for Cello and Piano
Prokofiev, Sergei	Sonata for Cello and Piano in C Major, Op. 119
Pucihar, Blaž	Summer Sonata for Cello and Piano
Puts, Kevin	Air for Cello and Piano
Rachmaninoff, Sergei	Sonata for Cello and Piano in G Minor, Op. 19
Rochberg, George	Ricordanza Soliloquy for Cello and Piano
Romberg, Bernard	Sonata for Cello and Piano No. 1 in E Minor, Op 38
Saint-Säens, Camille	Le Cygne from Le Carnaval des animaux for Cello and Piano
Schnittke, Alfred	Sonata for Cello and Piano No. 1
Schubert, Franz	Sonata for Cello and Piano in A Minor, Arpeggione, D. 421
Schumann, Robert	Fünf Stücke im Volkston, Op. 102 for Cello & Piano
Shostakovich, Dmitri	Sonata for Cello and Piano in D Minor, Op. 40
Sibelius , Jean	Malinconia for Cello and Piano, Op. 20
Smyth, Ethel	Cello Sonata
Steinberg, Carolyn	A Wintry Mix: Of Ice and Snow for Cello and Piano
Still, William Grant	Mother & Child for Cello and Piano
Strauss, Richard	Sonata for Cello and Piano in F Major, Op. 6
Stravinsky, Igor	Suite Italienne for Cello and Piano (after Pulcinella, trans. Piatigorsky)
Thomas, Augusta Read	Cantos for Slava for Cello and Piano
Tower, Joan	Très lent (Hommage à Messiaen) for Cello and Piano
Vaughan Williams, Ralph	Six Studies in English Folk Song for Cello and Piano
Vivaldi, Antonio	Nine Sonatas for Cello and Basso Continuo, RV 39-47
Walker, George	Cello Sonata
Watkins, Mary	Bus Stop for Cello and Piano
Webern, Anton	Drei Kleine Stücke, Op. 11 for Cello and Piano
Williams, John	Three Pieces from Memoirs of a Geisha for Cello and Piano

Williams, John	Theme from Schindler's List for Cello and Piano
Williams, John	Elegie for Cello and Piano
Zemlinsky, Alexander	Cello Sonata in A Minor

Concerto

Bach, CPE	3 Cello Concerti, WQ. 170, 171, 172
Barber, Samuel	Cello Concerto in A Minor, Op. 22
Bates, Mason	Cello Concerto
Bayolo, Armando	Orfei Mors for Cello and Orchestra
Beethoven, Ludwig van	Triple Concerto for Violin, Cello and Piano, Op. 56
Bernstein, Leonard	Three Meditations from 'The Mass' for Cello and Orchestra
Bloch, Ernest	Schelomo: Rhapsodie Hèbräquie for Cello and Orchestra
Boccherini, Luigi	Twelve Cello Concerti
Boëllmann, Léon	Variations symphoniques, Op. 23 for Cello and Orchestra
Brahms, Johannes	Double Concerto for Violin and Cello in A Minor, Op. 102
Bridge, Frank	Oration (Concerto elegiaco) for Cello and Orchestra
Bruch, Max	Kol Nidrei, Op. 47 for Cello and Orchestra
Chin, Unsik	Cello Concerto
Clyne, Anna	Dance for Cello and Orchestra
Daugherty, Michael	Tales of Hemingway for Cello and Orchestra
Dun, Tan	Crouching Tiger Concerto for Cello and Orchestra
Dutilleux, Henri	Tout un monde lointain for Cello and Orchestra
Dvořák, Antonin	Silent Woods, Op. 68, B. 133
Dvořák, Antonin	Cello Concerto in B Minor, Op. 104
Elgar, Edward	Cello Concerto in E Minor, Op. 85
Finzi, Gerald	Cello Concerto in A Minor, Op. 40
Golijov, Osvaldo	Azul for Cello and Orchestra
Goltermann, Georg	Cello Concerto No. 4 in G, Op. 65
Haydn, Franz Joseph	Cello Concerto No. 1 in C Major, Hob. VIIb: 1
Haydn, Franz Joseph	Cello Concerto No. 2 in D Major, Hob. VIIb: 2
Herbert, Victor	Cello Concerto No. 2 in E Minor, Op. 30
Jäel, Marie	Cello Concerto
Kabalevsky, Dmitri	Cello Concerto No. 1 in G Minor, Op. 49
Kernis, Aaron	Colored Field Concerto for Cello and Orchestra
Korngold, Erich Wolfgang	Cello Concerto in C Major, Op. 37
Kraft, Antonín	Cello Concerto No. 1 in C Major, Op. 4
Lalo, Édouard	Concerto in D Minor
Leo, Leonardo	Six Cello Concerti
Lutosławski, Witold	Cello Concerto
Milhaud, Darius	Concerto for Cello and Orchestra No. 1, Op. 136
Monn, Georg Matthias	Cello Concerto in G Minor
Montgomery, Jessie	Divided for Cello and Orchestra
Muhly, Nico	Cello Concerto
Penderecki, Krzysztof	Cello Concerto No. 2
Prokofiev, Sergei	Sinfonia Concertante for Cello and Orchestra, Op. 125

Respighi, Ottorini	Adagio con Variazioni for Cello and Orchestra
Rodrigo, Joaquin	Concierto in modo galante for Cello and Orchestra
Saint-Säens, Camille	Cello Concerto No. 1 in A Minor, Op. 33
Sallinen, Aulis	Cello Concerto
Schumann, Robert	Cello Concerto in A Minor, Op. 129
Shostakovich, Dmitri	Cello Concerto No. 1 in E-Flat Major, Op. 107
Stamitz, Carl	Cello Concerti for the King of Prussia
Strauss, Richard	Don Quixote, for Cello and Orchestra, Op. 35
Tavener, John	The Protecting Veil for Cello and Orchestra
Tchaikovsky, Piotr Ilyich	Variations on a Rococo Theme, Op. 33 for Cello and Orchestra
Tricklir, Jean Balthasar	13 Cello Concerti
Vasks, Peteris	Cello Concerto
Villa-Lobos, Heitor	Cello Concerto No. 2
Vivaldi, Antonio	Twenty-Seven Concerti for Cello and Orchestra, RV 398-409
Walker, George	Movements for Cello and Orchestra
Walton, William	Cello Concerto
Zwilich, Ellen Taaffe	Cello Concerto

Appendix B: Chronology of Works

c. 1687	Gabrielli, Domenico	Ricercari per violoncello solo
1703	Vivaldi, Antonio	Twenty-Seven Concerti for Cello and Orchestra, RV 398-409
1709	Vivaldi, Antonio	Nine Sonatas for Cello and Basso Continuo, RV 39-47
c. 1720	Bach, J.S.	Six Suites for Unaccompanied Cello, BWV 1007-1012
c. 1733	Barriere, Jean-Baptiste	Sonatas for Cello and Basso Continuo
c. 1735	Bach, J.S.	Three Sonatas for Viola da Gamba and Keyboard, BWV 1027-1029
1737	Leo, Leonardo	Six Cello Concerti
1740	Monn, Georg Matthias	Cello Concerto in G Minor
1750	Bach, CPE	3 Cello Concerti, WQ. 170, 171, 172
1765	Haydn, Franz Joseph	Cello Concerto No. 1 in C Major, Hob. VIIb: 1
1766	Dall'Abaco, Giuseppe	11 Capricii for Solo Cello
1766	Porpora, Nicola	Six Cello Sonatas
c.1770	Boccherini, Luigi	Twelve Cello Concerti
1772	Boccherini, Luigi	Six Cello Sonatas
1783	Haydn, Franz Joseph	Cello Concerto No. 2 in D Major, Hob. VIIb: 2
c. 1786	Stamitz, Carl	Cello Concerti for the King of Prussia
1792	Kraft, Antonín	Cello Concerto No. 1 in C Major, Op. 4
1796	Beethoven, Ludwig van	Three Sets of Variations for Piano and Cello, WoO 45, 46, Op. 66
1796	Beethoven, Ludwig van	Sonatas for Piano and Cello Op. 5, No. 1 and No. 2
1804	Beethoven, Ludwig van	Triple Concerto for Violin, Cello and Piano, Op. 56
1808	Beethoven, Ludwig van	Sonata for Cello and Piano No. 3 in A Major, Op. 69
1815	Beethoven, Ludwig van	Sonatas for Cello and Piano Op. 102, No 1 and No. 2
1822	Frank, César	Sonata in A Major for Cello and Piano
1824	Schubert, Franz	Sonata for Cello and Piano in A Minor, Arpeggione, D. 421
1825	Romberg, Bernard	Sonata for Cello and Piano No. 1 in E Minor, Op 38
1830	Chopin, Frédéric	Introduction et polonaise brillante, Op. 3
1830	Mendelssohn, Fanny	Zwei Stücke for Cello and Piano
1843	Mendelssohn, Felix	Sonata for Cello and Piano No. 2 in D Major, Op. 58
1846	Chopin, Frédéric	Sonata for Cello and Piano in G Minor, Op. 65
1849	Schumann, Robert	Fünf Stücke im Volkston, Op. 102 for Cello & Piano
1850	Schumann, Robert	Cello Concerto in A Minor, Op. 129
1853	Goltermann, Georg	Cello Concerto No. 4 in G, Op. 65
1857	Farrenc, Louise	Cello Sonata
1866	Brahms, Johannes	Sonata for Cello and Piano No. 1 in E-flat Major, Op. 33
1872	Saint-Säens, Camille	Cello Concerto No. 1 in A Minor, Op. 33
1873	Mayer, Emilie	12 Cello Sonatas
1876	Lalo, Édouard	Concerto in D Minor
1876	Tchaikovsky, Piotr Ilyich	Variations on a Rococo Theme, Op. 33 for Cello and Orchestra
1878	LeBeau, Luise	Cello Sonata
1880	Faure, Gabriel	Èlègie for Cello and Piano, Op. 24
1880	Bruch, Max	Kol Nidrei, Op. 47 for Cello and Orchestra
1882	Jäel, Marie	Cello Concerto
1883	Grieg, Edvard	Sonata for Cello and Piano in A Minor, Op. 36
1883	Strauss, Richard	Sonata for Cello and Piano in F Major, Op. 6
1886	Saint-Säens, Camille	Le Cygne from Le Carnaval des animaux for Cello and Piano
1886	Brahms, Johannes	Sonata for Cello and Piano No. 2 in F Major, Op. 99
1887	Brahms, Johannes	Double Concerto for Violin and Cello in A Minor, Op. 182

1887	Smyth, Ethel	Cello Sonata
1888	Franck, Cèsar	Sonata for Cello and Piano in A Major
1891	Dvořák, Antonin	Silent Woods, Op. 68, B. 133
1892	Boëllmann, Léon	Variations symphoniques, Op. 23 for Cello and Orchestra
1893	Popper, David	Hungarian Rhapsody, Op. 68 for Cello and Piano
1894	Herbert, Victor	Cello Concerto No. 2 in E Minor, Op. 30
1894	Zemlinsky, Alexander	Cello Sonata in A Minor
1895	Dvořák, Antonin	Cello Concerto in B Minor, Op. 104
1897	Strauss, Richard	Don Quixote, for Cello and Orchestra, Op. 35
1900	Sibelius, Jean	Malinconia for Cello and Piano, Op. 20
1901	Rachmaninoff, Sergei	Sonata for Cello and Piano in G Minor, Op. 19
1903	Beach, Amy	Five Compositions for Cello and Piano (transcription)
1905	Bonis, Melanie Helene	Sonata for Cello and Piano in F Major, Op. 67
1905	Coleridge-Taylor, Samuel	Variations in B Minor for Cello and Piano
1910	Janáček, Leoš	Pohádka for Cello and Piano
1911	Boulanger, Lili	Nocturne for Cello and Piano (transcription)
1913	Bridge, Frank	Sonata for Cello and Piano in D Minor, H. 125
1913	Pejačević, Dora	Cello Sonata in E Minor, Op. 35
1914	Boulanger, Nadia	Three Pieces for Cello and Piano
1914	Reger, Max	Three Suites for Solo Cello, Op. 131c
1914	Webern, Anton	Drei Kleine Stücke, Op. 11 for Cello and Piano
1915	Bloch, Ernest	Schelomo: Rhapsodie Hèbräquie for Cello and Orchestra
1915	Debussy, Claude	Sonata for Cello and Piano in D Minor (1915)
1915	Kodály, Zoltán	Sonata for Solo Cello, Op. 8
1919	Clarke, Rebecca	Sonata for Cello and Piano
1919	Elgar, Edward	Cello Concerto in E Minor, Op. 85
1921	Faure, Gabriel	Sonata for Cello and Piano No. 2 in G Minor, Op. 117
1921	Respighi, Ottorini	Adagio con Variazioni for Cello and Orchestra
1922	Hindemith, Paul	Sonata for Solo Cello, Op. 25, No. 3
1924	Bloch, Ernest	Prayer from Jewish Life, sketches for Cello and Piano
1924	Ireland, John	Sonata for Cello and Piano in G Minor
1924	Paradis Maria Theresia von	Sicilienne for Cello and Piano (published)
1926	Cassadó, Gaspar	Suite for Solo Cello
1926	Vaughan Williams, Ralph	Six Studies in English Folk Song for Cello and Piano
1929	Bridge, Frank	Oration (Concerto elegiaco) for Cello and Orchestra
1932	Barber, Samuel	Sonata for Cello and Piano in C Minor, Op. 6
1932	Stravinsky, Igor	Suite Italienne for Cello and Piano (after Pulcinella, trans. Piatigorsky)
1934	Milhaud, Darius	Concerto for Cello and Orchestra No. 1, Op. 136
1934	Shostakovich, Dmitri	Sonata for Cello and Piano in D Minor, Op. 40
1939	Casals, Pablo	Song of the Birds for Cello and Piano
1941	Maconchy, Elizabeth	Divertimento for Cello and Piano
1943	Still, William Grant	Mother & Child for Cello and Piano
1945	Barber, Samuel	Cello Concerto in A Minor, Op. 22
1946	Foss, Lukas	Capriccio for Cello and Piano
1946	Korngold, Erich Wolfgang	Cello Concerto in C Major, Op. 37
1948	Carter, Elliott	Sonata for Cello and Piano
1948	Kabalevsky, Dmitri	Cello Concerto No. 1 in G Minor, Op. 49
1948	Ligeti, György	Sonata for Solo Cello
1948	Poulenc, Francis	Sonata for Cello and Piano, FP 143
1949	Prokofiev, Sergei	Sonata for Cello and Piano in C Major, Op. 119

1949	Rodrigo, Joaquin	Concierto in modo galante for Cello and Orchestra
1950	Ginastera, Albert	Pampeana No. 2 for Cello and Piano, Op. 21
1950	Prokofiev, Sergei	Sinfonia Concertante for Cello and Orchestra, Op. 125
1951	Price, Florence	Adoration for Cello and Piano
1952	Martinů, Bohuslav	Sonata for Cello and Piano No. 3, H. 340
1953	Villa-Lobos, Heitor	Cello Concerto No. 2
1955	Crumb, George	Sonata for Solo Cello
1955	Finzi, Gerald	Cello Concerto in A Minor, Op. 40
1956	Walton, William	Cello Concerto
1957	Walker, George	Cello Sonata
1959	Shostakovich, Dmitri	Cello Concerto No. 1 in E-Flat Major, Op. 107
1961	Britten, Benjamin	Sonata for Cello and Piano, Op. 65
1963	Holst, Imogen	Fall of the Leaf for Solo Cello
1964	Britten, Benjamin	Three Suites for Solo Cello
1965	Moore, Dorothy Rudd	Baroque Suite for Solo Cello
1966	Pärt, Arvo	Pro et Contra for Cello and Orchestra
1970	Dutilleux, Henri	Tout un monde lointain for Cello and Orchestra
1970	Lutosławski, Witold	Cello Concerto
1970	Singleton, Alvin	Argoru II for Solo Cello
1972	Rochberg, George	Ricordanza Soliloquy for Cello and Piano
1973	Baker, David	Cello Sonata
1973	Perkinson, Coleridge Taylor	Lamentations from Black Folk Song Suite for Solo Cello
1974	Gubaidulina, Sofia	Ten Preludes for Solo Cello
1975	Rouse, Christopher	Morpheus for Solo Cello
1976	Sallinen, Aulis	Cello Concerto
1976	Walker, George	Movements for Cello and Orchestra
1977	Bernstein, Leonard	Three Meditations from 'The Mass' for Cello and Orchestra
1977	Pärt, Arvo	Fratres for Cello and Piano
1978	Pärt, Arvo	Spiegel im Spiegel for Cello and Piano
1978	Schnittke, Alfred	Sonata for Cello and Piano No. 1
1979	Ran, Shalumit	Fantasy Variations for Solo Cello
1982	Penderecki, Krzysztof	Cello Concerto No. 2
1982	Piazzolla, Astor	Le Grand Tango for Cello and Piano
1983	León, Tania	Four Pieces for Solo Cello
1986	Fine, Vivian	Cello Sonata (1986)
1986	Larsen, Libby	Juba for Solo Cello
1988	Steinmetz, John	Possessed for Solo Cello
1988	Summer, Mark	Julie-O for Solo Cello
1988	Tavener, John	The Protecting Veil for Cello and Orchestra
1993	Hoiby, Lee	Cello Sonata
1993	Vasks, Peteris	Cello Concerto
1993	Williams, John	Theme from Schindler's List for Cello and Piano
1994	Tower, Joan	Très lent (Hommage à Messiaen) for Cello and Piano
1995	Balentine, James	A Wiser Man for Cello and Piano
1995	Sheng, Bright	Seven Tunes Heard in China for Solo Cello
1996	Corigliano, John	Fancy on a Bach Air for Solo Cello
1997	Nyman, Michael	On the Fiddle for Cello and Piano
1997	Williams, John	Elegie for Cello and Piano
1999	Auerbach, Lera	24 Preludes for Cello and Piano, Op. 69
1999	Beamish, Sally	Cello Sonata

1999	MacMillan, James	Sonata No. 1 for Cello and Piano
2000	Dun, Tan	Crouching Tiger Concerto for Cello and Orchestra
2000	Kernis, Aaron	Colored Field Concerto for Cello and Orchestra
2000	Saariaho, Kaija	Sept Papillons for Solo Cello
2000	Watkins, Mary	Bus Stop for Cello and Piano
2002	Auerbach, Lera	Cello Sonata
2002	Bunch, Kenji	Broken Music for Cello and Piano
2004	Puts, Kevin	Air for Cello and Piano
2004	Snider, Sarah Kirkland	The Reserved, The Reticent for Solo Cello
2005	Pucihar, Blaž	Summer Sonata for Cello and Piano
2004	Walker, Gwyneth	By Land and Sea for Cello and Piano
2005	Williams, John	Three Pieces from Memoirs of a Geisha for Cello and Piano
2006	Fàbregas, Elisenda	Colores Andaluces for Cello and Piano
2006	Golijov, Osvaldo	Azul for Cello and Orchestra
2006	Higdon, Jennifer	Nocturne for Cello and Piano
2007	Dunphy, Melissa	Baroque Variations on "The Frail" for Cello and Piano
2007	Glass, Philip	Partita No. 1 for Solo Cello (Songs & Poems)
2007	Thomas, Augusta Read	Cantos for Slava for Cello and Piano
2008	Johnson, David H.	5 Melodies for Cello and Piano
2008	Steinberg, Carolyn	A Wintry Mix: Of Ice and Snow for Cello and Piano
2009	Ades, Thomas	Lieux retrouvés for Cello and Piano
2009	Bayolo, Armando	Orfei Mors for Cello and Orchestra
2009	Chin, Unsik	Cello Concerto
2009	Hailstork, Adolphus	Draw the Sacred Circle Closer for Solo Cello
2009	Shaw, Caroline	In manus tuas for Solo Cello
2010	Mellits, Marc	Book of Ruth for Solo Cello
2011	Prokofiev, Gabriel	Cello Multitracks
2012	Muhly, Nico	Cello Concerto
2012	Woolf, Luna Pearl	Helter Skelter arranged for Solo Cello
2013	Glass, Philip	Orbit for Solo Cello
2013	Maslanka, David	Remember Me for Cello and Nineteen Players
2014	Bates, Mason	Cello Concerto
2015	Alberga, Eleanor	Ride Through for Solo Cello
2015	Daugherty, Michael	Tales of Hemingway for Cello and Orchestra
2015	Dessner, Bryce	Tuusula for Solo Cello
2015	Esmail, Reena	Perhaps for Solo Cello
2016	Biedenbender, David	Light Over Mountains for Cello and Piano
2016	Joachim, Nathalie	Dam Mwen Yo for Cello and Recording
2016	Loggins-Hull, Allison	Stolen for Solo Cello
2016	Musgrave, Thea	D.E.S.-In Celebration for Solo Cello
2018	Frank, Gabriella Lena & David Fetherolf	Serenata for Solo Cello
2019	Clyne, Anna	Dance for Cello and Orchestra
2019	Prestini, Paola	To Tell a Story for Solo Cello and Electronics
2020	Casarrubios, Andrea	Seven for Solo Cello
2020	Roumain, Daniel Bernard	Why Did They Kill Sandra Bland? for Solo Cello
2020	Skye, Derrick	Hum for Solo Cello
2020	Zwilich, Ellen Taaffe	Cello Concerto
2021	Mazzoli, Missy	Beyond the Order of Things (After Josquin) for Solo Cello
2022	Canzano, Nicola	Partita No. 1 for Solo Cello

2022	Montgomery, Jessie	Divided for Cello and Orchestra
2022	Raitz, Kathryn	Not So Simple for Solo Cello
2022	Wiancko, Paul	Microsuite for Solo Cello
2023	Alexander, Eric	Symmetry of Trees for Solo Cello
2023	Canzano, Nicola Saraceni	Partita per Violoncello

Dates are approximate in some cases, and some reflect the year the work was published, if the date it was written is unknown. When more than one composer is listed in a year, they are listed alphabetically.

Appendix C: Other Cello Repertoire Resources

The following is a sample of some other places to find cello repertoire:

Feves, Michael and Henk Lambooij, A Cellist's Companion: A Comprehensive Catalog of Cello Literature (Lulu Books: North Carolina, 2007).
–very thorough catalog of cello music.

Homuth, Donald, Cello Music Since 1960: A Bibliography of Solo, Chamber, & Orchestral Works for the Solo Cello (Scarecrow Press: Maryland, 1994).
-catalog resource concentrating on a little over thirty years of solo cello music from the late twentieth century.

Markovitch, Dmitry, The Solo Cello: A Bibliography of the Unaccompanied Violoncello Literature (Fallen Leaf Press: Berkeley, 1989).
–a catalog focusing on unaccompanied cello music

https://www.cellobello.org/
—-has databases for Cello Music by Women Composers, Cello Music by Black Composers, Sphinx Catalog of Latin American Cello Works, 21st Century Cello Works

https://www.musicbyblackcomposers.org/
–compiled database of music for cello by black composers

University of North Carolina at Greensboro Cello Music Collection: https://library.uncg.edu/info/depts/scua/collections/cello/
–UNCG has one of the largest collections of cello music from some of history's greatest cellists, such as Luigi Silva, Elizabeth Cowling, Bernard Greenhouse, Laszlo Varga, and Lynn Harrell.